Dear Reader:

The book you are about to read is the latest bestseller from the St. Martin's True Crime Library, the imprint *The New York Times* calls "the leader in true crime!" Each month, we offer you a fascinating account of the latest, most sensational crime that has captured the national attention. St. Martin's is the publisher of Tina Dirmann's VANISHED AT SEA, the story of a former child actor who posed as a yacht buyer in order to lure an older couple out to sea, then robbed them and threw them overboard to their deaths. John Glatt's riveting and horrifying SECRETS IN THE CELLAR shines a light on the man who shocked the world when it was revealed that he had kept his daughter locked in his hidden basement for 24 years. In the Edgar-nominated WRITTEN IN BLOOD, Diane Fanning looks at Michael Petersen, a Marine-turned-novelist found guilty of beating his wife to death and pushing her down the stairs of their home—only to reveal another similar death from his past. In the book you now hold, BLOOD IN THE SNOW, Tom Henderson examines a tragic case of jealousy, deceit, and murder.

St. Martin's True Crime Library gives you the stories behind the headlines. Our authors take you right to the scene of the crime and into the minds of the most notorious murderers to show you what really makes them tick. St. Martin's True Crime Library paperbacks are better than the most terrifying thriller, because it's all true! The next time you want a crackling good read, make sure it's got the St. Martin's True Crime Library logo on the spine—you'll be up all night!

Charles E. Spicer

Charles E. Spicer, Jr.
Executive Editor, St. Martin's True Crime Library

BLOOD IN THE SNOW

THE TRUE STORY OF A STAY-AT-HOME DAD, HIS HIGH-POWERED WIFE, AND THE JEALOUSY THAT DROVE HIM TO MURDER

Tom Henderson

St. Martin's Paperbacks

BLOOD IN THE SNOW

Copyright © 2011 by Tom Henderson.

All rights reserved.

For information address St. Martin's Press, 175 Fifth Avenue, New York, NY 10010.

EAN: 978-0-312-94812-2

Printed in the United States of America

St. Martin's Paperbacks edition / May 2011

St. Martin's Paperbacks are published by St. Martin's Press, 175 Fifth Avenue, New York, NY 10010.

10 9 8 7 6 5 4 3 2 1

This book is dedicated to Alicia and Erik Standerfer, whose pain I can't imagine and whose help was appreciated and touching. And it is dedicated to Ian and Lindsey. No one should ever have to go through what they went through. Thank goodness for an aunt and uncle who fought to become their new parents.

PROLOGUE

Friday, February 9, 2007

Stephen Grant has a crush on the family au pair. His wife's about to arrive home from a business trip to Puerto Rico, but his mind's on the au pair. She's out dancing with girlfriends, and throughout the night, he texts her, flirting. He reminds her: she owes him a kiss.

His wife, Tara, is gone a lot, leaving him to run the house and be Mr. Mom to their two young kids. While he was the only dad at the kids' bus stop each morning, she'd worked her way through the ranks of Washington Group International, an Idaho-based engineering firm. She used to work out of the Troy office, but since October she's been working full-time in the company's Puerto Rico office. And then there are her business trips to London and Russia. When she is home on the weekends, he seems to alternately bore her and irritate her.

Verena Dierkes, the au pair? She's been with the Grants since August. She finds Stephen fascinating, an older man at thirty-seven, six feet tall, trim, a long-distance runner with a tight belly and nice legs. She's a nineteen-year-old German in the States for a year or two, a beauty, blond hair, nice smile. She's still a teenager, just graduated the year before from the Gymnasium St. Xavier, a school that caters to top students in her hometown of Osnabruck. Stephen seems to her a man of the world who has been making her feel like the woman she wants to be.

She is the latest, and best, in a string of attractive au pairs the Grants have got from Au Pair in America, a London-based company with U.S. headquarters in Connecticut. For a fee of $7,400, the company screened potential au pairs. Verena's contract calls for her to be paid $285 a week plus room and board for forty-five hours of work a week. The contract is for one year and can be renewed. If Grant has his way, it certainly will be.

Verena knows from his messages that Tara has been delayed in Newark. She's at Mr. B's, a popular nightspot in Rochester.

Stephen's messages to her, telling her he misses her, are cute, she thinks, but kind of annoying, too. She tells him to stop, her friends might get suspicious. They know it's him texting her. That isn't suspicious, but the volume of messages might be. It doesn't dawn on her to just ignore them, put the phone away, that not being part of her cultural vocabulary.

Things had started heating up between them in mid-January, though the crush, at least on his end, has been building for longer than that, and probably on her end, too. A friend of the family, Michelle, was coming by with her kids then, and Steve told Verena that Michelle's girl was going to play with his girl and Michelle's boy was going to play with his boy, and putting a smirk on his face, he mustered up his courage, decided to go for it, and said: "And you and Michelle can play. God, I'd love to see that."

No way she could miss his meaning, given the smirk.

He was instantly mortified. He'd gone too far. Verena was going to be mad. But after half a beat, she laughed, instead. She thought it was funny. She thinks Steve's funny. It makes him feel good. Tara used to think he was funny, too.

End of January, Tara was in London on business, and Steve and Verena were talking in the Grants' big, four-bedroom reddish-brown brick Colonial in Washington

Township, where what were recently cornfields twenty miles north of Detroit's northern city limit have been turned into outsized homes and overextended mortgages. They found each other fascinating, the way people do at that stage. Steve got a look on his face and told her he was thinking another bad thought, but this time, he said, he'd keep it to himself, meaning he wouldn't blurt it out like he did about Michelle and Verena.

No, said Verena, tell me. So he did. He told her he wanted to kiss her. "Oh, I can't believe you said that," she said, coy not mad. They kept talking for another twenty minutes, standing in the hallway.

The next night—or was it the night after?—she was in her room, getting ready for bed. Stephen came to the doorway. "You're so beautiful," he said. "I want to sleep with you."

She laughed. They started talking, talked for four hours before going to bed in their separate rooms at 2 A.M.

That's how it started. They'd sneak kisses, short kisses that became longer and more passionate.

One day she was at the computer, typing an e-mail to her brother, when she heard Stephen behind her. "I'm going to take a shower. Want to join me?" He was getting bolder, she more intrigued by the idea of consummating the heat growing between them.

"No," she said.

Another night, just after she went to bed, he texted her from another room in the house. "I want to have sex with you" was the message. She typed: "No."

On February 7, again just after she'd gone to her room for the night, he stuck his head in. "Good night. I love you." He came in and sat down on her bed. "I won't repeat those three little words again, but I am falling in love with you."

They hugged and cuddled for a few minutes. Wordlessly, Stephen stood up, took her by the hand, pulled her to her feet and led her to his room. He leaned her back on the bed, slid down her panties, and gave her oral sex, a gift she accepted with ardor and appreciation.

To show her what a giving and generous man he is, he ended their sexual encounter with just that act. He didn't, not yet, anyway, need to have it reciprocated. This is for you, he seemed to say. Your gift to me can come another time.

So that was what Americans meant by "swept off your feet." In a daze, she went back to her room. She couldn't wait to tell her best friend in America.

They haven't had intercourse yet, but it's been on Grant's mind since; that time is coming. Soon. About eleven-thirty, Verena pulls her car into the driveway. She walks in the side door. She hears someone coming down the stairs. It's Stephen. Racing to greet her? Coming to get the kiss (ooh, sweet double meaning there) that he's texted her that she owes him? No.

"What the fuck are you still doing here? Go! Just go!" he yells. Then realizing it's Verena, he apologizes.

"Is Tara still out there?" he asks.

"No. Where is she? She's not outside," she answers.

Stephen starts crying. It's horrible. Tara got home an hour earlier. She'd unpacked her bag. They'd got into a big fight over her constant traveling. And then she had called someone and said to come get her, that she'd be outside in a couple of minutes. And then she'd left.

Verena consoles him, tells him everything will be okay, Tara will be back. She goes into her room. There's a note on her pillow.

"You owe me a kiss," it reads.

She goes into his room. He's on the bed, naked. She gets in bed with him, holding him, consoling him, the teen girl mother to the man. Before the night is over, she goes back to her room. She wants to be in her own bed when daylight comes.

Stephen gets up before her, has business to attend to. When she wakes up, she can hear the kids down the hall. She had to get breakfast started for them. She loves those kids.

No Tara. She hasn't returned.

PART ONE

MISSING

THE CHATTY LITTLE GIRL
WITH THE BIG SMILE

Tara Lynn Destrampe, growing up in the little town of Perkins in the southwest corner of Michigan's sparsely populated Upper Peninsula was the last person anyone would have pictured running operations in the San Juan office of a worldwide construction and engineering giant.

The Destrampes were better off than most, in a place where hardscrabble is a very useful adjective. The UP has the highest unemployment year in and year out of any region in the state. Good jobs are scarce. Those lucky enough to mine or log or work for the county road department try to pass the jobs off to their kids if they can. Gerald Destrampe—no one knew him as Gerald, it was Dusty, friend, chatty Dusty, well liked by everybody who knew him—had by UP standards a great job, with security and full benefits as a wastewater-treatment operator at the Sawyer Air Force Base in nearby Gwinn.

When Tara was two and her sister Alicia one, the Destrampes bought a twenty-eight-acre hobby farm. Well, more than a hobby, but not something you'd support a family on. Mary Destrampe stayed home with the girls, grew vegetables in the garden, minded the chicken coop, and raised a wide variety of animals to supplement Dusty's paycheck.

Late in the winter, they'd tap the big, old sugar maples and sell off some of the syrup, too.

The girls had kittens and dogs and rabbits to play with. As they got a little older, bit by bit their parents assigned them various chores that were necessary to tend properly to the animals. It didn't seem like chores, or work.

Tara, twenty-one months older, was the more ebullient, chatty like her dad from the start. Still an infant, she'd say hi to everyone who came near. In elementary school, she couldn't keep quiet. From first bell to last, she yakked away. Her teachers would scribble on her report cards: "Talks too much." But she was so smart, and so cute, big smile, Shirley Temple head of curly hair, they couldn't get mad at her about it, just a bit frustrated.

In the fourth grade, realizing that telling Tara to stop talking was an unproductive way to string words together, her teacher had an epiphany: she told Tara that at the end of every day she didn't get in trouble for talking, she'd get rewarded with a piece of gum. Tara was soon a gum collector.

Winters are long and hard in the UP. It's not unusual to find snow in the woods in mid-May. It's far enough north that days are gloriously long in the summer, depressingly short in the winter. Laying in a supply of firewood to heat the house was a summer-long chore. Stacking it in the house to be tossed into the wood burner was the girls' work. Tara would throw the wood into the basement through a window, Alicia would stack it up neatly.

Not yet teens, the girls began raising sheep for the UP state fair. Tara was soon raising cows, pigs, rabbits, and chickens, as well. The girls joined the 4-H club, where her parents were group leaders. Her parents got her her own Appaloosa and she'd spend hours brushing him, before and after rides. Her career as farmhand had its peak in 1990 when she won the award for Grand Champion market hog.

Summers were a time for backpacking with her parents and the 4-H club, making trips to the spectacular Porcupine Mountains at the far northeast corner of the UP, along Lake

Superior. Its hiking trails were some of the most arduous in the state, and some of the most spectacular. If you got out early enough, and were lucky enough, you might spot one of the shy black bears out looking for thimbleberries or blueberries or raspberries. Or a bobcat lying on a rock in a patch of sunlight across a stream, sensing you weren't a hunter and posed no danger, so he didn't need to move.

Or to the equally spectacular Pictured Rocks National Lakeshore, also along Superior, just east of Munising, miles of easy trails along the lip of steep cliffs turned all colors of the rainbow over the eons by minerals leaching through the surface.

The 4-H club got Tara into shooting, too, and she took right to it. Soon after taking up the sport, she was competing in tournaments around the state, and bringing home what the shooters referred to as hardware—trophies and awards— with regularity. The club's four-member BB team took the state title one year, with Tara leading the way.

Every Christmas Eve, a family tradition, Dusty took the girls out with a group of his friends and a bunch of dogs to rabbit-hunt in the snow. Tara hunted ducks in duck season, deer in deer season. She and Alicia both made their father proud with their clean deer kills, not woozing out like little girls, but taking aim, calm, relaxed, breathing controlled, squeezing the trigger gently and bringing their bucks down with a single shot. No having to track a wounded beast through the woods and snow as it bled out.

Alicia and Tara got adept at tapping the sugar maples each March. The work in the snow was all the more fun knowing that the running sap meant spring was near at last. They started with a few trees at the back edge of the farm, but when Dusty bought more acreage down the road, the maple operation moved. The girls would come home, put on boots and strap on the snowshoes, and head out to collect what sap had drained into the aluminum pails affixed to the trees.

If it seems like an idealized pastoral childhood, in some ways it was. But there was a dark side, too. Dusty was known for his temper, and could be verbally abusive to their mother. Tara hated that in her dad, hated that her mother took it passively. Many years later, Tara would write about that aspect of her childhood and how painful it had been as part of an exercise during a training session at work. As a girl, she vowed it would never happen to her. She'd never have a husband who talked to her that way, and if she did, she'd put a stop to it.

Tara played on the varsity basketball team and ran track at Mid-Peninsula High School, which taught 275 kids from the towns of Perkins and Rock. Somehow, she found time to be a cheerleader for the boys' teams, too. By then, Alicia had caught up to her older sister in size and the two could pass for twins in their matching cheerleader outfits, same smile, same big hair teased high in front and worn long in back.

"Those were the days. The higher your hair was, the better," high school friend Melissa Hanson would tell the *Detroit Free Press*. A photo from the high school yearbook shows Tara and seven of her fellow cheerleaders all sporting the same look, achieved by lacquering their long bangs to a frozen frenzy with hair spray so they stood upright, aiming skyward. "We called it the wall," said Hanson.

Tara was first clarinet in the school band, too, and an excellent pianist, having taken lessons for years.

And just in case there was any worry about her being an underachiever, Tara had a part-time job, selling shoes at the local shoe store. She loved selling, started thinking of herself as a natural businesswoman. She wrote in her senior yearbook—there were forty-four in her class of 1990—that one of her goals was to "make enough money to buy everything I want. Live in a big house with a Jaguar parked in the garage."

Before graduating fourth in her class, Tara had her heart set on attending Michigan State University, the biggest school in the state, a long way away by distance in East Lansing, and a long way culturally from Perkins. Its forty-five thousand students would have made it a metropolis in the UP.

But Dusty and Mary weren't ready for such a move, yet.

They convinced Tara to stay at home a while longer, to spend two years attending Bay de Noc Community College, named for the deep, narrow bay on Lake Michigan they lived near, before giving the big world a try at MSU.

She studied marketing, fell in love with it, and, after she transferred to MSU in 1992, pursued a degree in business administration.

The next year, a handsome, tall, athletic former MSU student named Stephen Grant, a friend of one of her roommates, began pursuing her. Grant was a notorious partier, notorious womanizer, happily cheating on his current girlfriend if he had a chance to score with some drunken coed he'd just met. He'd tell friends he was an atheist, was going to go to hell anyway, might as well enjoy the ride there.

He and Tara met at a party, found out that by happenstance they both had apartments in a complex known as Cedar Village Apartments, which were wedged in between the Cedar River that ran along the northeast edge of campus and busy Grand River Avenue. For decades, Cedar Village had been considered MSU's party central. If the school wins or loses any big games or championships, East Lansing and campus police brace for the inevitable drunken riots and old couches set aflame in front of buildings and in front yards, a recurring theme.

He told her that having graduated from college, he was taking aim at a career in politics, that his temporary job as an aide in the Lansing office of state Senator Jack Faxon, a powerful Democrat from the Detroit suburb of Farmington Hills, was just the right foot in the door. Lansing is Michigan's capital; the job was to last through the fall elections of 1994. If Grant played his cards right, there'd be something better, permanent, once Faxon got reelected, which was considered a shoo-in.

Grant partied hard. He no longer had grades to worry about. Tara, always an achiever, was known as a hard partier, too, but unlike many of her peers at Cedar Village, fun never got in the way of school. Grant and Tara dated a couple of times. Tara was struck by his good looks and strong, confident manner, but for one reason or another, the relationship didn't take off. They remained platonic.

In August 1994, Tara's grandmother died, and the family united in the Upper Peninsula city of Escanaba for the funeral. Grant spent an entire day making the drive up from Lansing, surprising Tara, to say the least, when he called her to say he was in Escanaba, would be coming to the funeral home, if that was all right.

To his surprise, Tara was there with a boyfriend. To the boyfriend's surprise, something seemed to be clicking between Tara and Stephen. Tara was impressed that Grant had driven up. Maybe she'd underestimated him, after all. Or maybe he was just lucky, getting her when she was vulnerable, and impressionable.

Grant was invited out that night to a dinner with the family. They didn't take to him. Alicia, for one, was appalled her sister seemed so taken by him. There was something that struck her about him as entirely too worldly. He could sense their coolness. Feeling out of place, after dinner he got back in his car and started the long drive home.

Soon, they were boyfriend and girlfriend. Later, he'd tell friends that the day he'd got back to his apartment in Okemos, a suburb of Lansing that is something of a bedroom community for MSU professors and students, Tara had called him and told him she loved him. Grant tended to embellish things, though, so friends took it with a grain of salt.

After a couple of months, she moved in with him.

Faxon got reelected in the fall elections, but to Grant's dismay, the temporary aide job he had didn't materialize into an offer of regular employment with the senator or any of his political acquaintances.

So he gave up his apartment and moved back to Detroit, to work in his father's machine shop in Mt. Clemens. Tara made the move, too.

In September 1996, they were married in a little country church near her childhood home, a year after Grant had proposed on a bench in front of Detroit's world-renowned Institute of Arts, just yards away from one of the original casts of *The Thinker* by Rodin.

At the time of the proposal, Grant had embarked on a self-improvement campaign, soaking in culture, learning about fine wines, and becoming a talented amateur chef. His growing skills were well suited to Tara's existing talents, and their friends thought of them as the perfect couple.

Tara had trouble finding a job and Grant supported them, an irony considering the role reversal that was to come later. She finally landed a job at Kelly Services, a Detroit-based company that provided workers on a temporary basis to a wide variety of businesses and industries. One of Tara's placements was with the local office of Morrison-Knudsen, a legendary engineering firm that had built both the Hoover Dam and the Trans-Alaska pipeline. No longer thriving, Morrison-Knudsen was about to be bought by the Washington Group, a huge engineering and construction company with worldwide operations and more than twenty thousand employees.

Tara was determined to make the temp job permanent, which didn't take long, given her drive, work habits, gregarious personality, and, no small thing, big smile. And it didn't take her long to start working her way up the chain of command, either, despite taking short breaks to give birth to Lindsey in November 2000 and to Ian two years later.

In 2003, Tara was named a systems manager. In 2006, came the offer of a full-time posting in Puerto Rico at a salary of $168,000 a year. Soon, she got even more good news. She'd been accepted into a prestigious program with the company, geared at those with a real shot at upper management. It was called the LEAP program and was offered each year to just fifteen to twenty of the company's army of employees.

If there'd been any doubts in her mind or in that of her coworkers, there was none now: she was on the fast track.

* * *

Despite the demands of the job, Tara was a devoted mother, determined her kids should be as well rounded as she had been back in the UP. It upset her that Lindsey's elementary school didn't offer Spanish to first and second graders. She wanted her to get an early start on becoming bilingual. She was pleased when one of the au pairs was Spanish, so she could tutor the kids as part of her duties. Tara would check in from San Juan to make sure Stephen had, as requested, taken the kids to some performance at the ballet she thought would be culturally rewarding.

She wanted Lindsey to take dance lessons, and though Ian was just five it was time for him to start taking hockey lessons. As for Tara, she started taking golf lessons. A lot of business got done on the golf course, and with her about to begin the LEAP program, it wouldn't hurt to know a sand iron from a seven iron.

Tara would meticulously plan upcoming family events in a notebook, and compile lengthy lists of gifts both frivolous and practical to give her children at birthdays and Christmases, perhaps compensating for her long hours away from them. She was generous with Stephen, too. In 2007, although it was just February, she was already deep into the details of a special surprise for him, a combination birthday and Christmas present for him in December, a no-expenses-barred trip to the Napa Valley, where Stephen could indulge his taste for expensive wines, and they both could indulge their taste for luxury hotels.

Considering their expensive tastes—Stephen's mountain bike had cost $2,500, a marvel of light weight, incredible gear ratios, and ruggedness that could stand up to anything short of a roadside bomb—it was good that they had her salary to count on. In 2006, Grant made $18,900 at his dad's machine shop, less than Tara's year-end bonus of $28,000.

Perhaps thinking of that trip to the Napa Valley, eager perhaps for the renewal it might bring to a marriage that had been strained by her travel and her work, she wrote a long letter to Stephen. She apologized for always making him feel wrong, for not loving him as well as she should, for sometimes pushing him away when he was "the one person who has fully committed to me to love me unconditionally."

Tara wrote that she wanted them to renew their wedding vows so "she could have a clear mind and an open heart to fully love you for the incredible human being that you are."

It would have been a good letter to send with Valentine's Day coming up. Maybe she wanted to give it another read or two, polish it up in another draft. It was still in her notebook when she flew to San Juan on February 5, still there when she arrived back in Detroit on February 9.

VALENTINE'S DAY

A little before noon, Stephen Grant walked into the Macomb County Sheriff's Department just west of downtown Mt. Clemens, a down-on-its-luck town once known around the world for its mineral baths and elegant hotels, went to the Plexiglas window just inside the lobby, and told the desk sergeant he wanted to report a missing person, his wife of ten years.

The sergeant took his name, asked him what had happened, listened to his run-of-the-mill-and-odd-at-the-same-time story about a wife gone missing, and told him to wait in the lobby a minute.

The sergeant told one of the deputies working the front desk with him to go get Bill Hughes, a twenty-year veteran of the department. Hughes, like many others in Southeastern Michigan, was having a bad morning, him more than most. It had been a mild winter so far, people had gotten spoiled. But an Alberta Clipper had blown through overnight, dumping eight inches of snow and snarling everyone's rush-hour drive. First big blow of the winter, everyone acts like they've never driven in the stuff. Spinouts and accidents by the reckless, an overreacting crawl by the timid, all of it turning the roads and freeways into parking lots.

Hughes didn't start till ten, didn't have to come far, so his drive had been better than most. But his small cubicle off the desk sergeant's command center had sprung a leak overnight, up on the ceiling, right above his desk and computer.

He'd just finished moving his desk off to the side and out of the water, when a deputy helping work the front stuck his head in and told him he had company, some guy in the lobby wanting to file a missing person's report. Hughes would take the report, then pass it on to the detective bureau, which got all the missing persons cases.

There's always someone having a worse day than you, to put a leak in perspective.

Hughes opened the door to the lobby and invited Grant in. Hughes introduced himself, shook his hand, apologized for the mess as they entered his cubicle. Guy said his name was Stephen Grant. "Stephen" he called himself, not "Steve." Apparently the formal type.

Hughes jotted down notes longhand. He'd enter them into the computer later. He noticed right off a scratch across Grant's nose. Grant said the scratch came from a metal shaving at his father's tool-and-die shop in Mt. Clemens, USG Babbitt, where he worked a few hours a week making ball bearings. Mostly, he was a stay-at-home dad. Hughes made a mental note of a small scratch on one of Grant's hands, too.

Someone setting off a cop's suspicions isn't exactly news. Cops are suspicious of everyone. Nonetheless, Grant set off Hughes's suspicions right off, pulling out a little spiral notebook and referring to it before he started his story. Kept referring to it as he talked. You'd need a notebook? Wife's gone missing and you can't just tell the story? Hughes didn't like his voice, either, seemed jittery.

Grant was chatty, to say the least. He said he and his wife, Tara Lynn, lived on Westridge in the Carriage Hills subdivision in affluent Washington Township. That was a fast-growing community at the north end of Macomb County, population having doubled since 1990, median income up way more than that, cornfields rapidly being replaced by large

brick or frame Tudors and Colonials with oversized garages
on big lots.

The center of Southeastern Michigan's suburban building
boom, Washington Township would—though no one could
have imagined it then as housing prices were going through
the roof and everyone was scrambling to refinance and put
the equity to use—soon be the epicenter of economic col-
lapse, foreclosures and abandoned houses and extinguished
dreams. But at that time, on Westridge and the streets spreading out from it, it seemed the center of the American dream.

It was the kind of place filled with subdivisions named
by people who couldn't spell and didn't pay attention to the
meaning of the words they strung together. Where "Westridge"
became one word and could just as easily be to the east and
nowhere near a ridge, where the only trees in a "Forest Hill
Estates" would be a few saplings planted sporadically where
the corn once grew, or where no meadows were to be found
in or near "Meadow View." The subdivisions had winding
blacktop streets and no sidewalks and their silly names
missed their goal of lending an air of class. Carriage Hills?
How old was the last person to see a carriage around here
when he died?

Just as Grant was getting started, Sergeant Brian Kozlowski had walked in, hours earlier than he was scheduled,
there for a staff potluck lunch. Koz was walking past the
open doorway to Hughes's cubicle when he heard:

Hughes: "How long has your wife been missing?"

Guy: "It's been five days."

Five days? Who waits five days to report his wife missing?
Koz stopped outside the doorway and took the guy in. Might
be a good one. Had a feeling it would be. Took him in long and
hard. Later in the day, he'd find out everything the guy had
been talking about. He'd read Hughes's written report and
start planning what to do next.

First, though, he had a potluck to get to.

* * *

Kozlowski moved on, looking forward to reading Hughes's report later on. The report would tell the facts, dry and terse in the manner of police reports everywhere, but what was happening in Hughes's office was anything but.

Grant rambled on, all over the place, words tumbling out as if they'd been held captive. He said his wife had been late getting home the night of February 9, delayed by a big East Coast snowstorm. That he'd had a couple of beers while he waited for her. That they'd argued over the phone about her change in plans, she wanted to go back to Puerto Rico on Sunday instead of Monday. Had resumed the fight when she got home. After some yelling back and forth for twenty minutes, she'd made a call on her cell, told someone to pick her up, said she'd be out in a minute. Grant didn't know for sure, thought it was the limo service she frequently used to get to the airport.

Last thing she said to him on her way out the garage door? Don't forget to get her car, a 2002 Isuzu Trooper, into the dealership Monday to get a dent fixed.

They had an au pair; she got home ten minutes after Tara left.

Hughes asked, if his wife went missing on the ninth, why did he wait until the fourteenth to come in?

Her boss asked him to, he said. He'd left messages on her cell phone Saturday and Sunday, and when he didn't hear from her by Monday, he called her boss, Lou Troendle, in Puerto Rico. Troendle said Lou asked him to hold off a bit with the police, he wanted to have a meeting with her bosses in Puerto Rico to discuss it first.

Hughes didn't follow the logic of that, but let Grant continue. Hughes continued jotting down notes, Grant kept consulting his notebook.

Tuesday, he had called Tara's sister in Ohio, and her mother. Both said they hadn't heard a thing from Tara. Grant said he'd told the sister that he'd be happy to find out Tara was off with some guy in a motel. He thought, he confided to Hughes, that Lou and Tara's mom were lying to him. In fact,

Tara's family had voiced worries in the past that Tara and Lou were having an affair. He didn't believe it at first, but he'd been getting suspicious lately.

You know, said Grant, breaking off his timeline of events, he'd been talking to his dad and his dad told him the first person police always suspect in these things is the husband. Hughes read it as: "I'm cool about this. I'm not nervous that you'll be thinking I had something to do with it. See, I can bring it up."

He brought something else up too. He had, he told Hughes, a warrant out for his arrest for an unpaid traffic ticket. Pretty weird thing to tell a cop when you're visiting the jail. Usually that'd mean a quick arrest. Hughes figured it was Grant telling him: "See, I'm open and honest with you, telling you my secrets." Hughes let it slide. Detectives were going to want to talk to him soon, no sense in getting him on the defensive by arresting him and throwing him in a cell.

Back to the narrative. They'd been to marriage counseling, but it didn't seem to help, and he was thinking of hiring a divorce attorney. She didn't talk about her marriage problems with him, she talked about them with Lou.

You know, said Grant, Tara's company, Washington Group International, was involved in chemical weapons, and Lou was in charge of that project. Maybe Tara had been exposed to nerve gas. Maybe she'd been kidnapped by terrorists.

This was getting more entertaining by the second. Hughes stared at him, trying not to let him know he couldn't have seemed weirder now, if he'd been talking with a rat's tail sticking out of his mouth.

Well, then, let's call Lou, said Hughes. Grant gave him the number in Puerto Rico and Hughes called him in front of Grant. Be interesting to see how Grant handles that, probably last thing he was expecting.

Troendle struck Hughes as genuinely concerned, offered to help in any way he could. And he was emphatic: no way would Tara ever take off on her own. She wouldn't leave her kids, she wouldn't just not show up for work.

While Hughes jotted down notes as Troendle spoke, Grant sat there smiling at him.

When he got off the phone with Troendle, Grant asked him if he wanted to call Tara's parents now. No, said Hughes, he'd leave that to the detective bureau.

Grant brought up the au pair again. Hughes wondered why. Hughes asked him if he was having some kind of relationship with her.

"She'll never tell," said Grant, giving him a guy-to-guy smirk. Like he was being funny. Hughes didn't think it was funny, had a feeling he wasn't joking. In any event, pretty weird thing to say, you're in there reporting your wife missing.

"Is it all right if we send some detectives over to the house later?" asked Hughes.

"Sure."

His potluck eaten, this is what Kozlowski read from Hughes's report to start his official workday:

"Stephen Grant of 6686 Westridge stated that on 2/9/07, at approximately 2230 hours, his wife, Tara Grant, arrived home from Metropolitan Airport after being out of the country on business.

"Stephen stated that Tara, a division operating manager for Washington Group International, currently assigned to San Juan, Puerto Rico, changed her travel itinerary prior to her arrival home. Stephen stated that Tara called him from the Newark airport, during a flight delay, and told him that she decided to return to San Juan on Sunday, instead of Monday, as she had previously planned. Stephen continued to explain that he was upset about Tara's travel schedule and argued with her. Stephen further stated that he contacted Tara and continued to argue with her about 'family issues' while she was driving home from Metro Airport. Stephen stated that Tara stayed home approximately twenty minutes before leaving in a car-service black sedan, which she had called to their residence to pick her up. Stephen stated that

Tara had changed clothes before leaving (wearing black slacks).

"Stephen stated that he tried to contact Tara on Saturday and Sunday, and left several messages on her mobile, with no response from her. Stephen stated that he called Louis (Lou) Troendle, Tara's immediate supervisor in San Juan. Lou told Stephen that Tara had not reported in and he would tell her to call him when she arrives. Stephen stated that he also contacted Tara's mother and sister. Stephen further stated that he believes that Lou and Tara's mother was not being truthful about Tara.

"Stephen stated that it was unusual for Tara not to contact him and their two children while traveling. Stephen suspects that Tara is upset with him, due to their persistent arguing. Stephen stated that he contacted an attorney to discuss his possible options regarding a possible divorce.

"DISPOSITION: I contacted Lou regarding Tara. Lou stated that Tara has not reported in and expressed his concerns. Lou gave me the telephone number to their company's human resources department to assist in locating Tara.

"NOTE: Stephen's written statement attached. Stephen stated that his au pair was out when his wife arrived home Friday night. Tara's information was placed on LEIN."

The report described Tara as thirty-four years old, five six, 118 pounds, with brown hair and brown eyes. What it didn't describe was her vivacity, the light in her eyes and the life in her smile, the long, curly hair that at least some found particularly sexy in the way it framed her face, or her honed fitness from running miles on the trails of nearby Stony Creek Metropark, a huge park that practically abutted their home, just a short jog to the west. At 4,400 acres, it was the largest of the Huron-Clinton Metroparks that ringed Detroit, named for the Clinton and Huron rivers that formed the watershed that in turn created the lakes and streams the visitors came to play and fish in.

The report also described Stephen Christopher Grant as thirty-seven, six feet tall, 180 pounds, with green eyes and brown hair. It didn't describe his eyes, which would become more known than anything else about him in the weeks to come.

Attached was a three-page handwritten statement Hughes asked Grant to make.

"Fri Feb 9 at about 6 P.M. I spoke to my wife while she was delayed at Newark airport. Tara told me she was delayed about one and a half hours. She told me she was changing travel plans to fly back to San Juan on Sunday 11th instead of Mon 12th. I told her I was not happy with this and we argued a bit about her travel schedule in general. I said it was not fair to the kids that they would only see her for 1 day. She said 'tuff.'

"She arrived in Detroit. We talked three more times while she was driving home. The talks revolved around her committment [sic] to our family and to me but did not resolve the problem."

Grant wrote that after Tara got home, they continued the argument, and she told him she was going to try to go back to Puerto Rico in the morning, instead, if she could get a flight. "She also said that I could explain to the kids why she's not there in the morning. She left in a car service black sedan. She also told me I need still to take her truck to Tamaroff on Monday. Saturday, Sunday, no contact. I had phoned and left messages on her mobile phone and sent txt msg's. No response from her."

Grant wrote that he called Lou Troendle in Puerto Rico on Monday. "Lou said 'no worries.' Tara was not due in until later. He said he would tell her to call or call me, himself, and let me know she's there. I had not heard from him by 7:30 P.M. Monday 12th so I called him. He was at dinner but had not heard from Tara. I said that I needed to do something, call mother-in-law, call police, something. Lou said wait. He did not want me to do anything until Tuesday morning. He said it would only worry them."

Grant wrote that "Lou called me at 9:30 A.M. on Tue 13th Feb. saying he had not heard from her, she did not show up in

Puerto Rico office." He then left a message for Alicia Stand-erfer and called her mother, Mary, who, he wrote, told him "NOT to call police. She would send msg to Tara and have her call. Hearing this, I thought same as with Lou. Someone knew where she was. I told Mary if I heard nothing by 4 P.M. Tuesday, the 13th, I was going to police. I talked with my sister, who is friends with a Sterling Heights detective. She called him to ask what was the rule for reporting someone missing. Det. Jim Selewski told her I should wait until Wed 14th morning to report her missing."

Hughes's supervisor, Sergeant Larry King, formally signed off on Hughes's report at 3:35 P.M., which was official sanction for an investigation to proceed. For now, the incident was classified as: "Not a Crime/Other Service."

The stilted language of Grant's report caught Hughes's eye, it caught King's, it caught Kozlowski's. Who writes the date every time he mentions a day? The thing read like some prepared excuse you make when you call in sick to work before you head out to play golf. You never just say what you say when you really are sick, you have an elaborate story concocted with a timeline of everything that's happened to you healthwise the last few hours that now prohibits you from going to the office.

Got a live one, thought Koz.

And so it began.

BORN TO BE A COP

The son of a cop, Brian senior, a cop for twenty-six years, Kozlowski was born to be a cop, too. Koz, as he prefers to be called, as he practically demands, Brian being a name he was given but not one he uses or responds to, is a beefy, 250-pounder. Over the years, others have mistaken the beefiness for softness. As the son of a cop, arresting bad guys is all he's ever wanted to do.

Being a cop requires skills he has in abundance and some he doesn't have at all. The street stuff is where he's best. Working informants, sniffing out bullshit, duking it out with someone he's chased on foot down a dead-end alley.

The other stuff, office politics, schmoozing the chain of command, watching his mouth, suffering fools? Forget it. He grew up in the inner-ring Detroit suburb of East Detroit, one of the first suburbs to fill up following World War II, as the freeways were built and VHA loans were offered cheap to veterans. Later, the city, which bordered Detroit and wanted an identity of its own, changed its name to Eastpointe; the city fathers hoped some of the cachet of the affluent nearby Grosse Pointe might rub off on them.

Koz grew up near Nine Mile and Gratiot. Gratiot is a

main thoroughfare that once was the main highway between downtown Detroit and Mt. Clemens, the Macomb County seat where he now works. Nine Mile is a mile north of the Detroit border and the street that Eminem made famous.

"Born and bred for the job," is how Koz describes it. "It's all I ever wanted to be. I never had a thought to do anything else." When he was a little kid, Koz and his friends would spot his dad coming home after work in his patrol car, and they'd all chase it up the street to Koz's house. Koz used to sit in the car by himself, soaking in the atmosphere, the smell of his dad, the smell of his dad's cigars, no rules then against smoking at the station or in the car.

Koz was raised strictly, went to a small private Lutheran high school, and spent a year at Concordia College, a small school. School wasn't his thing, though. Soon as he was old enough, he applied for an entry-level job with the county sheriff's department and in 1990—"August 6," he says, an important date to him—he was hired as a jailer on the afternoon shift.

In 1992 he was promoted to day shift, then was accepted to the twelve-week police academy in 1993. Of the fifty-two in the class, he graduated third, a surprise to some of his academy mates, who mistook his grammar, which has a lexicon of its own, for intelligence.

In 1994, he was promoted to what he regarded as his first real cop job, riding the roads in a patrol car. He received training from several department veterans, though the training he got from one of them was hardly what the department had in mind, or what he appreciated.

This cop was just biding his time until retirement, taking it easy, ducking trouble, filling their days as much as he could with as little police work as possible. They spent a big chunk of the first day cruising garage and yard sales, his partner looking for bargains, and when he found them, jamming them in the police car.

If he drove past an interesting pile of garbage at a curb, well, that was fair game, too. Never knew what you might find. At the end of the day, Koz realized he'd chewed a groove at the edge of his mouth from literally biting his lip, trying to keep from blowing up at his first partner his first day on duty.

One day, dispatch told them of a suspected heart attack in progress at a nearby golf course. His partner took the long way around, going slowly, not bothering with flashers, timing it so he'd get there after EMS and not have to do anything. (These days, Koz has an image of another kind of field training officer on the wall in his office, a big poster of a nasty-looking Denzel Washington from *Training Day* as a funny reminder of his early days.)

In 1997, Koz was promoted to a multijurisdictional undercover surveillance team, working snitches for dope intel, bugging suspected members of organized crime, following home-invasion suspects, staking out businesses during sprees by rooftop B&E artists, busting prison guards selling drugs.

The work suited Koz just fine. You never knew when the monotony of sitting in a car, staring at a building, holding your pee, would erupt in the adrenaline buzz of chase and arrest.

"It's like bow hunting," says Koz. "You sit up in a stand for hours and nothing happens. Then, for five minutes, you better be on top of your game. Only it's not hunting deer, it's hunting human beings."

In 2000, Koz made sergeant, six months later a spot opened up in the detective bureau, and then in 2002 it was back to the multijurisdictional surveillance work, this time running a six-person street narcotics team.

In 2006, filling in gaps on his resume at the behest of bosses, he went back to uniform, working the front desk on the afternoon shift at headquarters. "I sat in a glass box, bored out of my mind. I was like a caged animal out at the front desk. It was well known I was unhappy. I was like a carpenter who builds custom cabinets and now he's pounding nails into two-by-fours."

First, he got into some disciplinary trouble, internal affairs slapping his wrist over what he considered a bullshit citizen complaint.

A guy claiming to be the son of Yahweh was arrested for disorderly conduct. He refused to be fingerprinted or give his name, beyond claiming to be God's boy. So, Koz helped put the guy into a restraining chair, strapped him into place and fingerprinted him. Turned out he had several warrants out.

The guy filed a formal complaint, internal affairs said he should have held off, kicked it upstairs, and waited for the chain of command to command. Fuck that, he thought. The guy turns out to be wanted, we restrained him in full view of a video camera that showed no undue force, and I'm the bad guy? Major bug up the ass.

Then, soon after, at a meeting, August of 2006, one of his command officers said something he considered dumb-ass about a task force. Koz bitched about it in front of everyone. After the meeting, a couple of officers up the chain of command came over to continue the discussion, ticked off at him. Ticked off they were ticked off, Koz let fly with an F-word or two, not that big a deal except it was at the front desk in the lobby of the sprawling headquarters and jail, the lobby always busy with citizens coming and going, paying tickets, making reports, queuing up for visiting hours and so forth. And when Koz let fly, plenty of heads turned, and his boss wrote him up on the basis that there was civilian staff in earshot. He was suspended for ten days, later knocked down to five.

"I was pissed off beyond belief," he said. " 'Fine, I'll just do my job. I won't bleed for you, anymore.' I resigned myself: 'I'll just put in my time and retire on afternoons.' "

Resigned to the idea that his career climb was over, he was surprised, shocked, really, when he got a call in November from one of his bosses, Detective Lieutenant Elizabeth Darga, who ran the detective bureau. It was the time of year officers put in for possible assignments in the new year, what was called the wish list.

"What are you putting in for?" she asked.

Nothing. Hadn't thought about it.

She liked Koz; she was one of the few who could get away with calling him Brian, thought he was a great cop. A hothead, impolitic, but a cop through and through. When they'd worked together in the past, he'd always treated her with respect, none of the subtle sexist shit other guys would think they were getting away with.

She knew Koz's reputation, had gone to her boss, Captain Tony Wickersham, asked him what he thought. She needed a detective on afternoons, she didn't care about Koz's beef, Koz was probably right anyway, she'd like to give him a shot. Wickersham told her to go for it, he hated to see Koz just putting in his time, punching the clock.

She asked Koz if he was interested in a new position, a spot they were creating in the detective bureau, working afternoons, alone, no partner. He'd be working the streets, out of the light of day, out of the sight of commanding officers.

Like offering a profile of a big buck to a bow hunter up a tree.

"That put a hop in my step. Someone wanted me," he said.

He put in for it, she pulled a string or two, and starting in January, the new job was his.

Six weeks later, it was Valentine's Day, and potluck.

A PAIR OF WHAT?

As Hughes was listening to Grant's one-hour tale, Lieutenant Darga, a twenty-year veteran of the department, was taking a call from a woman identifying herself as a sergeant at the state police headquarters in Lansing. She wasn't calling in an official capacity, but as a friend of a woman named Alicia Standerfer, sister of a missing woman by the name of Tara Grant. Supposedly missing five days, husband just now getting around to doing anything.

Darga is slender, cheerful, big smile, eager laugh, warm, not a bit of reserve, somehow not what one might expect from the head of the detective bureau for one of the most populous counties in Michigan.

She's local, grew up in Clinton Township just down the road from the sheriff's department, a jock who played softball, volleyball, and basketball at Clintondale High School, then went to Wayne State University on a scholarship to play softball, a sport she still plays regularly, still holding down left field. There are no cops in her family, she hadn't envisioned a career as a cop growing up, but she took a class in criminal justice as an elective, fell in love with it, and knew instinctively it was what she'd been meant to do.

After graduating from Wayne State in 1985, she took a job as a corrections officer in the jail, did that more than three years before being promoted to traffic cop. "I wasn't very good at that," she says. A soft touch for a story or an excuse, "I let too many people get out of traffic tickets."

She put in for evidence technician, an interesting job, not many dull days, worked the auto theft unit, and made detective in 1997. She got promoted to lieutenant in 2002, in charge of something called uniformed services. She was in charge of the road patrols and responsible for vehicles and cars and bored out of her mind. Always in the office, attending to details, a bureaucrat.

"I absolutely hated it. I had become an evidence tech so I'd always be in the mix, and now I was doing this," she said. "I'd go home and tell my husband, 'I'm not a cop anymore.'"

At the end of the year, she put on her wish list that she wanted to be detective lieutenant running the DB. Her wish came true. "This was always my dream job," she said.

The trooper from Lansing told Darga that according to Alicia, Tara's husband, Stephen, was planning to come in and file a missing persons report on his wife. "He's probably there right now," she said. According to Alicia, no way would her sister leave her kids, not answer her cell phone, not show up for work. Would never happen. Something wasn't right.

When Darga got off the phone, she stuck her head out of her office. Wickersham was standing there, his boss, Captain Rick Kalm, the chief of staff, was, too. "Hey, get in here. You guys gotta hear this," said Darga. She repeated what the state cop had said, the kind of story no detective is going shrug off. Her bosses agreed it merited major and immediate attention.

When Grant was done and Hughes had had time to finish his report, she called him in and asked him what he thought. He gave her his take on Grant's peculiarities and what he had had to say. Told her it was interesting Grant had a scratch on his nose. Darga didn't see a mention of the scratch in Hughes's report, told him to go back and put it in.

Most missing persons reports don't amount to anything. The person's got a reason to be gone, either comes back or stays gone, no foul play involved. Cops generally don't take them too seriously. With this case, they'd make an exception. Give it the highest priority. At 1:30 P.M., Darga told Koz and Sergeant Pam McLean to come into her office, filled them in, and told them she was assigning it to the two of them to co-manage.

She knew that Koz, from his years working narcotics, was street-savvy, a reader of people, a detector of bullshit. And a big tough-ass hombre who'd have the six-foot Grant feeling a little smaller than normal. McLean and Darga both had reputations as methodical, hard to rattle, hyperintelligent and organized. They had a lot in common and got along well. They even went to the same high school, McLean a freshman when Darga was a senior, and McLean had been a jock, too, playing softball and volleyball. McLean, at thirty-nine a sixteen-year veteran of the department, was also a good reader of people, couldn't be steamrolled, and it wouldn't hurt to have a woman with two young kids working a case about a young mom accused of leaving hers.

McLean is short, bubbly, looks girlish and younger than she is, more like a third-grade teacher than a veteran homicide cop. The daughter of an engineer at Cadillac and a medical assistant at Henry Ford Hospital, she'd planned on being an attorney. She took a criminal justice class in college, got hooked on a different part of the law instead, and was hired as a corrections officer at the county jail in 1991. She later made a name for herself working undercover—"I was twenty-eight and looked eighteen; I could always buy drugs, it was so easy it was disgusting," she explains—before making detective.

McLean had a bigger current caseload than Koz, including a double homicide, but Darga told her to put this at the top of her to-do list.

They divided up a list of people to call: Tara's family, her boss, her coworkers to start. Limo companies with contracts with the airport. Other taxi services. Darga called Alicia Standerfer's husband, Erik, to get a direct feel for how the family was taking this. Erik was emphatic. His sister-in-law under no circumstances would ever disappear for five days. Yes, she traveled a lot, but she kept in daily touch with those in her family. She would never stop answering her cell, she would never leave her kids wondering where their mother was, she was a dedicated executive who would *never* not show up for work.

He sold Darga. She told McLean and Koz to get out to the Grant house as soon as they could, today. "Look him in the eyes, see what he says, see what you think," she said.

Koz and McLean went over Hughes's report. First thing that struck Koz as peculiar? The word "au pair," not a noun he'd run into in his circles. He thought it was a typo, should have been "a pair." *A pair of what?* he thought.

At 4 P.M., Hughes finished a supplemental report and gave it to Kozlowski. The supplemental report contained more detail than the first report, primarily the scratch on his nose. "I noticed a red scratch on the bridge of Stephen's nose on the right side," Hughes wrote. "I asked Stephen did he get into a fight (physical alteration) with Tara on the night she left. Stephen stated no."

Hughes wrote that Grant told him he'd told Tara during their argument that the kids would be disappointed if she went right back to Puerto Rico, but also told him his two kids wouldn't miss their mother because he was the one who was involved in their soccer. And that he wasn't sure, at this point, if he even wanted Tara back.

The report said Grant told Hughes that while members of his immediate family thought Tara was having an affair with her boss, Lou, he didn't. He said he had called Tara's sister in Ohio to see if she had heard anything, that he'd told the sister that he was worried, that he'd even regard it as good news if he found out Tara was in a motel somewhere with a boyfriend.

The supplemental report ended with a line that caught Kozlowski's eye: "Stephen further stated that he owns a hand-gun."

Though the police would be extraordinarily busy for weeks on the case, filing reports daily, Koz made sure the rest of the reports, following Hughes's supplemental missing persons report, were kept out of the department's new computer system. From that system, any cop could access any report, and this case had all the makings of a big case, lots of media, so the last thing he wanted was someone leaking news. He put a lid on news getting out, at least to the extent he could. The various cops involved in aspects of the case would enter their reports into the computer system later. Weeks later, as it turned out.

Koz had worked missing persons cases and homicides. He was confident in his skills, cocky. He could get people to talk, he was persistent, he liked to think he could go at problems from different angles—"think outside the box," he'd say—to get what he wanted.

He called Grant. Voice warm and friendly, no cop edge to it, he told Grant he was on the case and wanted to come out and meet him. "I wanted to be his friend," he'd explain of his approach, meaning he wanted Grant to perceive him as friendly, not a threat, maybe not as smart as him, either. Think Columbo on steroids. "I wanted to be seen as on his side. It was like buying dope from a guy."

Koz called Lou Troendle. There'd been no plans for Tara to return early, on Sunday, he said. He'd worked with Tara for ten years, knew her, knew her family, said it was impossible to believe she'd take off on her own. Those ten years? She hadn't missed a day of work the whole time. He was, he said, very worried.

Washington Group's security chief, Joe Herrity, had checked out Tara's company cell phone records, her e-mail, the company credit card. No activity on anything since February 9.

Alicia Standerfer told them that Grant had called her at home the night before. She wasn't in, he'd left a message: "Can you call me when you get a minute? It's no big deal."

No big deal? Like, hey, Alicia, I had a peanut butter and jelly sandwich, and oh, by the way, Tara's been missing for four days. Talk to you later.

Alicia also told them that she had talked to her sister the night she went missing. Tara had called her from the Newark airport during her weather delay and they'd talked for forty minutes. Had Tara mentioned anything about her change of plans, returning to San Juan on Sunday instead of Monday? No, on the contrary, she had said she was going back to the island Monday. She was sure of it, could remember it distinctly.

They'd called neighbors and friends, too. No one had seen her, or heard from her.

In the midst of their calls, Koz got one of his own, about 3 P.M. It was Grant, wanting to know how the investigation was going. *Firing up harder and quicker than you can imagine,* thought Koz, keeping it to himself. Oh, getting started, he said. Be all right if my partner and I stop by for a follow-up tonight?

Sure, said Grant.

Next, Koz asked Sergeant Jeff Budzynowski, one of his fellow SWAT team partners and a member of a multiteam task force—"a manhunter," in Koz's words—to sit on Grant's house, see if he took anything in or out of the house, see who else might be coming and going.

An hour before Koz and Sergeant Pam McLean went out to Grant's house, Koz called Bud to see what, if anything, Grant had been up to.

"Shoveling the walk."

Had Grant spotted him?

"No."

Koz told him to pull the unmarked car closer to Grant's

house, make himself conspicuous. It was one of those un-marked cop cars that scream "Cop," a two-door black Ford Taurus with a big antenna and the cheapest wheel covers you could buy. Rattle Grant's cage. A version of good cop, bad cop. Koz'd come over and be soft and friendly, Bud having already played bad cop on stakeout, staring at the house.

At five or so, Koz and McLean headed out. Grant let them in, introduced them to the kids and Verena. First thing Grant said, once introductions were out of the way, was, "Do you have a guy on my house?"

Sure, Koz told him. Can't be too careful, he told him. You never know what might have happened to Tara, or what the motive was. They wanted to make sure no one was casing his house.

First question from Koz was, what's an au pair? Putting Grant at ease by telling him that at first he'd wondered what there was a pair of. Got a laugh, and an explanation. Verena, nice German girl, here to help with the kids, what with all his wife's travel and work. Arranged by an agency.

McLean thought it odd Grant was already drinking a beer, some brand she'd never heard of, Grant being a fan of expensive microbrews. A mom herself, she took it as a nega-tive that the kids were eating dinner by themselves, pizza at a kitchen counter instead of a real dinner with dad at a din-ner table.

While Koz talked to Grant in the kitchen, McLean talked to Verena, subtly guiding her away from Grant, ending up in the living room. The au pair was clearly nervous. Leery of eye contact, said she had plans, needed to get going soon.

McLean had her recount the events of February 9, her night of partying, then coming home to find Grant aban-doned. McLean had to work to keep the conversation going. Several times, Verena said it was time for her to get going.

She told McLean she thought it really unusual that Tara would have left her kids like that, and that she thought it odd that Tara would have called a service to take her to the air-port, that she always drove herself.

No kidding, thought McLean, remembering what Grant had told Hughes about his wife's travel habits.

After ten minutes, Verena insisted she really did have to go.

Lindsey and Ian were watching TV. McLean started talking to Lindsey, who offered to take her on a tour of the house. There was a family room, kitchen, laundry room, living room, library, and bathroom on the first floor, four bedrooms and a bath upstairs, a fancy wine cellar in the basement with a wooden and glass door with a lock. Must be some good stuff in there, you keep it locked up. Lindsey was engaging and charming, with a quick wit. "Hilarious," a charmed McLean would later describe her. Lindsey drew her a picture of a flower and gave it to her as a present.

"Mom's at work in another country," she said. But she'd be back home, soon. Said it cheerfully. One thing that struck McLean as odd? There weren't any family photos on display anywhere in the house, not of just the kids, not of just the parents, not of the four of them. Nothing. Struck McLean as particularly odd, maybe because her cubicle in the detectives' bureau was plastered with pictures of her grown son and her two young kids.

Meanwhile, Grant had taken Koz into the den. Everything was neat, the desk perfectly organized, nothing out of place. Nothing out of place with Grant, either. Stylish, expensive-looking haircut, clothes that fit just so. *Guy looks like the cover of* Men's Health, Koz thought, thinking of the contrast between the way Grant looked and the way he himself looked, a beefy cop, brush cut, wearing a shirt and tie but not the kind of guy or look that anyone would describe as stylish.

Grant was nervous, his eyes bouncing around, difficulty keeping eye contact, words coming out rushed, body stiff. Who wouldn't be nervous in his shoes, though, wife missing, cops at the door? But cops being cops, Koz took the nervousness for guilt. Guilt, and guilty until proven innocent.

Tara, Grant said, had decided to pack a bigger suitcase as she prepared to walk out that Friday night. Just before she left, Grant heard her say "Just a minute" on her cell phone, and a minute or two later did in fact walk out. Grant saw a black sedan, looked like maybe a Cadillac DTS. Koz asked if he could see the bedroom, get a feel for her packing, about to take off, see how it felt.

There was a computer in the bedroom. Grant, being helpful, logged on to their joint credit card account with Chase, then their checking account with LaSalle Bank. Nothing since the ninth. She wasn't using her credit card or her ATM card.

They walked out to the garage. There were two spiral notebooks and a blue file folder in the rear seat of Tara's Isuzu. Koz picked them up and examined them. One, marked "to-do," was a list of stuff for her to do at work. He asked Grant if he could take them. What was he going to say? No? Sure, he said.

Koz's mind was getting made up, now. She got mad and headed back to work early and left her work stuff in her car? Her to-do list?

Koz didn't make a point of it, but took in the entire garage, trying to fix it in his memory, getting a mental image of what was where.

Koz asked him about the scratch on his nose. A metal shaving at work got caught under his safety goggles, he said. He showed Koz a scratch on his hand, too, being helpful. And, just for good measure, he showed Koz a bruise and a scratch on his leg. That the way a guilty man would act? Helpful? Friendly? Yep, thought Koz. He wasn't in a line of work where the benefit of the doubt was very helpful.

Time to hit Grant with something out of the blue. Had either he or his wife been screwing around?

He'd been faithful, said Grant. Tara had strayed, but the affair was over. She was faithful, now, too.

They went back in the house. McLean was waiting for them and asked if she could take a closer look in the bedroom. There, she found a bunch of greeting cards in a drawer, an assortment of as-yet-unsigned cards for her kids that were for a variety of occasions, ready to be filled out when needed. Finding them touched McLean, made her sad. This wasn't a mom who would just take off. And if she had left, why not leave a card for the kids, say she was sorry, that she loved them? Instead of telling her husband it would be his job to tell the kids why she wasn't there when they woke up in the morning?

McLean also found in a nightstand next to the bed several envelopes filled with cash. Didn't count it, looked like a lot, at least a thousand dollars, she'd guess. They paid for everything with cash, said Grant, so they liked to have plenty around. Saying it fast, words spitting out, faster than he'd been talking before. Nervous.

She also found a loaded CZ75 9-millimeter Ruger with two loaded magazines in a black case, a roll of duct tape—interesting find in a bedroom whose occupant has gone missing; Grant said he'd set it down there a while back and had forgot to put it away—and a red photo journal. When she opened it up, it was filled with photos of the au pair and her friends. It was Verena's, Grant acknowledged. The unasked question McLean left hanging: in his and Tara's bedroom?

Something she didn't find made her suspicious, too. Tara had supposedly packed a bigger bag for her trip back to Puerto Rico. But her closet, a double-door walk-in that had a closet organizer to fit in all her business suits, regular clothes and shoes, was packed. There weren't any gaps you'd expect to see if someone in a hurry had reached in and grabbed some clothes.

There was a brownish stain on the floor by the bathroom. Tara's hair dye, said Grant. She'd spilled some recently and they couldn't get all of it out.

They went downstairs, got their coats on. Koz asked Grant if he'd come back in to headquarters tomorrow, they'd probably have some follow-up questions for him.

"You don't think I did something to my wife, do you?" he blurted out.

"If we thought you were involved with the disappearance

of your wife, we'd take you to jail right now," said Koz. He had him pegged as a wife killer, wasn't going to lose any sleep bullshitting him.

Grant visibly relaxed.

Oh yeah, tagging it on as an afterthought, just as Grant might have thought he was off the hook, he let him know he wasn't: can you take a lie detector test tomorrow, too? Just routine.

"Sure, no problem," said Grant. "What time?"

"Eleven," said Koz. He'd already checked, it was the first time available in the morning.

And another "oh yeah": "Do you mind if we send out an evidence technician tonight? We'd like to take some quick pictures."

"Yeah, sure," said Grant.

And then Grant started sobbing, great racking heaves, tears pouring out. He sobbed and he sobbed and the detectives said good night and left him to his dismay.

McLean and Koz looked at each other on the way down the driveway to their cars—she had started early and was going home, he was working an afternoon shift and was headed back to the office. "He did it," she said.

"We just don't know how," he answered. "Or where she is."

Back at the shop, Koz told evidence technician Adnan Durrani to grab a digital camera and go to Grant's, take a shot of the scratch on his nose, the scratch on his hand, and the bruise on his leg. Grant told him how he got the scratches, said he didn't know how he got the bruise. Back at headquarters, Durrani started what was called an ET file, for evidence tech, and put the photo CD inside it. Others would join it soon.

Koz went through Tara's notebooks. One was filled with letters she'd written as part of a training exercise she'd taken part in at a self-improvement seminar in Phoenix four months earlier. One was to her parents, one to her sister, and one to Stephen.

The one to Stephen caught his eye, in particular. She apologized for not getting over an old boyfriend named Pete and wrote that she needed to get over Pete so she could get whole with Stephen.

Was she having an affair? Had the notebooks revealed a motive?

LAWYERING UP

Thursday, the sheriff's department made up a standard missing persons flyer. It had a photo of Tara smiling straight at the camera—Grant had left it with police when he'd come in the day before—a physical description, time and place last seen.

Sheriff Mark Hackel asked those involved in the case so far what they thought. Did he do it? Most were sure Grant had killed her. A few had doubts. Sure, he looks good for it, but you never know, Tara may very well show up, having been driven to distraction by her husband to just get the hell out and stay away a while. The ones who were sure he did it were sure they knew why: no mother would just up and leave her kids. If she disappeared, foul play had to be at the heart of it.

Hackel knew the fallacy of that premise. He had lived its contradiction. When he was in the seventh grade, his parents divorced and it was his mom who moved out, leaving the children behind, leaving his father to raise them. It was a dominant fact of his life. Let others assume that no mother would leave her kids willingly; he wasn't going to manage this case on false assumptions.

If Grant's family had, in fact, now at its core a hole left by a mother who had fled, then the sheriff and Grant shared at least two things in their lives. The other? Stony Creek Metropark, the sprawling park that abutted the Grant home. Tara and Stephen had spent many hours there, biking and running those trails. Hackel put in long hours on the job, and he put in long hours at Stony Creek, too. He ran there, he mountain-biked there, he kayaked there.

He would soon know those trails and what bordered them better than he ever suspected.

Thursday morning, the sheriff's department got a surprise fax. It was from a prominent attorney Hackel and his staff knew very well, David Griem, pronounced "grim," as in "reaper." What do you know? Grant had lawyered up. Koz wanted to rattle his cage? Consider it rattled.

The fax read:

> Because of the tone of your February 14, 2007 interrogation of Mr. Grant at his home, it is my humble opinion that it is necessary for me to provide a buffer between your department and Mr. Grant.
> Just as Mr. Grant answered all of your questions, last night, he will continue to answer all of your questions in the future. I believe it is necessary, however, so there are no misunderstandings, that all of your future questions be submitted in writing, which will, in turn, be immediately answered in writing.
> David Griem

Two words stood out to Hackel—"interrogation" and "humble," Interrogation? Koz and McLean were fully capable of doing an interrogation. What Grant had had was a little talking-to. And there was nothing humble about the good counselor.

That clinched it for Koz and McLean. He did it. He murdered his wife. They're trying to find the guy's missing wife, the one he's sobbing over, and less than twenty-four hours after he asks the police to find her, he's got one of the highest paid attorneys in a town of highly paid attorneys telling them they can't talk to him in person?

The fax was a surprise. And that it was from Griem helped clinch it for him. Okay, I get it, he thought, you wanna make sure the cops don't steamroll you, run over your civil rights, fine, any half-assed low-end-of-the pay-scale attorney can handle that in his sleep.

But Griem? Dude doesn't start punching in buttons on the fax machine till he's got a retainer of $10,000 minimum, thought Koz, and then expressed it out loud. You're writing a big check for Griem at this point, something's up. Koz's hackles were too.

Griem was a heavyweight in Detroit legal circles. He had been the former chief trial attorney for the Macomb County Prosecutor's Office; he had also once headed up the U.S. Attorney's drug-enforcement team in southeastern Michigan and he had been city attorney for the large Detroit suburb of Warren.

He'd traded in the white hat—a metaphor widely used by relatively underpaid prosecutors for what they do, as in "I'm a career prosecutor, I love wearing the white hat"—for the black hat and high remuneration of high-profile criminal defense. He was widely respected for his skills, with a reputation as a defense attorney that matched the one he'd built up as a prosecutor. Unlike many high-profile defense attorneys—his clients included white-collar criminals, drug dealers, and well-known figures in organized crime—he wasn't particularly flamboyant, though he cut a certain figure with his longish silver hair and thick droopy mustache.

Griem was good with the press, too, and this was shaping up as a case that might require that skill, as well. He was a frequent commentator on legal matters for local TV and radio and knew all the on-air talent and their producers. And he'd been a recurring talking head for Court TV and Geraldo Rivera.

* * *

What happened was, Grant read Koz and McLean very clearly. They weren't buying what he was selling, and that being the case, he needed advice. He ruminated about it a little bit after they left, then called an attorney friend in Lansing, Tom Munley, for some advice. Grant told him his wife had gone missing, the cops for some reason seemed hostile to him. What should he do?

"You'll need to submit to the polygraph," said Munley.

"Okay," said Grant.

"I'll put you in touch with someone."

That someone was Griem. He had a habit, unusual for criminal defense attorneys, in a case like this of requiring his clients to take a polygraph first. Whether to avoid representing murderers, or just to cut through the bullshit and know what he was dealing with when he did represent them, no one was quite sure.

Thursday morning, Griem called Grant, told him to come see him immediately. Come straight to the office. Don't talk to any cops if they want to talk to you. Come right in.

"I just finished a trial. You're lucky," he said. In front of Grant, he typed up his note to Hackel and faxed it, started earning his money.

On the way home from Griem's, about one, Grant called Verena. She was in the garage, started crying. "These two policemen just scared me. They said they're looking for you." They were parked at the end of the street, she said, by the new bus stop. They'd stopped her when she drove into the subdivision, wanted to know where he was.

"Well, they know where I was. I was at the attorney's office," he said.

He called Griem. Griem told him they didn't have probable cause to arrest him but might be looking to execute a search warrant. Don't let them do it in front of the kids, he said. Searches can get ugly. Make sure you get the kids out of the house first. Hold off going home now, until you can figure someplace to bring Ian and Lindsey.

Grant headed to his father's shop. He hung out there a while, talked to his sister on the phone, decided to head home.

Just starting on his way, a few minutes after two, at the corner of Elizabeth and Groesbeck, a block from the sheriff's department, Grant made a turn, heard a siren, looked up, saw flashers in his rearview mirror and pulled over. Griem wanted to send a message? They were sending one back. They'd had an undercover cop on Grant since he left his house in the morning, to see where he went, what he was up to. The plan was, at some point, to pull him over, bring him in. Koz knew Grant had a warrant out for his arrest for an unpaid traffic ticket in nearby Rochester, and figured he'd rattle Grant's cage some more, and let Griem know he didn't have to depend on the written word to interact with his client.

So, they had the tail behind him, a patrol car parked up the road ahead of him. The tail called the patrol car, said he was handing him off, and as Grant passed the patrol car, it swung in behind him. Patrolman told Grant he'd made the turn without signaling. Maybe he did. Pretty convenient, considering they were going to take him in anyway, and had chosen that spot to start it rolling.

What was interesting, really interesting, was that Grant had gone to some trouble and a lot of expense, $900, the day before he reported Tara missing to pay off twelve unpaid parking tickets and two unpaid traffic tickets in several suburban cities. Which begged the question, why had he left one traffic ticket unpaid, and one warrant still in place? It wasn't that he had forgotten about the one he had mentioned to Hughes. The only explanation seemed to be that he wanted to be able to admit it when he reported Tara missing, to show how forthcoming he was, but wanted to clear up most of his record so as not to invite arrest.

In 1989, still a teenager, Grant had been arrested for reckless driving—doing seventy in a forty-five—and carrying a concealed Colt pistol without a permit. And his license was suspended five times from 2002–2005 for unpaid moving violations.

"I know why you're pulling me over," Grant said, pissed. "It's because of my wife." Two other cop cars pulled up as the first officer was back in his car running Grant's license number through the computer, just for show. What do you know? Gotta take this guy in.

A search of the car next was routine. What it found wasn't: one envelope with $1,145 in cash, another with $1,912.

Grant was arrested, cuffed, and taken to the jail, where he spent six hours before all the paperwork was processed, at freeze-frame pace, and he was able to post bail. One of the key components to the media frenzy that was slow to start but would soon build in a hurry was Grant's booking photo. It would become the iconic image of the case, a headshot of him staring straight at the camera, his eyes pop-eyed almost in 3-D at the viewer, a caricature of a deer caught in the headlights, except it was no caricature.

The picture would draw two universal responses: that guy's crazy, he did it. It wasn't his fault that's the way he looked, but people inferred fault nonetheless.

Griem went nuts. Called Hackel in a lather. Hackel played it cool. What were his deputies supposed to do? They knew Grant had a suspended license. They saw him driving down the street. You can't ask police officers to ignore scofflaws. Can you? Had nothing to do with his wife. Just the law being upheld.

In the following days, when the case would come to dominate local news like nothing in recent memory, Griem would rail to the media about the arrest. "Three police cars surrounded his car as he was driving home and arrested him over an unpaid ticket for driving fifty-five miles per hour in a forty-five-mile-per-hour zone," he would say. "Then they incarcerated him for six and a half hours and questioned him. Those are Neanderthal tactics and demonstrated bad faith on the part of the police."

Koz would swear later the only questioning happened when he stopped by Grant's cell, acting like it was just a coincidence Grant was there. "Hi," he said. "What's happenin' with ya?"

Should have put it in writing.

"I was just being a dick," said Koz later, smiling at the memory.

And in the ensuing days, Grant would tell the *Detroit News*: "I get why they stopped me. They thought I was going to be a little girl and go down there and cry and confess all my sins. But there's no sins, though. I'm a big boy, and I can take care of myself."

After Grant was released, Hackel got a call from Grant's brother-in-law, Chris Utykanski. He'd been enlisted by Grant's older sister, Kelly, to call Hackel, ask him to ease off. Chris Utykanski? Chris Utykanski? Why does that name ring a bell? Jeez! It hit him. Hackel went to high school with a Chris Utykanski. Good guy, quiet, they weren't quite friends but they were friendly. Chris'd tell people over the years, when Hackel was on TV or in the papers, hey, I went to high school with that guy. Now, Kelly thought Chris—he was her fourth husband—might help.

"Chris was tasked with asking me to go easy," said Hackel later.

Hackel, always smooth, was friendly with Chris, asked how he was doing. He made no promises, but Chris probably got off the phone thinking he'd made headway.

The police asked Grant to submit to a polygraph, but Griem would eventually turn them down. Defense attorneys know better than that, sure there is a built-in bias by cops to interpret results to a client's disadvantage. Amazing, though, how many ex-cops do polygraphs as a business or on the side, and how often they seem to see things in a different light once they're getting paid by the defense.

Griem had scheduled a polygraph for Grant for Friday, February 16, with a former Oakland County sheriff's deputy he often used. But Grant canceled it, said something had come up with the kids.

"You're throwing your life away," said Griem.

So Grant rescheduled it, took it, paid $600 to answer a few questions. Nice work if you can get it. The result? Griem and Grant weren't saying.

BORN TO BE SHERIFF? NO

Mark Hackel is boyish-looking, looks more like a new recruit than the top link in the chain of command. He is trim, a long-distance runner who has qualified for and run the fabled Boston Marathon, and he's a mountain biker and avid kayaker, as well.

For many years he played in area softball leagues, a nut for softball, playing in city recreation department leagues, church leagues, cop leagues, tournaments, pickup games, managing some teams. He still plays softball, filling in on an emergency basis when needed, but no longer has the time for a full-time commitment. He played soccer, too, both in indoor and outdoor leagues.

Hackel is the son of the popular longtime Macomb County sheriff William Hackel, whose career ended in disgrace and dispute, and five years in prison. William Hackel was sheriff from 1977 to 2000, resigning after he was charged with third-degree sexual assault. He'd been at a conference of the Michigan Sheriffs' Association at the Soaring Eagle Casino and Resort, one of the state's growing and thriving collection of Native American casinos in the midstate city of Mt. Pleasant.

A twenty-six-year-old woman took him up on his offer to come to his room, and they had sex. Later, she claimed he had forced himself on her. He said the sex was consensual. The jury agreed with her, a verdict that was highly controversial. Irony of ironies? It was Griem who handled the unsuccessful appeal of William Hackel's rape conviction.

Hackel's undersheriff and close friend, Ronald Tuscany, was selected by a three-person panel to replace him until the term ended that fall. In November 2000, Mark Hackel, then an inspector, beat out seven rivals to win his father's former seat. He's been a popular, effective sheriff, modernizing the department, starting a cyber unit to investigate computer crimes, installing computerized systems for taking and filing reports, insisting his deputies respond to citizens' e-mails.

The department has a Web site. They all do these days, but his department's is actually interesting, not just some boring static thing no one would spend more than ten minutes on unless they were desperate for a phone number they couldn't find elsewhere. "Welcome to your Web site" is Hackel's message to visitors. It's got a virtual tour of the jail, in case you're interested in your loved one's temporary new home; there's a kid's page and safety tips; residents going out of town can fill in a request to have deputies keep an eye on their houses; there are even links to local newspapers. Links to local newspapers? Legions of dead old cops are spinning in their graves at that one.

His dad killed the K-9 unit. Hackel brought it back. He brought in old folks to serve as volunteer greeters at the jail, take the edge off walking in there the first time to visit someone. And so forth.

Old-school policing was more about brawn. Today, he says, "It's more about service, and service is harder." His officers and the reporters who cover the department can call him twenty-four hours a day. At night, the phone is next to his bed. "I have to be available, and flexible," he says. Another word he uses frequently: "accountable."

Signs scattered around headquarters proclaim in big letters: DETERMINED TO KEEP YOUR TRUST. WORKING TO KEEP YOU SAFE. Hackel says it's no mere slogan, it's his personal mission statement. It might sound hackneyed, but when he repeats the slogan out loud, it comes out with passion that seems real, not rote.

Old-school cops bemoaned the U.S. Supreme Court decision that made *Miranda* the law of the land, requiring defendants to be warned of their rights and offered legal assistance. Beating on a suspect with a phone book served them well. Hackel speaks passionately about Sixth Amendment rights. How it is his duty to make sure they are protected, that his staff protects them, too. He would bristle, as the Grant investigation proceeded, at accusations that they were moving too slowly on Grant. It wasn't that they were indecisive, or weren't making progress on the case, or that he thought Grant might not have done anything wrong. It was that no matter what Grant had done, he had rights, too. You start abusing one person's rights, where does that slope take you?

A modern cop? He agreed as the investigation proceeded with Prosecutor Eric Smith's periodic pronouncements that they didn't have probable cause to search Grant's home, no matter how much the troops chafed at not being let loose to have a go at it. In due time.

You're just as likely to find him in a dark suit and crisp—*crisp*—white shirt as you are to find him in uniform. He's big on community outreach. It's his voice you get when you call the department's general information number, a blend of good policing and good politics. Nobody refers to him as Hackel's kid anymore. *He's* Hackel.

Although Hackel followed in his father's footsteps and has worked in the sheriff's department since he took a job in dispatch at eighteen in 1980, he didn't grow up wanting to be a cop. He wanted to be a businessman, maybe own his own franchise of some sort. He used to spend a lot of time hanging out at the local 7-Eleven in the Detroit suburb of Sterling Heights when he was a boy and thought it would be a pretty cool way to make a living, owning a store, meeting and greeting people all day.

As a kid, he was always making money. He cut lawns, he

had a paper route, he fished golf balls out of a drainage ditch at Maple Lanes golf course and sold them back to the golfers. He opened up his own bank account at fifteen.

He only took the dispatcher's job on the midnight shift for the $7 an hour it paid and for the flexibility it gave him to take some college classes during the day. "I never thought of it as a career," he says.

A call he took early in the morning on a hot summer night in 1981 changed everything. Changed his life. He'd never taken a call like that. Guy on the other end: "My neighbor says someone just killed his wife."

Hackel can hear sobbing in the background. Takes down the information. Detectives race to the scene, a big, expensive new house in a nearby township. The crying guy was a cabinetmaker named Robert Deroo. He's still crying. It's his house. Cops find the first body in an upstairs bedroom, a seventeen-month-old little girl named Jessica, dead in her crib, suffocated.

Second body is in the next bedroom, five-year-old Nathaniel, on the bed, peaceful in his blue pajamas except he isn't breathing.

In the master bedroom, Deborah Deroo, a twenty-five-year-old, is spread-eagled on the bed, nightgown up around her neck, which is already blue from bruising. There's a can of Mace next to her on the bed. There's a boy next to her, too, three-year-old Nicholas. His neck is blue, too, and he's motionless, but he's alive.

Cops suspect the husband, of course. They always suspect the husband, doesn't matter how much crying they do on the phone or at the scene. Had good reason to suspect him, too. Turns out the wife's been screwing one of the neighbors. And another neighbor says he heard a child screaming over and over earlier in the night: "Daddy, don't do it!"

For some reason, the prosecutor doesn't think he has enough to bring charges. The case remains open, but nothing happens for more than two years. The prosecutor decides he's not going to just let it go, charges him, takes him to trial. To nearly everyone's surprise, it takes the jury only four hours to acquit him.

Deroo then wins a court battle with Deborah's parents and gets custody of Nicholas.

The outcome pissed Hackel off. Motivated him, too. He'd started as a dispatcher in 1981 just to make a buck. By the end of the trial in 1983, "I realized it was an important job," he said, meaning being a cop. Let someone else serve up the Slurpees.

After he got an associate's degree in liberal arts from Macomb County Community College, Hackel took the deputy's test with the sheriff's department. He aced it, so the department sent him to the police academy, where he finished first in his class. He scored highest on the tests for physical fitness, too.

Deputies were hired in order of their class position. He graduated on December 3, 1983, his last day as a dispatcher. The next day, he was on the road in a patrol car, a uniformed deputy at twenty-two. At the next police academy class, he was an instructor. To his surprise, officials asked him to teach a course in self-defense and physical fitness. He's taught at the academy off and on since.

Hackel enrolled at Wayne State University in Detroit and got his bachelor's in criminal justice in 1991, taking seven years to get his degree, working more than forty hours a week, picking up classes when he could, approaching it the way he does the 26.2 miles of the marathon, one step at a time. Don't worry about outcome, just continue the process.

He got his master's degree in public administration in 1996.

Today, he is an adjunct professor at both Macomb College and Wayne State University in criminal justice.

On January 1, 2001, Hackel, having won election in November, took office as sheriff, at age thirty-eight. He could have easily passed for twenty-eight. Then, and now, he was as trim as the day he got out of the academy, thanks to his passion and commitment for running. That election was likely a tribute to the public's still high regard for his father. He easily won landslide reelections in 2004 and 2008. Those were tributes to him.

Hackel had been captain of the Sterling Heights High School wrestling team his senior year, in 1980. As a senior, he was first team all-conference and all-county. "It was the first time I had my name in the paper," he says. He was skilled, but more than that, he was a tenacious trainer. He won by dominating his matches in the third and final period, and he did that by always being in better shape than his foe.

And that meant pounding the roads, always by himself. The cross-country coach would see him out on the roads and kept trying to recruit him for that team, too, but Mark loved the solitary joys of running alone, not having to make small talk, getting into that Zen place where your mind and body are on autopilot and the endorphins have kicked in. It would have marred its perfection to be doing it as part of a team. He was greedy about wanting to keep his running *his*.

He has run five marathons, with a best time of three hours and two minutes at the *Detroit Free Press* marathon. He missed his target of breaking three hours, so close to, yet so far from, that magic number for marathon runners, but it qualified him to run the 101st Boston Marathon in 1997.

Hackel couldn't have been blamed for wondering, when the Grant case broke on February 14, why me? He likes the limelight. He is extremely media savvy, and a born politician if not a born cop; he's been known during a 5K race to ask a friend running at his side to switch positions with him because he's spotted a TV crew at the side of the course ahead, and he wants the cameraman to get an unimpeded shot of him. But now? At this time? He didn't need the aggravation and stress this case had all the potential of blowing up into.

Stress? Hackel had had his fill of it earlier in the month.

He was coming off the saddest case of his career, one that literally kept him awake at night, so disturbingly heart-wrenching it had been. Same damn month, one following right after another.

It was February 4, Super Bowl Sunday. What could be finer for a sports nut like Hackel than to be at a buddy's annual Super Bowl party, getting ready to watch Peyton Manning and his Indianapolis Colts take on the bad-ass Chicago Bears?

Game started with a jolt, Bears returning the opening kickoff for a touchdown. Hackel's cell phone rang; not one of his buddies, a Bear fan needing to chortle. It was a deputy back at headquarters, low seniority, pulling duty on Super Bowl. There was bad news, more bad news than Hackel ever heard of, not counting terrorists in airplanes.

Jennifer Kukla is thirty-one, a hard thirty-one, raising two kids alone, living in a trailer, trying to pay the bills working at McDonald's up the road. Voices have been talking to her in her head. Telling her bad stuff, stuff it's getting harder to ignore. Telling her to kill her kids. Kill Alexandra, who's eight. Kill Ashley, who's five. Kill them now, and save them from all the pain later.

Sunday, 7:30 A.M., she takes out the butcher knife and comes at the kids. They see the look in her eyes, they know to run. She runs after them. Ashley gets it in the chest, pulls away, gets under the kitchen table. Alexandra's screaming: "Mommy, don't do it." She swirls, slashes Alexandra across the neck, nearly cuts her head off. Turns back to the table, reaches down, drags out Ashley and slices through her neck, too, the floor a lake of blood.

Next it's the family dog and its two pups. She disembowels all three, says later it was to keep them from eating her kids. Then the girls' pet mouse, she takes it from its cage and snaps its neck.

The killing over, she drags her kids into their bedroom and places them, just so, on the bed.

Kukla starts pacing. Eleven hours later, her sister, Lau-

ren Russell, drops by to take Jennifer to dinner. Door's open, trailer's dark, but she can make out her sister, walking in circles in the front room.

Jennifer sees her, comes to the door. I just killed the kids, she says. Lauren runs to her car, to her kids inside, scared for them. She drives off, pulls over a safe distance away, calls 911.

"I think my sister may have harmed her children," she says. "She said she killed them. She said she was going to the deep ends of hell."

Sergeant Lori Misch gets the call, bad day now for her, too. She gets there, Jennifer is sitting on the front steps, smoking a cigarette. Jennifer looks up at her. "I'm waiting for a hearse," she tells Misch. "One made of bones, to take me to hell."

Hackel got to the scene fast as he could. Looked at the mess and the girls in their winter coats lying on the bed, butchered, blood everywhere, up till then toughest thing he'd ever done. Couldn't even be mad at their mom, tortured as she is.

Darga showed up, too. "It was a house of horror. It was like out of a movie. The kids are laying there, the dogs. I saw the mouse last. I saw this little mouse cage and I looked in and the mouse is dead, too!" The capper.

Darga, warm, quick to smile, eager to laugh, all of that, for sure, and a core of solid alloy that might come as a surprise if you think her only smiley, laughy, and warm. The Kukla scene was a nightmare. A bunch of cops helped process it. The department had a debriefing afterward.

It surprised Darga, the reaction of many of her fellow officers. Shaken, not getting over it. "I was shaken," said Darga. Not by the horror-movie scene, not by the blood on the floor, the dogs or the mouse. By her fellow cops. "I was taken aback," she said later. "This is what you signed on for. This is what you do."

And what you do is, you gather the best evidence you

can, you work the scene as hard as you can, you don't fuck up, and if you do all that you're supposed to do, you put people away and you keep them away. That's the benefit to society, and that's why you get paid.

Jennifer's sister came to Kukla's arraignment, there to support her no matter what she had done. Hackel was there, too. Lauren told him there was no money to bury the kids. Hackel had been haunted by their photos, by how adorable the little girls were, how happy their smiles despite what little they'd had in their lives.

"Can I have some photos of the girls?" he asked.

Sure.

He took them to a friend at Warren Bank, they set up an account. At a press conference about the case later, Hackel said he'd answer every question they had but first he wanted their help. He held up the girls' pictures and said there was no money to bury these poor girls. Not yet, but if you'd help me get the word out, we'll bury them properly.

The bank was besieged. Elementary school classes organized fund drives. Old ladies came in with change purses. Little boys came in and broke their piggy banks, literally, on the bank's counter. A week later, they had $40,000. The girls got buried and got nice headstones, and Hackel put in a playscape at their school, Ojibway Elementary, with a big plaque in their honor. There was some money left over which they gave to another charity.

He thought the media went a little crazy, then? No. Tara went missing, and he found out what media crazy really looks like.

He'd find out, too, that the Kukla case and the Grant case would link together in an unimaginable way.

ABOUT THOSE CALLS

The detectives started checking out Grant's story before they went out to his house. And they checked it out harder once they'd been there. A lot of it was routine, and easy. Grant had told them Tara had changed her plans, intended to go back to Puerto Rico a day early; airline records told them she'd done no such thing. She'd kept the same booking, kept the same seat, didn't use it.

Cell phones are a wonderful thing. Ask any cop. Best thing that's happened to detective work since DNA solved its first murder case in England more than twenty years ago. As fast as a computer can multiply two times four, you can get a person's cell history, who they called when and for how long. You can use his or her phone to pinpoint where he or she is in real time. Same way people wonder how they looked stuff up before Google, cops wonder what they did before cell phone towers.

Tara's cell phone records didn't show any calls to anyone she worked with that weekend. Seemed she would have called someone about a change in plans, tell them she'd be back a day early or something. And the records didn't show any calls since.

Grant told them Tara left their home in a black sedan,

after making a call to be picked up. But her records didn't show any calls around the time she would have had to have made that one, much less to any of the services permitted to shuttle passengers to Detroit's Metropolitan Airport. Her last call had been that eighteen-minute call to Grant at 9:47 P.M.

Eventually, they found out that in the last year of weekly travel, she had only used a service once. Every other trip, she drove herself. So much for Grant's assertion that she frequently got to the airport by shuttle.

Credit-card records would normally take a while to access. They'd have needed to petition the court for a search warrant, but Tara only used a company-issued card and the Washington Group was happy to monitor its use: nothing since 9:32 the night she arrived at Metropolitan Airport, when she'd used it to pay to get her car out of the parking deck.

What tales did Grant's cell phone records tell? Sandwiched around the call he got from his wife were four calls to the au pair, starting at 9:08 and ending at 10:32.

There were logical explanations other than murder for all of this. Tara was extremely savvy. If she did want to disappear for a while, sit with a lover on a beach somewhere while she figured out what to do with her life, she'd have likely known using her cell phone or credit card could help trace her. Maybe she had an affluent boyfriend in Puerto Rico, or had met someone in London, and the lover was taking care of all her expenses.

The possible explanations didn't matter, the way Koz looked at it. There was a resonance between this case and his own life. Koz's first wife had been an executive with General Motors. Like Tara Grant, she traveled the world on business. Like Tara, she was wed to her cell phone and her laptop. If she had ever taken off on him, she'd have been easily trackable through phone records and e-mail history.

Tara's phone had gone dead, and so had her computer and her cell phone.

There was one difference between his wife and Tara—Tara had two kids she loved, too.

This is not a woman who took off, Koz thought. *This is a woman who met her demise.*

The timing of calls between Tara and Steve on the day she went missing was interesting. Hardly incriminating in a legal sense, but incriminating to Koz and McLean. They were back and forth on the phone all day. Short calls. You could picture an angry outburst and a hang-up, the hung-up-on person calling back, yelling his or her bit and hanging up, too. Back and forth. That's what Koz and McLean figured. They weren't picturing love-you, can't-wait-till-you-get-home calls.

They wrote on a white board in the detective bureau a log of the calls.

11:00—Steve calls Tara, 1 minute.
11:04—Tara calls Steve, 5 minutes.
11:32—Steve calls Tara, 3 minutes.
12:00—Steve calls Tara, 6 minutes.
12:47—Tara checks voice mail.
13:00—Tara Flight 476 leaves PR.
16:20—Flight arrives Newark.
16:21—Tara checks voice mail.
16:27—Tara calls Steve, 2 minutes.
16:29—Tara checks voice mail.
16:34—Steve calls Tara, 6 minutes.
17:11—Tara calls Steve, 3 minutes.
17:55—Tara calls Alicia, 42 minutes.
18:03—Tara checks voice mail.
18:38—Tara calls Steve, 1 minute.
18:41—Tara calls Steve, 7 minutes.
21:08—Steve calls Verena, 1 minute.
21:10—Tara checks voice mail.
21:10—Tara calls Steve, 1 minute.
21:29—Steve calls Verena, 30 seconds.
21:32—Tara pays parking Metro Airport.

21:32—Steve calls Verena, 4 minutes.

21:44—Steve calls Tara, 1 minute.

21:47—Steve calls Tara, 18 minutes. Last call either to be
answered by or made by Tara's cell.

22:07—Steve calls Verena, 2 seconds.

22:32—Steve calls Verena, 2 minutes.

On Saturday, Steve called Tara's cell six times, without
response. Thanks to the modern miracle of data storage,
Koz and McLean were able to get transcripts. From a jaded-
cop point of view, they indicated an actor covering his ass.
Yet, assuming that Tara had taken off and was still alive and
Stephen was guilty of absolutely nothing, wouldn't his words
be exactly what one would expect?

2:17 A.M.—"Tara, it's Steve. It's after two by now. It's
quarter after two and I just want to know what the fuck's
going on. Um, I think you owe me and your kids at least, at
the very least, um, call me. Um, bye. Uh, just call and let me
know what the hell's going on."

9:29 A.M.—"Hey. It's me. I'm just trying to find out what's
going on this morning. Uh, uh, if you're still leaving today,
if you're leaving tomorrow. Um, what's going on, and if
you're planning on coming by. Just tell me ahead of time
so I can make plans. Make sure the kids are here 'cause they
want to see you. Uh, give me a call. Bye."

11:56 A.M.—"Hey, I get that you're pissed at me. Um, I
just left the house. I have to go to the bank for my dad. Um,
Verena's at the house with the kids. Please at least call your
kids. Um, it's ridiculous, Tara. It's not right. Just call. Please.
So I can talk to you. They didn't get to see you last night.
Please. Bye."

6:03 P.M.—"It's me. It's, um, you need to call us. Just let us
know what's going on. Um, the kids and I would like to talk
to you. Please. I just don't know what the deal is, so call me.
We're here. Um, we're just ordering pizza for dinner, so we'll
be here. I'm just gonna have it delivered, I think. So, call us.
Bye."

11:11 P.M.—"Hey, I get that you don't want to talk to me, but you don't have to hit the ignore button every single time I call. Um, I was simply calling to let you know that you left your glasses here. Um, and if you need me to ship them down there . . . I just need, ah, your FedEx number or whatever the hell you want me to do with this. Um, and I need to know if you need me to go buy that bottle of wine, or if you did it. You said you would, but I don't know if you [did] . . . You owe your kids phone calls. They keep asking. Call. Bye."

Grant called Tara's cell once on Sunday, at 1:43 P.M. "Tara, next time I call you, pick up your phone. Please do not hit ignore. It's bullshit. It's absolute bullshit that you can't call me or your kids. It's bullshit. Pick up your phone or call the house. Call somewhere. Call me. Call my cell. Call the kids. This isn't this bad. I know you're mad. I'm mad. This is not right. Just call me. Bye."

He called her at 7:49 Monday morning. "Hey, it's me, once again. If I don't hear back from you in fifteen minutes, I'm gonna call Randy, get Lou's cell number, and find out what the fuck is going on. This is nonsense, Tara. You owe me a phone call. You owe me to let me know what the fuck is going on between us. Please call."

He called once more Monday and once Tuesday.

Interestingly enough, or so McLean and Koz thought, he never called her on Wednesday, the fourteenth. That's the day he reported her missing. Wouldn't you think he'd have left a message or two warning her that if he didn't hear from her he was going to the police that day? Or a message later saying he'd reported her missing and it was now a police investigation?

Grant knew nothing of the cops' progress. Neither did Griem. Obviously, neither did the reporters, who lived in a short-term world. The beat reporters had access to copies of police department reports, but Koz hadn't been filing them, wouldn't for weeks. He was keeping the lid on as much as he could.

Soon, the media and critics of the department would start wondering, then bitching, about the lack of progress.

MEDIA MANAGER

Like so many involved in the disappearance of Tara Grant, Captain Wickersham was a lifer with the Macomb County Sheriff's Department, starting as a jailer in 1985. His parents owned three restaurants in the area, all called the Nugget. They were clean, brightly lit places you could go into before work or after a night of drinking and get the same reliable, well-proportioned plate of bacon, eggs, and hash browns, big, hot burgers or a variety of dinner entrees.

They were twenty-four-hour-a-day, seven-day-a-week operations, and if you were in the family, it often meant twelve-hour days. After three years, Wickersham had had more than enough. It became clear to him: either he did something better with his life, now—"I said, 'Phew, I got to find something else to do'"—or this was going to *be* his life. And since he didn't know how to do anything else, that meant going back to school.

He enrolled in the law enforcement program at Macomb Community College, later getting hired to the entry-level job at the jail.

By the time Tara went missing, he had risen to captain, third on the chain of command behind Hackel and Captain Rick Kalm, the chief of staff.

Wickersham led the staff briefing every morning on the case, making sure they were all on the same page, reporting developments to Hackel, preparing updates for the media. He also served as liaison with Griem, keeping him off Hackel's back. Wickersham might be preparing the media, but nothing prepared him *for* the media.

Mt. Clemens is the county seat of one of Michigan's biggest counties and is just a few miles up Gratiot Avenue from Detroit, so it gets its share of crime and bad news and local media attention. So he was used to that.

And it wasn't as if Wickersham hadn't worked monster cases before. In May 1996, an attractive woman named Deborah Iverson, an ophthalmologist at Beaumont Hospital, one of Michigan's best hospitals, had been kidnapped in broad daylight from a downtown parking lot in the affluent, low-crime suburb of Birmingham in Oakland County.

She'd had a 9 A.M. appointment with her psychiatrist, cashed a check for $1,000 at the drive-up window of a local bank a little after ten, and cashed a second check for $300 at another branch at eleven.

The next morning, her Toyota Land Cruiser was found in a rural area in Macomb County. Iverson was facedown on the floor in the back, strangled. Clutched in her hand was a photo of her two young boys, Ricky, four, and Colin, two.

Had her death occurred a few miles south in Detroit, it would have been headlines for a day or two. That she was kidnapped in Birmingham in a seemingly random act made it huge news. It was in the headlines and on TV for months, as leads popped up and petered out.

Iverson's husband, Robert, also a doctor, was the prime suspect, despite passing two lie detector tests. On December 30, 1996, the case broke open with a call from an attorney representing an anonymous client. The day before, a woman named Anitra [sic] Coomer had called his client and said her live-in boyfriend, McConnell Adams, had severely beaten her. She'd also told the friend that Adams was the one who had killed the doctor that was in the news.

What happened was this: Coomer and Adams had a two-year-old son, were $480 behind on their day care, and had got an eviction notice from their landlord. They headed to Birmingham to look for a suitable candidate to rob. Iverson, impeccably dressed, getting into her $40,000 SUV, was perfect. After they forced her to cash the checks, they drove her into the boonies. Iverson, pleading for her life, told her about her kids. Coomer went through Iverson's wallet, found the photo of the boys, and told Iverson to hold it. It'd be a comfort. She then handed the belt from her coat to Adams, who wrapped it around Iverson's neck and killed her.

Big case, big news, but most of the focus had been on Birmingham, where Iverson had disappeared, and not on Macomb County, where she'd been found, so Wickersham had escaped much of the press crush on that one.

Another big case? It wasn't nearly as juicy, didn't have the elements that attracted the press, no beautiful doctors impeccably dressed and found strangled in the back of a luxury SUV.

It was 1998, two eccentric sisters, Josephine Vereller, twenty-eight, and Jacqueline, twenty-two, were living in deplorable conditions in a dilapidated house filled with garbage in Macomb Township. Protective services got involved, took Josephine's two kids away from her. Later, a social worker named Lisa Putnam went to the house for an inspection. One of the sisters hit Putnam over the head with a hammer, they beat her to death, then drove her hours north and dumped her body in a field, fifteen to twenty yards from the road.

Putnam's fiancé reported her missing. Obvious place to start the investigation was her last known visit. Evidence tech found bloody clothes in the garage. Later, the body was found.

Weird case, big for Wickersham, not for the media. Not like *this* was about to become. The beat reporters for the dailies would soon be replaced by stars from downtown. Local TV crews would set up shop in the parking lot. As the days went on, national print and cable TV media would descend. It would be a pack that kept multiplying, and it would be a hungry pack, in need of food, in need of news, in need of *developments*.

THE MEDIA SWARM

It all started so slowly.

Friday morning, February 16, John Cwikla, a former radio newsman and savvy, well-respected, longtime public information officer for the sheriff's department, sent out flyers about Tara's disappearance to the local media, by fax and by e-mail. They were understated, brief, and to the point.

On Saturday, one paragraph on the case ran as filler on an inside page of the *Detroit News* Metro section. The headline read:

Missing Woman Reported in Washington Township

Followed by this:

The Macomb County Sheriff's Department is investigating the disappearance of a 34-year-old Washington Township woman. Tara Lynn Grant was last seen at the family's home during the evening hours of February 9, according to sheriff's officials. The circumstances of her disappearance are unknown. Grant is white, 5-foot-6 and 120 pounds, with brown hair and brown eyes.

That caught the notice of local beat reporters. On Saturday, Griem told them he'd hired an ex-FBI agent to investigate Tara's disappearance. They were going to help the police get to the bottom of this. (In the coming weeks and months, there would be no further word of the agent.)

Griem also posited a theory: Tara had been in the process of laying off some fifty employees in San Juan. "That's something to take into consideration," he said.

Hackel was criticized by many—by Griem, certainly, and even by some of his own cops—for seeming to feed the media beast, instead of fencing it off and letting it froth. Some thought he enjoyed the limelight a tad more than seemly. Some saw him as a politician taking advantage of face time.

There's some truth to both. But the real truth is that Hackel prides himself on being a new-era, twenty-first-century cop. He embraces technology, and whether his deputies embrace it or not, they better get used to it, and get good at it. Kozlowski got in the habit of checking e-mails while duck hunting.

Hackel grew up in a cop family and is old enough to serve quite well as a bridge between the old way of doing cop work and the new. He's seen the old and understands it, but he thinks what he does works best. That includes knowing how to use the press. Call it manipulation if you want, he'd call it strategic. Reporters are a perpetual fact of life for the top cop in one of the most populated counties in Michigan. You can look at them as the enemy or try to figure out a way to make them friends, or at least useful.

Hackel handled the growing media throng on the Grant case to perfection, with an able assist from Wickersham. Let Koz snarl and grumble, and McLean refuse to return phone calls and e-mails. That was their right, and their way of doing business. Early on, Hackel began daily press briefings at 11 A.M. There were two large cardboard posters of Tara on easels to his left and right. He found a way to keep things fresh, a bit of news released here, a pointed comment there, a hint here and there that reporters would try to interpret. The conference worked in another way—he could deal with the growing crowd all at once instead of having a pile of message slips on his desk or recorded phone messages to respond to.

Hackel had the kind of savvy and charm that left many of the reporters feeling *they* were the one with a special relationship with him. You'd see him charm someone and think, boy, he's laying it on a bit thick, no? And then you'd be the one being charmed and liking it just fine.

He got the press he wanted just about the time he wanted it, and he drove Griem up a freaking wall.

By the time the investigation came to its denouement in early March, local radio and TV were on the story 24/7, ever more breathless; headlines in the dailies trumpeted Tara's disappearance and developments in ever larger headlines; and satellite trucks from all the national cable TV channels massed in the sheriff's department's parking lot like a gathering of tanks getting ready to invade Iraq.

During the last week of February, alone, the log kept by John Cwikla that kept track of national TV interviews contained these names: *Inside Edition,* Greta Van Susteren, Catherine Crier, *America's Most Wanted,* Nancy Grace for CNN headline news, *Larry King Live,* NBC's *Dateline, The Today Show, Hardball, The Abrams Report, Good Morning America, 48 Hours,* and the *CBS Morning Show.*

"It was my first time with all that media. I think we pulled it off fairly well," said Wickersham when it was over. An understatement.

TARA'S FAMILY: ON THE HUNT

On Saturday morning, February 17, Tara's sister, Alicia, her husband, Erik, and Erik's sister, Jeannie, began their five-hour drive to the Detroit area. Seemed more like fifteen. Alicia was frantic, the miles going by in less than slow motion. She needed to be there, to be active once she got there, to be a participant, do *something,* instead of just sitting at home, or standing at work, waiting for news, waiting for Tara's voice.

Chillicothe had been good to the Standerfers, a riverside town in southern Ohio, a bit of Tennessee leaking its culture northward. Erik, an engineer, had been a manager at the paper mill in town since 2002; Alicia landed a part-time job soon after that gave her flexible hours to attend to her children.

In 2004, they were joined there by Alicia's parents, in sad circumstances, a family pulling together. Dusty had suffered a stroke and could no longer work, and the Standerfers urged the Destrampes to come and be near them. They did, moving into a small ranch house less than two miles away.

But the sad news was tempered by good. Alicia gave birth to her first child, Alex, the same year, and to a daughter, Peyton, the next. And life had been pretty much good ever since.

The Standerfers were used to the ride up I-75. They spent

summer vacations in Michigan's northwestern Upper Peninsula, meeting in large family gatherings on Platte Lake around the Fourth of July, and Erik's immediate family was from Mt. Morris, north of Flint. But those drives north had been filled with happy anticipation. This one? Desperation and dread.

Finally they arrived at their first stop, the sheriff's department. Koz updated them on the investigation and gave them a stack of flyers with Tara's picture and police contact information.

The three retraced Tara's likely route to Metro Airport, stopping at gas stations and convenience stores along the way to post the flyers. They then drove back north to the Grants' house. As Erik pulled the SUV into the driveway, Grant came out to meet them. Clearly, he'd been waiting for them. He reached out and gave Alicia an awkward hug, she bracing and leaning back from him, him fighting to hold her tight. She wanted to believe his story—it was infinitely better for her sister's well-being than the alternative—but deep down, or not so deep down, she was sure he was lying. Last thing she wanted was to be in his embrace. Grant started recounting his tale of recent events and broke down in sobs.

Erik had never liked Grant, not from the time he first met him at the funeral for Tara's grandmother in 1994. Didn't like his imperious attitude, didn't like his work habits—or nonhabits, was more like it—didn't like the way he could snap churlishly at Tara in front of others, trying to show everyone how smart *he* was. What had clinched it for Erik was one time Tara and Stephen were visiting them in Ohio. Erik walked into his son's bedroom, and there was Stephen, yelling at Alex, just a toddler, about something stupid.

Erik had told him to get out of the room and had never trusted him since. Neither had Alicia. She adored her sister almost to the point of idolizing her, and she couldn't stand the way Stephen would lash out at her verbally. Worse, she couldn't stand it when her sister took it.

Tara would ask the Standerfers to go in on family gifts or try to plan outings or family vacations or other get-togethers.

It had got to the point where often Erik and Alicia would either cancel plans that had been made, or come up with some excuse to get out of it.

The day Tara went missing, her forty-minute call from the Newark airport had been, in part, to ask Alicia if she and Erik were interested in making plans for the two families to go in on a vacation rental together. They weren't.

They went inside. The Standerfers wanted to brainstorm ideas for what to do next. At the very least, they were going to go and put out flyers in the neighborhood. And try to figure other ways to get the word out. Do something. Anything. Grant, from his body language and his tone of voice, was clearly disdainful. Nothing they said interested him in the least. Same old Steve, thought Erik.

Sunday, the Standerfers and Jeannie went out in a radius of fifteen miles from the Grants' home, taping up flyers at hotels, gas stations, party stores, and on poles. Grant stayed hunkered down at home. He ignored the Standerfers. And he ignored the calls that started coming in from reporters wanting to know if there'd been any news, looking to make some.

In the afternoon, Alicia met with Kozlowski at the police headquarters. She told him her version of events so far, that Grant had left her a voice message on February 13 saying that Tara had left him. That she had called Lou Troendle in Puerto Rico, who told her that he had argued with Grant about his not having filed a police report, and that Lou said he told Grant that if Stephen didn't file it, he would fly back to Michigan and file it himself. That after she had got off the phone with Lou, she'd called hotels in Puerto Rico and rental-car services in Michigan trying to track down her sister, without success.

When the Standerfers got back to Grant's house that night, there was another couple there. The woman, first name Simone, confided to Alicia that Stephen had asked her and her husband to be there, telling them he was afraid of Tara's sister and brother-in-law.

THE FATHERLAND BECKONS

Also on Saturday, the seventeenth, Sue Murasky, a counselor with Au Pair in America, came to the station, Verena in tow. A lawyer for the agency joined the conversation on speaker phone. Koz told Murasky about Tara's disappearance and that they were conducting an investigation. He told everyone he needed to know a little more about Verena.

Verena was born in a little village in the Rhine Valley named Aulhausen, and was a recent high school graduate on her first trip abroad. She had been placed in the Grant home the previous August. Hoping to become a teacher, the au pair was taking classes at Macomb Community College. She was one of seventeen au pairs in what was called the Rochester cluster that Murasky oversaw. Other au pairs came from Thailand, Austria, Brazil, South Africa, Chile, and Peru.

Erik Standerfer would tell Koz later that it had been Stephen's idea to hire an au pair, after the birth of Ian. Despite his minimal work schedule, he insisted Tara get him some help with the kids. He may not have liked her work schedule, but he enjoyed its fruits.

There hadn't been any complaints against the Grants, said Murasky, but it was interesting that they'd gone through seven in five years, some quitting after just a few weeks. She provided a list of names and contact information to Koz.

Verena told him that she had got along fine with Tara and Stephen. He had never done anything to cause her concern. She said that after Tara's disappearance, Grant had made a bunch of calls in front of her and the kids to his wife's cell phone, urging her to call home. And she wasn't aware of any marital problems in the home, said that Grant was a good father and husband.

She told him she returned to the Grant house after her night out dancing, getting there between 11:30 and 11:40 P.M. That timing set off an alarm for Koz. They'd got search warrants for Stephen and Tara's phone records and they showed that the last call Tara's phone ever received was at 9:47 P.M., fifteen minutes after the last purchase on her American Express card, paying for her parking at the airport. The call from Grant ended at 10:05, then he'd called Verena on the house phone two minutes later and again, on his cell phone, at 10:32.

Meanwhile Koz had driven the route Tara would take to get home from the airport, and it was just about an hour on the dot. So she would have got home about 10:30, just about the time Grant was calling Verena. And Verena got home an hour after Tara arrived, not the fifteen minutes or so Grant had claimed.

His version was that Tara had got home at 10:30, left in the black car about 10:50 and Verena had walked in a couple of minutes later, soon enough, he said, that he thought it was Tara coming back for something. A half hour wasn't much time to get in an argument, kill someone, and get rid of the body. But Verena walking in at 11:40 gave him an hour and ten minutes.

Given all the calls Grant had made to Verena the night Tara went missing, Koz had to ask: was she romantically or sexually involved with Grant? No, she said, quite firmly.

Verena never looked Koz in the eye. There was something going on. What? He had no idea. He suspected the worst, but was willing to think he just wasn't seeing things right. "I can't figure out forty-year-old women, how am I going to figure out a nineteen-year-old?" he would say later. "She was nineteen. Who knows what was going through her mind? Maybe Grant swept her off her feet. Maybe she was just scared."

But he was sure she was being evasive on some level. He had a sense that pressing her would be a mistake. If he wanted to get more from her, it would be better to back off and wait.

Murasky and Koz agreed the Grant home was hardly a fitting place in the meantime for a nineteen-year-old. Koz didn't express his feelings about Grant, he didn't have to. It was clear from his tone and inflections that he had his suspicions.

That afternoon, Murasky helped Verena pack her bags. Verena wasn't happy about it, but reluctantly agreed to move out. Grant convinced her to stay one last night, which they spent in his bed.

Police started calling the former au pairs, who were willing to register complaints now. One told him she thought Grant had gone through her things, another said she had been afraid of Stephen's angry outbursts. He left messages for others to contact him.

On the twenty-first, to Koz's surprise, and the agency's relief, he lost a witness and it lost a headache. Verena got on a plane at Detroit Metropolitan and went back to Germany. Murasky called him to give him the news.

Verena continued to call or e-mail Grant each day, and he called her and e-mailed her, daily, as well. Grant told her they had to make up new e-mail addresses, that the cops were on to their old ones.

What Grant didn't know was the cops were on to their calls, too. One of the periodic tails on him saw him making a call from a pay phone one day, ran to the phone when Grant was done and called his own home phone number. Koz then got the phone company—a private company, it was happy to cooperate, didn't even ask for a search warrant—to give him a copy of that phone's calls. The call immediately before the call to the cop's home was to Verena in Germany.

HOT E-MAILS

On Tuesday, February 20, things started heating up. They got hot and they got juicy, and the hot and juicy got the media hot and bothered. It was stuff you just can't make up.

One of Grant's ex-girlfriends, a nursing student in Lansing named Deena Hardy, called the sheriff's department, got through to Sergeant Larry King. A friend of hers named Tom Gromak, a staffer, interestingly enough, at the *Detroit News,* had convinced her she had no choice. She said she wanted to pass something on about Grant. King passed her on to Koz, Koz did a little internal "hoo-rah!" when she told him what her "something" was.

That "something" was eight e-mails passed back and forth between Hardy and Grant in ninety minutes in the morning of Thursday, January 25, fifteen days before Tara went missing, while Tara was in London on business.

Stephen was on the make, reveries of his time with Hardy apparently moving him to action. He didn't exactly segue into it, spend a few days in casual back-and-forth—what have you been up to, how you doing, long time no see, jeez, that's interesting, me, I've been . . . No, Grant got right to it, man of action.

Grant sends her an e-mail telling her he has suspicions

Tara is having an affair with someone he calls the Geezer, and then he writes: "I hope you keep at the nursing thing. You never know when I might need a sponge bath. If you want to practice, let me know."

Hardy counters: "You are married. You shouldn't talk like that. How would you feel if Tear-ah"—apparently her dismissive term for "Tara"—"was talking like that to the old Geezer?"

Grant: "I was only being helpful with the offer to be a test subject . . . I was just being supportive, not dirty. I don't care about being married. I never have. It is that no-conscience thing."

Hardy: "You have not changed a bit. Don't you worry about being burned eternally by the devil? Why did you get married in the first place? Seemed like the cool thing to do?"

Grant: "The answers in order are NO, love and No. I think you misunderstand, though. I like being married. I just think of marriage vows like speed limits. Sometimes you have to break them, and sometimes you get caught. You just need to keep an eye on the road to avoid detection." (And sometimes you get pulled over for warrants and they take your ass to jail, but he didn't get to that part of it, that chapter in his life not lending itself to seduction.)

Hardy asks him if he's on the home or work computer. Grant says he's at work, then complains about his Internet access there. "My work computer sucks. It is actually the connection. At this site, I have no high-speed access. I was using one of the neighbor's connections via wireless, until their IT guy saw a slowdown in the DL speed and put up a firewall. BASTARD!"

"Funny, you are still a little thief. Some things never change," says Hardy. "So, what are you going to do about the cheatin' wife? Also, would you mind changing your e-mail setting so it includes the thread? I sometimes forget what I said.

"Hey, that rhymed.

"I am so frickin' bored today."

"Don't know, yet," Grant writes back about the Geezer. "The problem is she says things in code. And because of that, I don't know what is actually going on."

But not wanting her to think him a man of no action, he brags about being able to read Tara's e-mails because of a guy he knows. "Bryan is a vice president at a computer company and one of his techs helped out a bit, if you know what I mean. Straight-up NSA shit, if you get my drift. Actually, he had some software, over-the-counter stuff U can buy at CompUSA that did the trick. It just sounds cooler the other way."

The software was called Spector Pro 3.1. Literature for the software bragged that it recorded e-mails, keystrokes, instant messaging, and chat conversations for AOL, MSN, Yahoo, and other services and all Internet domains that had been accessed. It could also take literal snapshots of the computer screen, up to one a second.

In fact, Grant had caught Tara sending e-mails to an old boyfriend named Pete, nothing serious in them, nothing to prove she was having sex with him, which was what Grant feared and alternately assumed to be true and knew to be impossible. He'd send the ex-boyfriend e-mails pretending to be Tara, trying to get him to say something incriminating, prove his worst-case scenario for him, but either nothing was happening, or something was happening but she was too smart for him. Poor Grant, trapped in another either-or.

"If you are sooo bored, I am still in need of some excitement in my life. Wink, wink. Tara flew to London yesterday till Friday night, and I am all alone with no one to play with . . . I do want to see you naked. Naked women are always good to see. Especially if you haven't seen them in a while."

Koz found the e-mails interesting, funny, and pathetic. What a dweeb! But he found them intriguing, too. Grant had told them that Tara was being faithful. He'd told Hardy he thought she was sleeping with her boss. Motive is key to any murder prosecution, and for the first time they had a strong one.

"She was a stand-up person," Koz said later of Hardy. "She walked into this hot potato and came through for us."

Hardy even agreed if they could work it out, she'd be willing to have a phone conversation with Grant while Koz listened in, see if she could entice him into saying something incriminating. But it never came to pass.

Koz and other detectives worked the angle of an affair by Tara hard. Possibilities included a boss, a coworker, and the former boyfriend, who was the guy Tara had written about in the notebooks Koz found in her car. All led to dead ends. Pete was nothing more than the one who got away, the high school sweetheart you never quite get over and never stopped wondering, What if?

"We investigated the possibility of an affair in every way, shape, and form. We didn't find anything," said Koz afterward. "The only intimations we found came from Grant himself. Basically, I think she was just too busy. She didn't have time."

"I went through thousands of her e-mails and thousands of everything on her computer. There was nothing," said McLean much later. "She was *not* having an affair. *Not*. That I can tell you."

Grant, though, remained suspicious in the weeks before Tara disappeared. Later, detectives would find an e-mail he had sent to Tara the evening of February 1, an e-mail he called "Sorry!" in the subject line that managed to be both apologetic and accusatory, while at the same time coming up with a cover story for how he could have found out what she was saying to Pete without having planted a bug in her computer.

"I am sorry! I keep fucking up and don't know why," he began. "I was not looking for anything on your old computer, I swear . . . What happened was I was going through 'documents and settings' for work-related stuff to delete. For some reason MSN LIVE kept popping up. Every time I hit 'X' or 'CLOSE' it would come back," he said.

Grant told her that the last time he tried to close out, the window that popped back up was one of her old e-mails. "I am sure you can figure out my next course of action. SORRY! You had said when we talked about me taking it to CompUSA that YOU were afraid it might have private info. I took that to mean confidential/work related, but seeing the login, I wondered what else might be there. So, I looked.

"I love you Tara and I was HURT by what I read. I know we have gone through this already, but I was NOT expecting to read what I read. REALLY! I was simply overwhelmed. I could not even think when you called that night. I really couldn't.

"I will never—this is in writing—say anything about him or that situation again. I did not and had not thought about IT in a long time. REALLY! I trust that you are true to me, but I do worry.

"But YOU must help me a bit. I know you HAVE to travel for work. I get that, and I am PROUD OF YOU for all you have done and earned in this job.

"But you are on the road a LOT. And you do drink sometimes too much when you go out. I of all people am not pointing a finger about the drinking, but when people drink—everyone—they sometimes forget who they are for a time and do things they might not otherwise do. Do I think you have? I DO NOT know. I am only being honest, but in reality, I can NEVER really know EXCEPT in my HEART. And there the answer is NO!

"I LOVE YOU? I was just hurt by what I read and had to tell you."

It was a stroke of fortune for Hackel and his detectives that Hardy's friend worked at the *Detroit News*. It was to their delight that George Hunter broke the story of the e-mails the next day. The *News*'s front-page story Wednesday had this big, bold headline: SEX, LIES, SPYING

Not even Hackel imagined the upshot. *Good Morning America* aired an interview with Hackel. CNN did a report on the case. All the local radio and TV stations and reporters for the other dailies clamored for copies of the e-mails and fresh quotes. WJR-AM, the clear channel behemoth, beamed the news out repeatedly to its millions of listeners across a huge swath of the Midwest and Canada; WWJ-AM, the local all-news radio station, trumpeted the story every ten minutes; the rock radio jocks had a salacious field day.

And, wonderful, unintended consequence, Grant decided to fight fire with fire. He stopped ducking the media. He embarked on a campaign to be the best friend to everyone who had access to a notebook and pen, microphone or camera.

He became ubiquitous.

"I hope Tara walks through that door," he told the crew from Channel 7, now welcome in his house. He sobbed, on the verge of hysterics. "God, please call. Please. Call anyone." Squeezing out the high-pitched words to his wife, looking straight at the camera, eyes bugging out. EYES BUGGING OUT.

Griem, thinking he could play the media game with Hackel, probably even thinking he could win it—maybe being the former Macomb County prosecutor that he was, he was one of those who still thought of Hackel as Bill's kid—arranged a group photo op and interview session with his client at his office.

Grant told the reporters his wife had taken off before, but this was the first time he was scared. So scared, he almost hoped she was off with another guy. "If she's with somebody else, okay, I can understand that. But I wish she would at least call home. Her kids are worried about her."

He denied any involvement with Tara's disappearance but said: "I understand why I'm a suspect. I get it. The police always look at the husband."

Griem had made his move. Hackel made his. Looked straight into the camera and told as bald-faced a lie as he could with a straight face. "Stephen Grant isn't a suspect. We haven't even established that a crime has taken place."

Not a suspect? No one believed it, of course. But he said it with such a straight face, who knows, maybe it would give Grant pause. At the very least, it would have to confuse him. The more confused he was, the better. They were still in the first period. Hackel was just getting warmed up. Let's see what Grant and Griem have left when we get to the third.

Grant's sister was recruited into the media wars, too. A short redhead who was in sharp contrast to Grant's lean, muscled hardness, she said she had been busy circulating Tara's flyers, too, while Stephen was trying his best to shield the kids from both the media and what they were writing and saying.

"They obviously know Mom is lost," she said, "and that police are looking for her. But we're trying to shelter them from this as much as we can."

As lame as Grant's lines might seem to an outside reader, they had worked. Hardy told Koz she and Grant had made plans to meet the week of January 30, but Grant canceled because of something with his kids. As the story turned overnight into a monster, Hardy would thank God she and her former boyfriend hadn't hooked back up again.

ODD DUCK

Undercover cops tailed Grant off and on to learn a little more about his habits. His work habits were sporadic, couple hours here, couple of hours there, dad a believer in flex time, apparently.

Grant's food habits ran to bottled water and candy bars in the morning, regular stops at two Buffalo Wild Wings, one just down the road from his dad's machine shop in Mt. Clemens, the other near his house, at 26 Mile Road and Van Dyke. One day, surveillance trailed him first to one, then later in the day to the other.

The cops didn't follow him inside, but if they had, they would have quickly learned that the waitresses could count on him ordering boneless wings with the blue cheese dip, and an expensive microbrew from Kalamazoo, Bell's Oberon Ale. Regulars at the bar could count on generally pleasant company. Grant was conversant about sports and current affairs, chiding those who weren't keeping up on news of the day.

In fact, they could also count on getting beat by Grant at the bar's electronic trivia game.

Grant was a rabid fan of his alma mater, often wearing green and white on days of big games and rooting avidly if

State's usually powerful basketball team was kicking some-one's butt on TV. He made sure everyone knew he was an MSU grad. And visitors to his house would see his diploma proudly displayed in a prominent spot in the den. What no one but Grant knew, not even Tara, was that the diploma was a fake, cobbled together through a combination of ingenuity and Kinko's technology. Grant was, in fact, a dropout, per-haps a victim of his partying days at the Red Cedar Apart-ments. MSU records show that he transferred to the school as a junior in 1991, studied history for two years, but was still a junior when he enrolled in his last class in 1993.

Two other things the Wild Wings regulars could count on? Anecdotes from a proud, beaming dad about his kids, and anecdotes about the Grants' string of au pairs. For those who knew he was married, it might have struck them as un-seemly the relish with which he showed photos of the au pairs that he'd taken on his cell phone, comments he made about how hot they were or how hot, they in turn, thought him.

They were all young and pretty, he picked them out per-sonally, he bragged, and to hear Grant tell it, they were all enamored of him. He liked to tell the story of how one time, one of them saw him outside the house caught his eye, did a striptease in her bedroom window for him. Though when he found out another of the au pairs was screwing some young American, he canned her ass, sent her packing. He'd show their pictures and brag them up, but he wouldn't think any-thing, either, of calling the current au pair up on his cell and screaming at her over some imagined slight or chore she'd botched.

Certainly it came as no surprise to the regulars when they read in the papers or heard on the radio that Grant had been zinging salacious e-mails to an ex-girlfriend.

Then, along came Verena. He talked more about her then he had the others. He took a lot of pictures of her, usually smiling that smile of hers at him, easy to call it sexy, that smile, and showed the pictures to everyone. About mid-

January, folks noticed him talking about her even more, showing more photos of her. Couldn't keep quiet about her. It got to be annoying. He talked to Verena a lot on the phone, too, but never raised his voice. Apparently, she was good at chores.

Lest anyone thought Grant was bullshitting about how attractive he was to Verena, he'd flash around his cell phone, let people read her text messages to him. They were open to interpretation, nothing X-rated, but they were clearly flirtatious, meant to be come-ons, hinting at pleasures to be had. Clearly this was one teenager with the hots for an older man, many of them thought.

Grant had been a teller of tales his entire life. In high school, he'd try to pick up girls by telling them he was *the* star of the basketball team at Henry Ford II High School in Sterling Heights. Some star. One girl from a nearby high school, who worked with him at a Chi-Chi's restaurant, was impressed by his stories and agreed to a date. Afterward, she bragged to her father about having gone out with Grant, sure her father, who unbeknownst to Grant was a counselor at his high school, would be impressed by her catch. Not only is Grant not the star, he told his daughter, he's not even on the team.

Grant would tell the guys in high school about his hunting and fishing exploits, how he was a slayer of deer, catcher of trophy trout, but other than a semiautomatic rifle he kept hidden in his bedroom and would take into the woods nearby to shoot at trees and impress his buddies with his firepower, there wasn't much evidence of those skills, either.

Grant was a fan of exotic sports cars in high school, and used to prowl Ferrari and Porsche dealerships to touch and stare. He was a fan of glossy car magazines, as well.

David Buss was one of those Grant would show off his semiautomatic rifle to. Years later, in 1996, Buss got a call out of the blue. As he would later tell the *Free Press,* Grant was looking to reconnect.

"Remember me?" he began the conversation.

They hit it off and were soon hanging out again, at least for a while. Buss was surprised to find that Grant had become quite the cook. "He would have us over for dinner. He would make these elaborate meals. He really liked to entertain. He would have these, like, French delicacy recipes that he would make, but he would never look at a recipe book or anything. He would just know how to do it. He would just make it up on the fly."

About the time Tara got her Puerto Rico assignment in October 2006, Buss ended his friendship with Grant, tired of his overbearing ways. "He's always had this personality where he has to be the center of everything. Narcissistic is a good word for it. He was always right, no matter what."

Other friends and couples grew tired of him, too, and found reason to beg off on suggested get-togethers. He could be funny and charming and witty, but he always wanted to be in control, planning every detail of a night out and getting upset if anyone had any variations in mind.

The regulars at the Mt. Clemens Buffalo Wild Wings knew Grant worked down the road; they didn't know it was a tiny, two-man, messy shop, the last link at the bottom of the auto-supply chain, a few machines, Grant and his dad grinding out ball bearings and other parts for larger suppliers.

Grant told them his family business was a major auto supplier, major in Detroit usually meaning something akin to Delphi or American Axle, with thousands of workers and multiple plants.

The family business was growing, too, he'd brag. In addition to helping run one "major" supplier, he had added two other businesses to the umbrella of supplier operations— Grant Bearing Specialists L.L.C. and Precision Centerless Products L.L.C. He didn't like the way his father ran the business, so he'd show him where he had gone wrong by running the new ones much more efficiently.

There was a catch that Grant didn't bother explaining. He'd registered those business names, it was true, but that's all they had remained, or ever would remain, letters on paper.

If he was feeling particularly garrulous after two or three Oberons, he'd open up, maybe with one of his favorite barmaids, or one of the regulars sitting next to him. He had a secret line of business, couldn't tell them much more than that. Connected through his wife, doing secret stuff, dangerous stuff, don't ask, for her employer, the Washington Group.

Can't talk much about it, saying too much already, but it involves undercover work, company gives me bodyguards, that's all I can say.

Grant had been president of the Carriage Hills subdivision, the guy residents would go to if they thought one of their neighbors was violating zoning codes or if they wanted him to warn someone about driving too fast on the winding streets. When he stepped down in 2004, he told incoming president Frank Perna that he had to resign because he'd be leaving the area soon for job reasons.

The job, if there really had been one, didn't materialize. When Perna ran into him later, Grant told him things hadn't panned out. Still, Perna remained impressed by what seemed to be a happy couple. He envied them as he'd see them jogging in the neighborhood, one or the other of them pushing a baby jogger in front of them as they went by.

The Grants had moved to Carriage Hills following the sale of their former home in nearby Shelby Township to Barbara Horn in 2001. The house had been advertised as having three bedrooms, and it did. But it turned out, Horn found to her dismay, that the third bedroom, over an attached garage, had been converted by Grant himself, and none of the work, particularly the electrical wiring, was up to code.

Horn won a suit in small-claims court but had trouble collecting. Once, Grant came to her office to make a payment, then created a loud and embarrassing scene over the receipt. He was told not to come back to the office again.

Horn started showing up after work to collect payments, but on her scheduled visits the sidewalk was increasingly littered with obstacles like sleds and kids' toys that she felt had been deliberately put in her way to trip her up.

She arranged once to meet him in a restaurant parking lot and was so leery of him, she backed her car into a spot in case she needed a quick getaway. Grant, recognizing her car, pulled in perpendicularly in front of her, blocking any departure.

PRELUDE TO A SEARCH

Anyone mistaking Hackel's new-era sensibilities for weakness was, well, mistaken. Just as those describing him as gaunt are mistaken—that ain't gaunt, it's stripped-down hard, the six-percent-body-fat kind of hard with muscles that'll fire hard for hours.

On Tuesday, February 20, Grant, through Griem, formally turned down the sheriff department's request that he submit to a lie-detector test. Griem said they'd consider it if it wasn't administered by Hackel's troops, and he said his client was being harassed by the sheriff and his department.

Coincidence, or planned response, on Wednesday, Hackel held the first of what he said would be a daily morning press conference to keep the media apprised of developments. They showed up in throngs, young kids from suburban weeklies and shippers, veterans of the dailies, TV crews, radio guys from fifty-thousand-watt clear-channel stations that beamed their signals throughout the Midwest and from little stations that got lost in the static a few miles away from their transmitters.

Was or wasn't Grant a suspect? That became a central question. Hackel played it both ways. No, he isn't. Followed by explanations for why he was.

"It's become very clear at this point he doesn't want to cooperate with us," Hackel said one day. "You would think he'd be right there at our side, wanting to get all the information he could from us. But he hasn't called us once. Think about that. He called us and said his wife is missing, but since then, he hasn't called to ask how the investigation is going, or if we have any new information.

"We're getting information from other family members, and from Tara's workplace. The only person who is not cooperating with us is Stephen Grant."

Hackel made a surprise announcement at his press conference on Wednesday, February 21, that blew up the already fervid media interest, and would over the next few days bring criticism raining down, even from his own cops.

Talking to reporters who had gathered well in advance of the scheduled press conference, for the first time Hackel referred to Tara's disappearance as a possible crime of violence. "We are focusing our investigation into the possibility of foul play. This is day thirteen of her disappearance, so it makes you stop and think," he said at the briefing. "If she's no longer alive, there's a concern about the body as evidence, and extracting evidence from the body. This is a difficult thing to discuss, but, unfortunately, in our business, it's something we have to consider."

Hackel then said his department was going to conduct a search at an undisclosed wooded area on Saturday for Tara's body. A warm front was moving through, he said, and if her body was buried where they were going to be looking, the thaw should make the search a little easier to find it.

The news went around town instantly. TV stations broke into their regularly scheduled broadcasting with the news. Print reporters got it up on their Web sites. The radio folks trumpeted it breathlessly. It was big headlines in the dailies Wednesday morning.

It wasn't the coming warm weather that prompted the

search, though. That morning, Hackel got a call from Chad Halcom, a reporter at the *Macomb Daily,* a struggling paper based in Mt. Clemens that, like its brethren across the U.S., was trying and failing to figure out how to compete with free news on the Internet, its sales plummeting by the week, month, and quarter. At least until the Grant case broke. It had been a boon for circulation, and the *Daily,* like the *Detroit Free Press,* like the *Detroit News,* was playing it for all it was worth, and then some. There hadn't been anything like it in town since Hoffa went missing.

Halcom, like his peers and competitors, was working all the angles, trying to come up with something fresh and trying to keep his byline on page one. He called Hackel about something Grant had said to him in a recent interview, thinking he might be able to stretch it into a feature, probably not worth a call, anyway. Pretty thin stuff, but you never knew.

Grant had told Halcom that he'd been out mountain biking at Stony Creek last summer, maybe the summer before, and Sheriff Hackel had gone past him on a trail, in the other direction. Interesting thing? Hackel wasn't wearing a bike helmet, in clear violation of the rules posted on big signs at all the trailheads. The park police generated revenue writing tickets for bikers without helmets. Kind of funny to have the sheriff out scofflawing on his bike. Grant told Halcom he even hollered out at the sheriff: "Why don't you have your bike helmet on?" But Hackel had just kept on, ignored him.

To say that Hackel is media conscious is like saying bees are pollen conscious. His first reaction was, Shit, last thing I need is a story about the sheriff not wearing a helmet. A rule-breaker, doesn't practice bike safety. It was true, sometimes he wore a helmet at the park, more often than not, he didn't. He wasn't one of those crazy kids on the trails there, flying down hills and around turns. He was a slow descender. He was out there pushing big gears, ripping into ascents, working his legs and lungs and building up his endurance. He wasn't taking chances, he wasn't worried about taking a spill. Plus, he liked the wind in his hair.

But nonetheless, bad for the image.

But Halcom wasn't looking at it from the law-breaking point of view. It was: sheriff and suspect share a hobby. Right, pretty thin. He got off the phone with Hackel and gave up on the story. There'd be other, better angles.

Something about it got Hackel to thinking, though. It worked at him, that *something*. He couldn't articulate it, not right away. But it felt odd. Hackel believes in his sixth sense, believes in listening to it, believes in letting those things that don't *seem* right percolate away. Something to be said for being a twenty-first-century cop; something to be said, too, for trusting your instincts, the way people have been doing since they were sensing predators on the savannah.

"It's weird," Hackel told Wickersham. "Why is he talking about me and my bike helmet? Why is he talking about me? Why is he talking about Stony Creek?"

Wickersham thought he was making too much of it. So what? He said something to a reporter. Who cares?

The more Hackel worked it, the more convinced he was that the mention of Stony Creek had importance well beyond its context in some story of seeing the sheriff biking. Was Grant subconsciously expressing something about the park itself? Or somehow, for some reason, dropping a hint to Halcom about something?

He called Kalm and Wickersham into his office. "Let's do a search of the park. Where you can easily drop a body."

Kalm and Wickersham weren't sure. It would be a logistical nightmare, the kind of big-ass search Hackel was picturing. And it was going to get Griem in a lather. Besides, what were the chances? Grant didn't seem the kind of dumb you'd have to be to discard your wife in a park adjacent to your house, even a park the size of Stony Creek.

Hackel insisted, for several reasons. One, they weren't making much headway doing what they were doing. It would ramp up the pressure on Grant when he announced it at the daily press conference, and maybe Grant would do something stupid in response. It would help raise awareness in the community, get people to keep an eye out. People in any of the other large metroparks that ring Detroit might be a little more observant. Tara might be in one of them, instead of Stony. And at the least it would give him and the detectives a sense of doing something.

Finally, he thought, What if April comes and the snow melts and she had been out there all along? Find her now, *if* she's there, the body will be preserved. Wait till spring, it could decompose, or coyotes could strip the bones. They'd look awfully stupid for not doing a search now if the body showed up then, and Hackel hated the idea of looking stupid.

So that was that. They'd do a big, public search on Saturday.

Hackel had decided to hold off a while on the location of the search, play it for all it was worth. Not so much for ongoing media play as for ongoing Grant play, a cat batting a mouse from paw to paw.

Hackel made sure that right after he announced the search of an undisclosed wooded area he mentioned Grant, reinforced the linkage between the husband and the missing body they hoped to find in the snow.

He pointed out discrepancies between what Grant was now telling the press and what he had told Kozlowski and McLean at his house a week earlier. (Could it have been just eight days? Seemed like a month.)

Grant had told them, for example, that Tara had never taken off before. Now, he was saying she'd taken off two other times, but this was the first time he was scared about it.

And discrepancies between what he'd told police and what the facts told them. For example, Grant said he heard Tara tell someone on her cell that she'd be right out. But the last call ever made on her phone had been at the airport at least an hour earlier.

Hackel bemoaned the lack of simple cooperation from Grant. Was it too much to ask, to be allowed to look at the home computer, see if there were any clues in its files about Tara's whereabouts? Was it too much to ask, that they be given some of Tara's clothes, so the K-9 dogs could fix her smell and maybe help track her?

They didn't have probable cause for a search warrant of the home, he said. So they needed Stephen's cooperation, but for some reason he just wouldn't give it.

Hackel wasn't playing to the press, or the audience watching on live TV. He was playing to Grant, whom Hackel assumed was watching, self-absorbed as he was. For days now, Hackel and his detectives had kept the TV on, looking for what had seemed to have become an endless series of interviews with Grant on the local news. Same story, same tears, same bug eyes, same pleas for Tara to please come back.

If Hackel was in a meeting, it was John Cwikla's job if he spotted Grant on TV to record it so Hackel could watch it later. It was telling that Grant invariably asked the reporter interviewing him: "What are people saying about me?"

Grant would take their business cards and, to their surprise, at first, call them later just to chat. Hank Winchester at Channel 4, the local NBC outlet, was a favorite. Grant took to calling him regularly, setting a record with five calls in one day, all times of day or night. Winchester's first interview with Grant was on February 19. Grant told him which four questions he was allowed to ask, but then got on a roll and talked to the newsman for forty minutes. One talk they had, Winchester asked him if he could borrow any home movies Stephen might have of him and Tara, family gatherings, birthdays, Christmas, that sort of thing.

Grant gave a coy look, a smirk. Well, there were intimate movies he and Tara had shot, he said. Winchester was taken aback. "Hank," said Grant, "I'm having guy talk with you. Don't take it the wrong way."

Griem counterattacked. Reporters were suddenly offered intimate, one-on-one time with Grant. Joe Swickard, the veteran crime reporter for the *Free Press,* interviewed Grant for ninety minutes that afternoon in Griem's downtown Detroit law office. Grant was histrionic. He clutched Swickard to demonstrate how he had held Tara while pleading with her about her excessive travel during one dustup. Grant acknowledged being what he described as the number one suspect, but with his now famous bug eyes, he looked Swickard in the face, reached across the table, and took his hand and told him in a breaking voice how he had begged Tara for strength, love, and honesty.

Swickard later made a note: "His hands were soft, moist and cold," wrote Swickard.

At the 11 A.M. press conference on Thursday, Hackel ratcheted things up even more. This time, he disclosed that the search would be at Stony Creek, that it would start first thing in the morning Saturday, and it was going to be a big mobilization involving many of his troops, members of the department's reserves, Stony Creek's police, and throngs of volunteers.

More Web postings by the print folks. More radio flashes. More breaking into regular programming on TV. Much of it, Hackel assumed, being digested by Mr. Grant. And Mr. Griem.

Hackel caught flak for that announcement. Many in the media, happy to have breaking news, nonetheless wondered why Hackel would blow it up on Thursday. Wouldn't it make more sense to just quietly start the search on Saturday? If Grant did murder his wife and, moreover, actually buried her where they were going to be looking, why tip their hand? It seemed to confirm suspicions that Hackel had become as insatiable for press as the press had become insatiable for him and the case. His own detectives, many of them, thought it was out of line. Some of them told him to his face.

"People said I was doing it for attention," he would say

later. "I *was* doing it for attention. This was a missing persons case and it needed all the attention we could get."

It got Grant's attention. It got Griem's.

Grant told the *Detroit News* in a story that ran Friday that he wanted to help out on the search. He ran there and biked there all the time. He knew it intimately, despite its size. He'd be a great asset.

Griem called Wickersham on Friday and reiterated what the *News* had to say. Grant wanted to be there, wanted to help out, said the attorney. Wickersham thought it was weird, a dumb idea. No way, he told the attorney. It's a public park, he's got a right to be there, countered Griem. They went back and forth.

Hackel got on the line. "The only thing we'd need him for is to tell us where the body is," he said, getting in the last word. Griem went off on him. "Went absolutely berserk," was how Hackel described it later. Griem called back. Grant had changed his mind. He didn't want to be there, after all.

At the 11 A.M. press conference on Friday, Hackel responded publicly to the *News* story. "We don't need him there," he said. "Unless he knows where she is." Great line. Boy, did that play well on TV.

Getting in a jab at Griem, Hackel went further. Besides, he said, Grant's attorney had told them they weren't allowed to talk to his client. What good would Stephen be on a search if none of the police could talk to him?

Oooh, that was it. Griem got that fax machine cranking. "I'm bewitched, bothered, and bewildered," he wrote, either a fan of alliteration or old songs, "why the sheriff would say such a thing. Mr. Grant wanted to do anything and everything he can to help find Tara."

And, about to pick up his marbles and take them home,

Griem finished by saying: "I will fire him as a client if he participates."

Hackel almost busted a gut. Bewitched, bothered, and bewildered? That was rich.

Hackel got more of a reaction to the announcement of a search than an offer to help from Grant. Friday afternoon, to everyone's surprise, Grant showed up at the sheriff's department, good citizen doing his part, bringing in two laptops to hand over to detectives.

By happenstance, a Channel 7 TV truck was there on other business when Grant walked in. By then, Grant had the most recognizable face in town, and the crew spotted him walking across the wide expanse of driveway and sidewalk from the parking lot. Within seconds, the image of Grant opening the door and walking in was going out live and was repeated relentlessly.

Kozlowski let Grant into the detective bureau. Not only did he have the laptops they wanted, but, he said, he wanted to volunteer his services for the hunt. Who better? He was always out there, biking and running, knew it cold. He wanted to run it by the boss.

"I'd like to talk to Sheriff Hackel," he said.

"Just a minute, Steve," said Koz. He went down the hall to Hackel's office. He was in a meeting with Kalm and Wickersham. "Sheriff, Stephen Grant's here and he wants to talk to you. He wants to join the search Saturday."

Kalm interceded. No way, he said. He told his boss he flat out couldn't talk to him, not the way Griem was acting, not after everything he'd said about how they could interact with his client.

Hackel went along with his chief of staff. Koz thought it was senseless overreaction. Grant came in on his own accord, was the one who asked to talk to Hackel. If Hackel responded, so what, it wouldn't violate Grant's rights. Fuck

Griem, why worry about him so much? Koz bit his tongue, went back and told Grant no-can-do.

Within minutes, the other radio and TV crews in town were careening into the parking lot. A flock of reporters with microphones waving were waiting for Grant when he walked out twenty-five minutes later. What was up? Any news? What do you think about the search? Are you going to help out?

He had, he told them, dropped off two laptops the police wanted, so much for allegations he wasn't being cooperative. One was a work laptop that Tara had used until a month ago, the other an older machine Stephen had, by coincidence, taken in for repairs the day before she went missing. He said he didn't think the old one would be of value, they hadn't used it in years. But whatever the police were looking for, *if* there was anything to be found, would certainly be on the work computer.

It was a charade, the move not mollifying police but pissing them off. They would have their forensics people look at them, but didn't expect to find anything.

Koz looked out the office window as the charade was playing out and saw Grant on the sidewalk in front of the entrance, holding court. *Fucker won't talk to us,* he thought, *but he's out there yapping up a storm to the press.*

Hackel told reporters it was "a staged event." Both Griem and Grant knew which computer the police wanted, and it was the PC at home, not the laptops that had been tossed in the closet. "Unfortunately, it's been made clear to us we aren't going to be allowed to see that one," said Hackel.

Absent a search warrant, he was up the creek in his kayak without a paddle.

THE SEARCH

Saturday, February 24, an army of cops and volunteers gathered before dawn at their staging area, the Powell Middle School, not far from Stony Creek's nature center, and close to park trails that Grant was known to use regularly and which were very close to secluded public dirt roads that abutted the park. If someone wanted to hide a body, that seemed the most obvious way. You wouldn't have to enter the park proper in your car, passing the manned entrance booth. You could just pull up to the edge, carry or drag your load just a few yards, and be on trails.

Hackel and Wickersham shared memories of the killing of Lisa Putnam, the social worker beat to death by two sisters in 1998 and then dumped in a field. Bodies are hard to carry. The sisters had dumped Putnam's just a few yards from a road. Chances were that if Grant had killed his wife, and in the small likelihood that he had decided to dump the body close to home, it would be at the park—and given the deep snow and thick woods, not far from a trail heading in.

Hackel was playing a hunch, no better place to play it. Both Steve and Tara ran there regularly, it was close to their home, it was deeply wooded and interspersed with swamps and bogs. You couldn't find any place nearly as fine as this for miles around to hide a body. During the search, there would be cops and park rangers in planes, on all-terrain vehicles, on mountain bikes. On horses and on foot. Counting the scores of Explorers and other volunteers, there would be about 150 searchers in all.

They were looking for Tara, of course, but they were looking for evidence of her, too, a cell phone, a purse, some clothes. There were more than four thousand acres and many miles of trails in the park. They could properly search the whole park in weeks. Hackel charted a manageable amount of terrain, and just after sunrise, they headed out.

It was still black out when Hackel arrived, first on the scene. Cops and volunteers started to arrive, slowly at first, then en masse. The department's mobile command center, a converted mobile home loaded with police gear and communications equipment, pulled in. Area roads were sealed off with yellow crime tape or cop cars parked sideways. The entire area was off limits to the media, which stayed back at the school.

Stephen Grant didn't show up. His sister Kelly and her husband, Chris, did. She chatted with investigators at the mobile command center, exchanged brief hellos with some of the media, who said they'd be calling her later. She left after the searchers headed out for their various assigned starting positions, took calls later at Grant's house, telling reporters he was fine, wasn't mad, no problem, everyone had to do what they had to do.

The Standerfers and Alicia's mom, Mary, had driven up from Ohio the day before. Hackel had them stay with him throughout, as he roved from place to place to offer encouragement and see if anything had turned up. "I wanted to be able to put a human face on the search. When I'd introduce Alicia to them as we went around, it was a way of saying, 'This is the sister. She's suffering, too. There's another victim besides Tara Grant,' " said Hackel later.

Early on, Hank Winchester, who was hanging with the press near the command center, got a call on his cell phone.

It was Grant, asking for some advice. Did Winchester think it would be appropriate if he went for a jog while the search was going on?

Mid-morning, a sheriff's deputy in a helicopter radioed word back to the command center that he'd spotted what looked like a body in a grassy area. The chopper circled back, dropped in close, everyone's adrenaline surging. It was a deer carcass. "I didn't know whether to feel happy or disappointed," said Hackel later.

At 12:30, Hackel called it off. They'd covered all the ground he'd mapped out. They'd come up empty. "It was a crap shoot," said Wickersham.

It was so anticlimactic. Even Hackel, who knew he was only playing a hunch all along, was deflated. His sixth sense had been acting up. It was a sense he believed in. Senseless, his critics—and their numbers were growing—might have put it.

Hackel had to look at the disappointment in Alicia's face. Erik's and Mary's. In the faces of his men and women. And now he had to troop back and face the media beast, face their questions and second-guessing. He tried to put a chipper tone in his voice, and failed.

More than a few reporters muttered to each other or themselves, some cops, too: what the fuck was *that* about? This swarm-of-attention search? Many had thought Hackel was surely playing coy, that he had to have known something, must have got a tip, something, that led him to that specific place with that kind of an army. They were sure they'd see him coming back, the look on his face making it clear they'd found Tara. Instead, *had* he really been playing a hunch? Just picked out a small portion of a mammoth park and devoted those kinds of resources to it, and he really had had nothing to justify it?

"I have a completely empty feeling inside. Now what?" Alicia told reporters.

Exactly.

Kozlowski was deflated, too. He'd had his doubts about

the search but had been hopeful. He was the sometimes loose cannon, not necessarily the most popular guy with some of those up the chain of command. And, aware of the pressure, political and otherwise, this case was engendering, he had had the feeling lately, rightly or wrongly, that if anything went wrong, he'd be the fall guy. He was the lead detective, and they weren't detecting much.

It'll come down on me like a load of bricks, he thought.

He'd been waking up every night, usually a few times, wondering, *What do I do, now? What do I do?* He was hoping that would end. Apparently not.

Hackel wanted to keep Grant guessing. He had no plans for another search, no intentions of mobilizing another one on hunch alone. But when asked about another search, he said it was a possibility, they might. He'd see.

Hackel wanted to salvage something else from the morning. He looked into the cameras, knowing they were sending out live shots, and said: "I want people to keep their eyes open. If you're out walking in a park, not just Stony Creek, but any park, if you see something suspicious, even a little suspicious, take a closer look."

At home nearby, a dental technician relaxing on her day off made a mental note to do just that.

Saturday had its rewards, nonetheless.

Sue Murasky, the Au Pair in America counselor, called Koz with big news: She'd been told by another of the agency's au pairs, Rebecca Ramcharan, that Verena Dierkes had confessed to her that she had been having an affair with Grant, starting before and continuing *after* Tara's disappearance.

Murasky gave Koz Ramcharan's phone number and told him she had told the au pair to expect his call. When Koz interviewed her two days later, she confirmed that Verena had told her about the affair, and had told her that she and

Grant were in love. They'd been flirting around, and the flirtations had turned to sex, and she had started sleeping with Grant while Tara was away.

Ramcharan provided Koz with a string of e-mails that had gone back and forth between her and Dierkes going back to the latter's arrival in Germany.

On February 22, the day after Dierkes had flown home, Ramcharan sent her a note: *"Just e-mailed to say that I miss you a lot. I hoped you arrived home safe. I bet your friends and family are excited to see you.*

"I'm thinking how boring my weekend is going to be now that you are not here. I guess all I can do is pray that you do return as soon as possible so I will have someone to go clubbing with in spring.

"Take care of yourself,

"Rebecca."

Dierkes, homesick for her new home in America, heartsick for Stephen, wrote her right back:

"I miss you, too!! Everybody is glad that I am home except for me. I wanna go right back!! And I will, but I probably have to wait a month. I safed [sic] a lot of money so I will come back, and then we'll see how things go on.

"I so don't want to be here, and that's not fair to my parents 'cause they really missed me a lot, and they were crying when they saw me. I was not crying, 'cause I was just thinking of . . . That actually makes me sad!! It was nice to see my family again, but if somebody would offer me a ticket to come back tomorrow, I would take it. I already talked to my parents, and they know that I really wanna come back, and I think they are kind of fine with it, but they are just worried.

"Nobody knows what's going to happen to Steve, and they don't know him, so they cannot say for sure that he didn't do anything. But I know it!! So they just have to trust me!!!

"God, I miss you guys a lot. I didn't sleep for thirty-four hours, so I'm kind of tired, but I don't really wanna sleep. I

*wanna go out with your and have some fun!!! But soon we
will have fun, again. So hope you enjoy your weekend. I
will, cause I can drink legally!!!:-) Miss you!*

"*Verena.*"

The last in the chain came from Verena late on Sunday,
the twenty-fifth.

"*How are you? I'm OK. Still miss you a lot!! What did
you do tonight? You are probably still out with the other
girls . . . It's so sad, and I hope I can come back as soon as
possible!!*

"*I got an e-mail today, and the police might wanna talk
to some au pairs. They will probably ask what I told you
about my host family. You know, I always told you good
things!! But please, don't forget about that ONE thing. You
have to promise! You can't say anything!! 'Cause if you do,
you know what's going to happen to him!!!!!!! I don't even
know if the police is going to ask some questions. I just
know that they wanna talk to me, again, and to all the former au pairs the Grant family had in the past. And other au
pairs in the area. That means my friends. Just don't forget
about it, I'm scared!!!! Miss you!!!*

"*Verena*"

Koz asked Ramcharan: what was the one thing?

She answered: her promise to Verena that she'd never tell
anyone about her affair with Steve. Verena had confided
details about it to her. It was too exciting to keep to herself.
But she made her promise never to tell.

Juicy stuff, though. But more than that. It was another
motive. Maybe motive enough to kill his wife and hide the
body.

READING HIS REVIEWS

The drama of Saturday having fizzled without a closing act, both sides resumed sparring the following week. Hackel complained that the two laptops Grant gave them were old and likely useless, what they needed was the home computer.

We can't do that, said Griem. The home computer had, he said, communications on it between him and his client, and turning it over to the police would violate attorney-client privilege. Beside, Griem claimed, since Tara hardly touched the home computer, it wouldn't have anything of value on it. (The same computer that Grant's friend had installed spyware on so he could surreptitiously read Tara's e-mails, so much for its being valueless.)

In any event, how could anyone accuse his client of not wanting to help solve this mystery when on his own dime he'd hired a private eye to help find Tara? And not just any private eye, said Griem, but a former FBI agent.

Grant confirmed he'd brought in his own guy. He was working hard, working all the angles, called Grant daily. Problem is, said Grant, he needs to talk to the cops, needs their help, and they won't talk to him. They're keeping him in the dark, treating him like a schmoe, what kind of crap is that?

Private eye? We never heard from one, don't know anything about it, countered Hackel.

Meanwhile, Grant's media spotlight was growing far beyond the off-Broadway stage of southeastern Michigan. He cried on Fox's *On the Record with Greta Van Susteren,* he pleaded for Tara's return on ABC's *Nightline,* and there he was on MSNBC, too.

The more some national TV folks got, the more the others wanted their fair share, too. Griem told Amber Hunt of the *Free Press* that it was getting out of hand. Someone from CNN's Nancy Grace show had, he told Hunt, called three times in one day, "and they told us that Sheriff Hackel is appearing, that Tara's sister is appearing, and more or less threatened us to appear. We're not going to add to this media feeding frenzy," he said.

The irony apparently escaped him, that he was claiming to take the high road of not feeding the media frenzy while complaining to a member of the media who is taking notes for a story that will be prominently displayed the next day. The local media was working hard to keep the story alive and center stage, and Griem was doing his bit to help.

Grant kept his busy schedule with the media. "I want people to get to know me a little better. I think people have the wrong impression," he'd tell reporters.

If his frequent trips past the sheriff's department were any indication, he must be putting more time in at his dad's shop nearby, too. Even so, it struck some that there was a taunting aspect to his making a point of stopping at the BP gas station kitty-corner from the police station every day to pick up his newspapers.

John Cwikla, the department's media liaison, stopped at the BP every morning to get the latest edition of the paper. One day the store owner told him, that guy in the news, the one with the missing wife, comes in every day to buy the paper. Three papers, actually.

No shit, thought Cwikla. He told Hackel when he got into the office. Hackel thought no shit, too. Hackel went across the street asked the owner if he could look at the footage from his surveillance camera. No problem. Hackel looked. Sure enough, there was Grant, every morning, buying a bottled water, a Reese's peanut butter cup—creature of habit—and the *Free Press,* the *News* and the *Macomb Daily.* Couldn't hardly get out of the store for reading all about it. Staring transfixed at the stories about him, looking for his quotes.

Grant was feeding the press. And it was feeding him. It wouldn't get enough of him, and he, apparently, couldn't get enough of it.

On Monday, February 26, police established a hotline, 800-690-FIND, and a Web site was set up to accommodate tips, generating more headlines, of course. Sergeant King called the National Center for Missing Adults and had Tara's information entered into its data base. He e-mailed her photo and it went up on its Web site, too.

Grant had kept Ian and Lindsey out of school since the story had broken the weekend after he reported their mother miss-ing. He had been afraid of what the other kids might say to them, or in front of them. Obviously, given the coverage, most, if not all, of them would have known what was going on in their classmates' lives.

But he couldn't keep them out forever. On Tuesday, Feb-ruary 27, he drove them to school. As the days had turned into weeks, and their fears about their mother grew—it was clear she wasn't on a normal business trip, so where was she?—Grant tried to put them at ease.

The family's beloved golden retriever, Bentley, had gone missing the year before and was gone a few days. The fam-ily had worried and grieved but the dog had returned. In his best Mr. Mom, Grant told the kids their mom being gone was just like when Bentley was gone. He was gone for a while, and she was gone the same way.

* * *

On Thursday, police in the Upper Peninsula searched a cabin Tara's parents own not far from her childhood home, on the odd chance she was using it as a place to get away from it all. They found no sign of her.

ANOTHER AU PAIR

Koz got an interesting e-mail on Tuesday, February 27. It was from one of the Grants' former au pairs, a young Ukrainian woman named Viktoria Prokhoda.

"Hello!

"I am an ex-au pair of the family Grant. I've been with this family from February 2006 to May 2006. If you have any questions to me, your [sic] *welcome to call. My year in U.S. is over and I'm in Ukraine, now. I will be glad if I can help you."*

Koz called her the next day. She told him about her time with the Grants, Stephen in particular, and had requested another assignment after three months.

What was so wrong at the Grants'?

It wasn't anything concrete. Grant struck her as creepy. He was too nosy, far too interested in what she did after her workday ended and who she was going out with. Was she going on a date? Who was the lucky guy? That kind of thing. It had been none of his business but he always kept at it.

What really got to her, though, and was the reason she quit, was the feeling she had every time she was in her bedroom at night. She had no proof, she'd never spotted him, but she had one of those feelings you get that someone is watching you. It wasn't just a feeling. It was a conviction. She had been sure of it. Every night. And she had quit because of it.

"I could always feel he was watching me when I was in my room," she said.

Koz remembered the layout of the house and the second-floor bedrooms from his visit there on the fourteenth. The Grants' master bedroom was on the other side of a wall from the au pair's. There was a large closet that lined that wall in the Grants' room. The closet had one of those closet organizers you see advertised on cable TV, an ingenious contraption that filled every square inch of the closet with shelves and hangers and had been jammed with Tara's stuff.

Had there been a peephole in the closet, too, hidden behind Tara's things?

Another thing to think about, in case they ever got a search warrant.

A SCARY FIND

Sheila Werner, a thirty-four-year-old dental hygienist, loved the Stony Creek area, with its lake and forests and dirt roads, in close proximity to the subdivisions rising out of old corn-fields. She hated litterbugs, how they fouled such a pretty area. About 1 P.M. on Wednesday, February 28, she went out her front door for a walk along the shoulder of Mt. Vernon Road, picking up trash as she went, as she often did.

About three hundred feet south of Imwood Road, she veered off east into the woods, and into a little frequented corner of Stony Creek Metropark. Just a few yards in, barely off the road, she spotted a large, gallon-sized Ziploc bag jammed between several fallen tree limbs, something red inside it in sharp contrast to the snow. Everyone who lived anywhere near the park had been transfixed by the search on Saturday, and she remembered what Sheriff Hackel had said on TV about looking more closely at anything that seemed the least bit suspicious.

She reached down and picked it up. There was what looked like blood pooled at the bottom, and inside it there were other plastic bags balled up, a pair of latex gloves, and what looked to be metal shavings.

This was litter enough for one day. She turned around,

walked briskly home, the top of the Ziploc pinched between her fingers. She set the bag down in her garage and went inside to call the police. Officer John Warn took the call and got directions to her house. It looked like blood to him, too, nothing much else had the same viscosity and hue. He then followed her in her car the short distance down the road to where she'd found the bag.

Warn called Koz, who told him he was sending Deputy Ron Murphy, an evidence tech, to meet him. Warn looked around the area in the twenty minutes it took Murphy to get there but found nothing else. Murphy tested a spotted piece of the plastic with something called MacPhail's Reagent. If the object was blood, the test solution would turn a bluish green. It did. Murphy then took pictures of the scene with his Canon digital, focusing on a set of deteriorating footprints that headed away from the tree limbs and deeper into the woods.

Okay, it was blood. But that didn't mean it was human blood. It would need to be sent to the state police crime lab in Sterling Heights to determine what kind of blood. The hunters on her team told Lieutenant Darga not to get too excited. Stony Creek is lousy with deer, they practically overrun the place, and poaching is rampant. It was common practice when you were cleaning deer to stuff shit in bags when you were done. Clean up the area. The Ziploc was probably remnants poachers neglected to pick up from a recent kill and butchering.

And just what would cause poachers in the field, asked Darga, to deposit metal shavings in the bag? No one had an answer for that. She didn't want to get her hopes up, but Grant worked in a machine shop that made ball bearings. The place was probably full of metal shavings, a messy ubiquitous byproduct of shaping spheres of steel to the proper size.

There were a few strands of longish, light-colored hair in the bag, too. Maybe human. Maybe not. Grant had a dog. It had longish, light-colored hair.

There is a perpetual and enormous backlog of tests to be

done at the state's crime labs, much of it a result of law requiring DNA analysis of all convicted felons. Waits can run to a year. Now, though, given the notoriety of the case, the nearest lab went right to work.

Jennifer Smiatacz, a forensic scientist with the state police, called King the next day. The blood in the bag was human, all right. The bag contained four clear plastic garbage bags, one pair of latex gloves, one 7-Eleven bag, and another Ziploc bag, and they all had human blood on them. And those were metal shavings. There was no identification, yet, on the hair

All of them, Hackel, Kalm, Wickersham, Darga, McLean, Koz, and King were sure they finally had probable cause for a search warrant. The bag was found not far from the Grant home. It had metal shavings similar to what would be found in the kind of shop where he worked. It had hair similar to his dog's. It had human blood, his wife was missing, and he'd had visible cuts on his nose and hand the day he reported her gone.

Hackel told Koz to write drafts of search-warrant requests for both Grant's house and his dad's small machine shop, a dingy little place with metal shavings all over the floor and whose name, USG Babbitt, gave it a grandeur far beyond what it deserved. USG Babbitt sounded like some conglomerate. A more appropriate name would have been: "Al's Joint." (Stephen Grant, who used to bristle at suggestions his wife was the breadwinner, would protest that he made a good living at a major auto supplier, "major" being open to interpretation, if not hallucination.) USG Babbitt shared a gray cinder-block building with several other small businesses; it was the last business at the east end of the building, barely big enough to house a few machines, what seemed like years' worth of dirt and grime, and a couple of workers.

Koz did the drafts that night on his home computer. He'd written up hundreds of them in his career, had it down pat.

Friday morning, while Darga reviewed Koz's drafts, he and a group of ten or twelve detectives went out to Stony

Creek to see what else they could find. They fanned out
from the site of the Werner find, came up empty, and headed
over to Grant's dad's machine shop in Mt. Clemens. It abutted some woods and wetlands along the Clinton River,
which might be a good spot to hide or dump something.
They searched the woods and wetlands, went through a
Dumpster, came up empty again, and returned to the department about noon.

Darga signed off on Koz's warrant requests, and told him
to take them over later in the afternoon to the prosecutor's
office for review, Prosecutor Eric Smith was assembling a
team to meet him.

Smith and a bunch of his staff were there, including two
of his top trial attorneys, Bill Cataldo and Therese Tobin,
and the staff member who specialized in appeals-court issues who would make sure all the dots were over the i's and
the t's were crossed. The appeals attorney made some suggestions, as did Smith's chief of staff, Ben Liston, an Ivy
League graduate who had a reputation as a wordsmith.

Smith got on the phone to Richard McLean, a magistrate
in the Forty-second District Court in Romeo—the Grant
home was in that district—and filled him in on developments.
Koz signed the requests and they faxed them over to McLean.
He read them, got Koz on the line, swore him in, and got his
pro forma promise that what he had claimed on the warrants
was true, signed the papers, and faxed them back.

It was closing in on 5 P.M. Koz led one small group of detectives over to the dad's shop nearby. Another group headed
to the Grant house. On the way, an anonymous caller phoned
in a tip that a bunch of women's clothing was in a ditch at
Van Dyke and 26 Mile Road, just a few blocks from Stony
Creek. That caused a tizzy but proved a false alarm. There
were clothes, but they weren't Tara's.

No one was at the shop, so they broke down the door with
a battering ram. The place was dark, even with the lights on,
dirty and in disarray. There were several metal lathes and
drill presses, a sand blaster, and a band saw. Tools had been

left out, and there was litter on the machines and a coating of metal dust almost everywhere, except for a large clean patch on the floor. The overhead lights cast creepy shadows. Koz, not the skittish type, got the willies. It had the feel of a slasher movie, They saw what looked like a couple of drops of blood on the floor in a doorway, under the door handle, took photos of them. Probably nothing. Easy place to cut a hand.

The shop had a small, enclosed office, its roof beneath the higher roof of the shop proper. Koz found a ladder, leaned it against the office roof, and climbed up. There were footprints in what looked like years' worth of dust, and a big cleared spot where something had sat until recently.

Other than that, after a half hour, forty-five minutes, diddly. They could always come back later with evidence techs and spend more time on a thorough search. Now, though, the techs were converging on the house, and so were Koz and King. They headed west to Van Dyke and started driving north. Van Dyke is one of the busiest surface roads in Michigan and at 6 P.M., it was jammed with traffic.

Koz heard something whirring, looked up, saw they were racing helicopters up Van Dyke. Shit! The news must have got out. Bloodsucking TV guys were on the way.

"I WAS THE PERFECT MOM"

After two weeks of nonstop attention, Stephen Grant was known by the media members who covered the story closely as a nonstop yakker and publicity hound. He was chatty and available, often seeking out his favorite print and TV folks with phone calls at all hours.

George Hunter, a reporter for the *Detroit News,* asked Grant for some sit-down time for an in-depth interview Friday. Grant, always happy to oblige, on a first-name basis with Hunter by now, as he was with all the familiar faces covering the melodrama, agreed to meet with him at the house at noon. They chatted, or rather Grant talked, words flying out, flitting from topic to topic, voice high-pitched and eyes popping.

A story on the interview would be, although Hunter didn't know it then, part of a big package of stories the *News* would run on Monday, under the headline: I WAS THE PERFECT MOM—NOT TARA

No, Grant said, Tara wasn't the perfect mother the media and her family were portraying. She was far from perfect, both with the kids and with him. She was a bad mother for the kids, and a worse wife with him.

In fact, said Grant, the last words Tara had said to him before she left the house the night she disappeared were: " 'Don't forget to take my truck in Monday.' That really took the wind out of my sails. She was telling me that's all I was. It was like: 'You be the valet and take my car in.' "

Grant told Hunter he resented the time Tara spent away from the family. They often, he said, argued over who was the boss in the family, who'd run the household.

They'd fought the night she disappeared after she told him she'd decided to return to Puerto Rico a day earlier than previously planned, he admitted, but nothing out of the ordinary.

"In a lot of households, when there's an argument, that means fists are involved," he said. "But Tara and I never did that. It wouldn't come close to happening. I wouldn't do it."

So, they got in a yelling match, and after she ordered him to take care of her truck, she walked out, got in a dark car that had pulled into the driveway and left, Grant watching her from the door that led to the garage, through the open garage door.

"She left the house angry," said Grant. "My biggest concern was that I was going to have to explain to the kids the next day why their mother wasn't going to be there like she said she would. All I could do was close the garage door. I was done."

Grant told Hunter how he'd swept Tara off her feet when he showed up, unexpectedly, at her grandmother's funeral in Escanaba in August of 1994. The rest of the family had been cool to him but "the next day," said Grant, "she called me and told me she was in love with me."

Grant recounted a history of their marriage, her rise up the corporate ladder punctuated by the birth of their kids, and the frequent travel that began in 2003 when she was made systems manager, Lindsey just three, Ian one, no matter to Tara.

"She's been traveling all over the world for four years. It became difficult, but I learned to live with it," he said. She'd changed, he said. Changed in personality, changed in looks. That loose-curled hair she had now? The look made so famous by the photos the newspapers kept running and the TV news kept airing? That one? Grant didn't like it. It seemed to symbolize how she'd changed.

"Tara looked completely different when we met. She was beautiful," said Grant. "It's hard to explain. She just looked a lot different. She had the big hair."

Big hair, indeed. Long and big. Photos of her taken then, you'd think she was a country-and-western recording star, not a college coed at Michigan State. He loved that look.

They'd had their rocky times as man and wife, and although they'd continued to fight over the travel, things were better now. They'd gone to marriage counseling in 2005 and 2006 but as a couple they had more or less got past the need. The secret? Communication.

Grant disputed Alicia's contention to the media that her sister was a good mother who often flew home to attend important school events.

"That's not true," said Grant. "I don't recall one time when she did that. She was there on weekends, but it wasn't out of the ordinary for her to come in, kiss the babies, and then leave, again."

Grant said he didn't think Tara had been unfaithful, but he had reason for doubt. Over the last year, she'd been text-messaging one of her old bosses, back and forth, like they were fourteen-year-old girls. They'd be texting and Tara'd be giggling. One time, the Grants were in the car on the way to Alicia's, and Tara and the old boss were texting. Grant put up with it for a while, but was steaming. Finally, he reached over and grabbed the phone. *"I'm P-ing,"* she had typed. He yelled at her: "What the hell would you tell somebody you're going to the bathroom for?"

But that wasn't it, she told him, her dismissive tone letting him know he was a child, a dummy, having to have it spelled out. She didn't mean it literally, she meant it in the context of "I'm laughing so hard I'm peeing." Her and Mr. Witty on the other end had been cracking each other up. Except she wasn't really laughing, not so her family could hear. Imaginary laughter, in her head. Texting to some coworker far away and ignoring her family in the car. Does that sound like the perfect wife?

"I was a better mom than Tara was. There's no other way to put it," he said. "I was the mom in the house. She was gone all the time. If the kids needed someone to take them to swimming, or school, or soccer practice, I took them. To be honest, as weird as it sounds for me to say this, I was the perfect mom, not Tara."

Grant was parroting one of his recurring themes: how such a good Mr. Mom wouldn't be capable of the violence people were suspecting him of. He had once told Hunter he was such a good stay-at-home mom that a trained private investigator he claimed to have hired to find Tara *knew* he didn't do it.

"When I first sat down and talked with my private investigator, he said, 'I can't believe the police are looking at you as a suspect, because you're not that guy,'" Grant told Hunter. "He said, 'Someone who would harm his wife isn't the kind of guy who helps clean the house and cooks dinner. That guy is not you.' People who know me—even if they've only known me a short time—they know I didn't do anything wrong. They know it's not me."

The private investigator never surfaced. Nothing he found—if he existed and if he found anything—was ever revealed.

Now, Hunter asked about the scoop he'd had in the *News* back on February 21, that fifteen days before Tara's disappearance, he had sent extremely suggestive e-mails to an ex-girlfriend, telling her he thought Tara was having an affair, that he was frustrated in his marriage and wanted to see her, the ex-girlfriend, naked?

"I did say, 'I want to see you naked,' but that's because I'm a guy. Men always want to see women naked," he said. "There are a lot of things people say just kidding around that they wouldn't want to see on the front page of the newspaper."

Grant acknowledged that people suspected him of his wife's disappearance and said he understood why. "When Laci Peterson came up missing [in California in 2002], I was sure her husband did it. But now, I'm on the other side of it. I know people think I had something to do with why Tara is missing, but I didn't do it."

These days, he said, life was disjointed. "Surreal, like I'm walking around in a daze."

They shook hands, Hunter hoping the case didn't eat into his whole weekend, Grant heading over to his dad's shop for a bit and then over to his sister's. He wouldn't stay long at Kelly's. His buddy from Channel 4, Hank Winchester, his phone pal, was coming by the house later for an interview, and Grant wasn't one to keep him waiting.

A WALK WITH THE DOG

Just as the first cops start arriving at the Grant house to execute their search warrant about five, word comes from the surveillance team that had been on Grant for a week that he has just left his sister's and looks to be headed home.

A Channel 4 TV truck, with telescoping monster antenna folded down on the roof, pulls up. Hank Winchester is there for his interview. The cops want to know what he's doing there. He wants to know what they're doing. Search warrant? Ho, boy, this is going to be better than any interview. They start broadcasting live as cops and evidence technicians keep arriving. There will be five techs in all, two from the sheriff's department, three from the state police crime lab.

Hackel has stayed back at the office, to monitor developments, to see how to play the media angle if anything pops. It's already popped. Captain Kalm, who's running the show at the house, calls him, tells him about Winchester. Shit! Hackel turns on Channel 4, sure enough, there's his men and the Grant house, lit up in the TV klieg lights.

Instantly, the incoming phone lines light up. It's reporters and producers at the other stations calling in a lather, bitching about getting cut out of the loop, why is Hackel playing favorites, why is Winchester getting spoon-fed the scoop? Oh, they're pissed.

Hackel tries to placate them, tells them he had nothing to do with Winchester being there first. No one buys it.

Wickersham tells Deputy Tom Szalkowski to head out onto Van Dyke and stop Grant just before he can pull into his subdivision. They don't want him seeing all the activity and bolting. Let him know what's going on, follow him in. With him coming, they won't need to kick in the door. He can let them in. Meanwhile, the techs start unloading their gear.

Szalkowski pulls over onto the shoulder on Van Dyke, has only a few moments to wait, pulls Grant over. Grant gets in the scout car. Hackel knows Grant's in the car because he's watching it on live TV, as are hundreds of thousands of others, TV helicopters arriving, one of them beaming shots of Szalkowski and Grant.

The deputy tells Grant about the search and that he'll need to keep out of the way, but to follow him to the house. And just to be on the safe side, please hand over your driver's license. Grant hands it over. At the house, he sees they're just starting. He parks his Jeep and gets out.

"He's getting out of the car! He's getting out of the car!" hollers a member of Winchester's crew. The camera swings his way and beams the image of Grant—he always looks pop-eyed, but now it's somehow even more exaggerated, like deer-in-the-headlights pop eyes, given the circumstances, the klieg lights on him, the commotion in front of him, Wickersham walking up to him.

They talk for a minute or two, Wickersham explaining they've got their warrant, what they'll be doing, how long it might take. They would have rammed in the door if they had to but they knew Grant was coming, Wickersham doesn't tell him that.

"You're not going to tear out the ceiling tiles, are you?" he asks, polite, doesn't act put out at all. Strange question, thinks Wickersham. Should they? He's noncommittal. He tells Grant they'll treat the house with respect.

Grant hands over the house key, gets back into his Jeep and pulls it into the driveway. He goes in the house, calls Griem on his cell, explains what's happening, hands Wickersham the phone. "My attorney wants to talk to you," he said.

"Do you have an arrest warrant?" asks Griem. Griem is having a cow. Apoplectic. Wait till he finds out, any second, that it's all happening live on TV.

"No."

In that case, says Griem, please release my client. Not that anyone is holding him. Smith has already told Hackel that they have no grounds to keep Grant, until and unless they find something in the house and can get an arrest warrant approved. Griem is a respected adversary. They are determined not to give him any issues to appeal, later, if it comes to a trial.

Grant says he needs to get his Lab/shepherd mix, Bentley, out for a pee. Gets the leash, puts it on the dog, out they go. They walk down his driveway. The media has converged en masse, by now, Winchester having lost his exclusive. The photographers click off shots of man and beast off for a stroll.

Winchester's cameraman keeps Grant in his sights. Daylight is nearly gone, snow is blowing sideways. Viewers watch Grant walking into the distance and quickly disappearing into the dark, there one second, gone the next, the effect exaggerated by the TV lights, the snow between the camera and Grant, and the darkness down the road.

If this were a novel, critics might criticize this passage as heavy-handed dramatic foreshadowing. But this was real life, the kind of stuff, it's true, you can't make up.

"WHAT THE . . . !"

Moments later, Griem pops into view on Hackel's office TV. He's giving an impromptu press conference, telling the reporters around him that the warrant is never going to hold up. "I'm going to take that warrant and stuff it where the sun doesn't shine," he says.

Cheeses Hackel off. Amuses him at the same time. Griem has no way of knowing about Werner's find. Let him spout.

Koz and King pull up at the Grant house. By now, at this point in the investigation, King, Koz, Hackel, McLean, all of them are sure Tara is dead. She was too good of a worker, too good of a mom, too good of a sister and daughter to have disappeared from everyone. Her husband, sure, she could have disappeared from him, but someone else would have heard from her.

"Everyone's thoughts were, she's definitely dead somewhere," King said later. Still, there was hope that this was some elaborate plot she'd carried out, that she was hiding in the Upper Peninsula, figuring out what to do with the rest of her life, or off on some Caribbean island with a secret lover, deciding how to reconcile him with the rest of her life.

The main object of the search is to get the home computer Griem had so assiduously kept them from getting. The techs would search painstakingly for trace evidence. Maybe some blood spatter on a wall that has gone undetected. Luminol everything; under ultraviolet light that'll show if any blood had been spilled and cleaned up recently. Maybe they'd get lucky evidence of a scuffle. But so much time had passed, they weren't expecting a lot. This likely would be methodical, tedious, time-consuming, and, except for the computer, fruitless.

To Koz, the feeling he has is that most of those at the scene look at the search as CYA time, cover your ass. Do a search because it's something at this point you need to check off a list, but not holding out much hope that anything would come of it. Maybe later, when the tech guys got into the computer.

Koz and McLean, though, they have a feeling. "I thought we'd find something. Pam and I were both convinced," he'd say later. McLean had taken the day off; her parents were up from Florida for a long weekend, and her and her mom planned on shopping. But when Darga called her to let her know they were going to execute the warrant, McLean made apologies to her parents and raced over to the Grants.'

There are twelve members of the sheriff's department at the scene and three state police forensic scientists, who are setting up shop in the kitchen and getting ready for their hours of painstaking work, which will mean going over literally every square inch of the house. Not much to look at or do for the detectives on the scene, so they're just milling around, wanting to be at the center of things, basically just getting in the way. "Just bullshitting, doing what cops do. Waiting for the techs to tell us to do something," Koz would describe it later.

"Hanging around, telling jokes," was the way Darga described it. She has lab people setting up, her own evidence techs starting to film the house. She turns to the other cops, the bullshitters and jokers. "Out, all of you. Out of the house. Go sit in your cars or whatever," she said.

Koz suggests they go to the garage, bullshit there. They close the garage door, keep the wind out, keep the press from staring at them, keep the frickin' helicopters from beaming their images across the airwaves. There are so many helicopters out there now, hovering back and forth, it's a miracle none of them have collided.

Koz looks around the garage. He was in there the night he and McLean first interviewed Grant, and he tries to remember what it looked like then, if there is anything different now. He walks over to a tool chest and opens it. A bunch of tools are lined up neatly on a sheet of rubber. There are two empty spaces. He wonders what those tools are. Where they are. One of the spaces is pretty big. Hacksaw, maybe?

A large green Rubbermaid storage container with red handles and a blue lid catches his eye, crammed in with a bunch of other stuff along the wall, a black mesh tarp folded up on top of it. The garage is cluttered, hard to remember if anything is different. Had the Rubbermaid been there before? He can't remember, but that of all the things in the garage is bugging him.

No one notices till later there is a tag taped to the Rubbermaid bin. It says, "Boy's Clothes." It had been Tara's container. She'd used it to store clothes Ian had outgrown, to give to Alicia.

Koz goes over to the container and tries to pop the lid. It doesn't want to come. So he gets a good grip with what he calls his big Polack hands and gives it a tug and off it pops. There's a black garbage bag inside. He thinks, *Dog food.* That's all it is, the dog food container. Almost puts the lid back on. Instead, he leans over, grabs the bag with two hands and rips a small hole. Inside? Another black garbage bag. He rips a small hole in that one. There's another black bag. Rips it. Jesus Christ! A fourth garbage bag.

Koz rips a small hole in this bag, too. He can see colors inside that one, light's not real good, hole's small, but he can see a flash of red and some plastic. Not another bag, not sure what it is. He thinks, *Deer carcass.* He's a hunter, he's stuffed deer carcasses in garbage bags, and the image pops into his mind. He sticks his hand into the bag to get hold of what he's looking at and . . .

And it's wet! He yanks his hand back out of the bag. His fingertips are red.

"What the fuck!" he yells.

The other cops have been off to the side, bullshitting. They hear Koz and run over. Detective Sergeant Mark Grammatico shines a flashlight into the bag. "That looks like blood," he says.

There's blood, A lot of blood. A lot of blood for a goddamn Rubbermaid bin in a garage in Washington Township.

"Get the techs!" hollers Koz. He pokes his head in the house. "Lieutenant, you better come here," he hollers to Darga.

Someone yells out a warning from the house. They've got the TV on inside so they can half-ass follow what the TV guys are up to outside, and right now, there are live shots from a helicopter of the detectives inside the garage. They're shooting through the windows. Thank God you can't see what the cops are all interested in.

They open the big garage door, back the cars out to give them some room, close the door. Luckily, there's a four-by-eight-foot sheet of plywood leaning against a wall, and they use it to block the windows.

Koz is still thinking that somehow it's a deer carcass. It's the only thing that makes sense. Don Murphy, one of the evidence techs, has a knife and slits the bags wide open. They're all leaning in to get a better look. There's an audible collective gasp. A couple of "shits."

There's skin, a dull, oddly white look to it. Wearing a black bra. Unreal. Koz thinks of Resuscitation Annie, a mannikin they do mouth-to-mouth training on, or CPR. Annie's got skin that color. This isn't registering. They rip the bags all the way open.

Koz turns to Lieutenant Darga. "Is that her?"

Darga leans forward, moves a step closer, leans lower.

She sees a woman's suit, or part of it. She nods. "Yeah, I think so. I think it's her."

Not entirely. It's a torso. A freakin' torso. No head, no arms, no legs. Just a torso. And some clothes. Technically, maybe it's not Tara. They'd need to run tests to confirm the identity. But this isn't a time for technicalities. It's 8 P.M. The search for Tara is over. Or at least for this part of her.

PART TWO

HUNT

"WHERE IS HE?"

They're all shocked, of course. It's completely surreal. Why is there a torso here? Who would leave a torso in a garage? Cops have been on you for weeks and there's still a torso half-assed hidden in your garage? "We all thought she was dead, by then. Everything had led to a dead end. She hadn't touched her money. She hadn't shown up for work. She hadn't used her credit cards. She hadn't used her cell phone or her e-mail accounts. But *nothing* prepares you for *that*," King would say later.

"Did any of us think we'd find a torso?" Wickersham would ask. A rhetorical question.

There, in the garage, he says to himself, *Holy shit!* Feels deflated. Then a surge. "Okay. Now we got him. Let's go *get* him."

It's freaky. It's shocking and scary. It's also like winning murder-detective lotto. What were the chances? The evidence techs start shooing everyone away from the scene, worried about someone contaminating it and the evidence. McLean isn't happy at what they found. But she's happy about: "We got him." She thinks, *We got him.* An investigation that had taken over their lives, that seemed to be going nowhere, that seemed to be going in a direction where the guy they know did it is going to get away with it, and: "We got him!"

Kalm calls Hackel and gives him the news. "We got her," he says.

Hackel would say later that everything came to a stop. Just froze. "What the hell are you talking about?" he says.

"We've got her body. Actually, we think we have her torso."

The hair on Hackel's neck literally stands up. "You've got to be shitting me!"

"I had two conflicting emotions," the sheriff would say later. "I didn't know whether to be happy or sad. We'd broken the case, so you've got those emotions. But I was still hoping she just took off somewhere, left that asshole. She's a person you felt like you've gotten to know. And she's dead. You feel like crying."

Hackel tells Kalm to lock it all down. No one talks on their cell phone. No one says a thing. This isn't getting out until he can break the news to Alicia. He tells Kalm he'll be right there.

Wickersham calls Griem, tells them his client has fled and they need to talk to him. Tells him nothing about the torso.

"If you catch him, promise me you won't question him," says Griem.

"Of course."

"If you find him, call me."

Meanwhile, Koz is switching gears, from stunned observer to pissed-off hunter. "You had to wrap your mind around what you were seeing," he would say later. And once he wrapped it, the gears switched.

He turns to Wickersham. "Where is he?" Meaning Grant. Knowing they had a surveillance team on him, figuring they still do.

Wickersham turns to Darga. She's been running the team. "We dropped him when he got home," says Darga.

The crew had followed Grant home. But there seemed to be no need to stick around when he was surrounded by enough cops for a softball game. For another, with Winchester's crew there and the helicopters filming from overhead, they didn't want any of the undercover guys' faces showing up on TV. How were they to know he was going to take the dog for a walk? A long walk. An ongoing walk, apparently.

"I'm going to go get him," says Koz.

He runs out of the garage to his car. It is snowing hard, now. McLean stays behind. She'll head up the crew at the house till they pack up in the wee hours of the morning. She feels a sense of relief, a sense of adrenaline surging through her *and* a sense of sorrow. She'd never met Tara but felt she knew her. Felt sisterhood with her. "I compared myself to her a lot," she'd say later. "I want to be the perfect mother. The perfect spouse. The perfect boss at work. You know, if I work an afternoon shift, I'll take off in the middle of the day to go home and make dinner so my kids will have a hot meal. Heaven forbid they have to eat pizza. So, I understood her. She was an amazing person, and this psychopath killed her."

A little later, one of the crew finds what looks to be part of a spinal cord in the freezer in the basement. Fuck! That sends a chill through everyone. "My God! Is he fricking eating her?" McLean wonders. "Do we have another Jeffrey Dahmer?" They hadn't seen the entire torso. Maybe some of it had been broken off. What in the fuck is going on here?

They're all sort of freaking now, but the county medical examiner, Daniel Spitz, calms them down when he gets to the house a little later. He looks at the spinal cord. "It's an animal," he says.

At the least, Grant isn't a Dahmer.

Grant disappears into the snow and deepening twilight with Bentley. When he can no longer see anything of his house or the action there, he calls a friend, Michael Zanlungo, who lives two miles or so away. Zanlungo had met the Grants shortly after they moved to the area four years earlier, and liked both Tara and Stephen. In 2005 and 2006, Grant had been the head coach and Zanlungo the assistant coach of their daughters' soccer team.

Zanlungo was one of those firmly on the side of: there's no way Stephen could have done it. There has to be a logical explanation, even a tragic one, that doesn't involve him.

Grant tells Zanlungo the police are in the middle of carrying out a search warrant at his home and, while they have temporarily impounded his car, too, told him he was free to leave. He is, in fact, out for a walk with the dog. Any chance Zanlungo can come pick him up?

Zanlungo doesn't ask why, says sure, he'll pick him up in a few minutes at a nearby intersection. He pulls up, Grant and Bentley hop into his car. Grant was calm on the phone, is anything but calm now. He looks behind them, he looks to the side, he looks back behind them again.

We being followed? No. What about that Taurus? Don't think so. Zanlungo notices Grant is sweating, despite the cold he's just come out of. For the first time, Zanlungo is having doubts. Grant sure doesn't look like an innocent man.

He even says, "What's going on? You're not acting like an innocent person."

Grant has a confession for him. The cops have his computer, and they're sure to find compromising e-mails from him to their former au pair. He thinks they're going to arrest him, now that they believe he has a motive. But before they do, he needs to get to his kids first. They're at their aunt's.

Grant asks Zanlungo if he can borrow his car. Last thing Zanlungo thinks he should do. Can't work up a flat-out no. Tells him it's the company car, can't lend it out. But, he says reluctantly, you can borrow my truck. A few minutes later, Zanlungo pulls into his driveway, next to a bright yellow Dodge Dakota Sport Quad pickup. He hands Grant the keys, Grant and Bentley get into the truck, and Grant once again disappears into the night.

*   *   *

Koz has a hunch. Knows one of Grant's favorite hangouts is the Buffalo Wild Wings a few blocks away, at 26 Mile Road and Van Dyke. Has a feeling Grant has gone there to wait out the search, knowing they wouldn't find anything in the house, cocky fucker thinking he'll pull it off, no one will think to look for Tara in a Rubbermaid bin.

"I thought for sure I'd see him sitting at the bar at Buffalo Wild Wings and end it right there," he said.

He races in. Grant's not at the bar. Isn't there. There's a strip mall at that intersection, couple of gas stations, a McDonald's. Koz cruises them all. Nothing. He knows from the surveillance team the Grant kids are at Kelly's, so he drives over there, racing through the snow.

Meanwhile, one of the other cops calls Grant's cell, gets the recording to leave a message, says they're about done. Tells him he might wanna come home and lock up the house.

Hackel arrives at the house. He goes straight into the garage, opens up the Rubbermaid bin to see with his own eyes. Only then will it be real. In addition to the blood and clothes and the shock of her torso, he sees twigs and leaves.

He turns to Kalm. "I'm telling you, he retrieved this thing from the park."

Bill Robinette arrives from the county Medical Examiner's Office. Well, doesn't arrive at the house, arrives at a Meijer's store in a nearby strip center at 26 Mile Road and Van Dyke. They didn't want live TV shots of someone from the coroner's office carrying out body parts. So Grammatico had put the lid back on the Rubbermaid bin and carried it out of the house, to the peering eyes of the media, just something they were taking for later examination. Nobody thought anything of it.

Robinette took possession of the bin and took it back to

the lab. He inventoried its contents; taken one way, just a short list of stuff, taken another, a sorrowful reminder that the bloody thing in the bin had once been a vibrant, stylish, sexy woman in the prime of life:

1. *An extra-small shirt from Ann Taylor.*
2. *A black Gillian & O'Malley bra, size unknown.*
3. *Black V-shaped bikini underwear from Victoria's Secret.*

At the Utykanskis', Kelly and Chris are polite enough to Koz. They invite him in. Grant's not there. His kids still are. So is Bentley. Koz is allergic to cats, hates cigarettes some, there's cat dander so thick in the house he can almost see it. Some skinny-assed friend of theirs is chain-smoking, Koz can't breathe. He doesn't say anything about the torso, of course, just that they're looking for Stephen, need to talk to him.

He was there, a little while ago, had borrowed a white truck from a neighbor and stopped by, just after they'd got back from a church fish fry. Koz tries Grant's cell phone. It's *there,* in the front room, ringing. Sister explains that her brother didn't want to get hassled by the cops, no offense, traded phones with Chris so he'd have some peace.

Koz calls in the news Grant's not on foot, he's got wheels, a white truck. Later he'll wonder how Kelly could have mistaken that bright yellow truck for white.

Back in his office, Hackel turns on the TV. Griem is back on; this time it looks like a street in Greektown, a two-block area in downtown Detroit, just around the block from police headquarters. Griem's wearing a knit cap, says DETROIT POLICE DEPARTMENT. Pisses Hackel off. He knows what Griem's message is: I like cops, I just don't like your cops.

Hackel hears Griem say it again: "I'm going to stick that search warrant where the sun doesn't shine."

Ohmigod, thinks Hackel, you have no idea. He tells Cwikla to call a press conference for 9 P.M. He isn't going to say anything about what they found—he still hasn't called the Standerfers. The media arrive, hoping for something big. They get what they already knew. A warrant had been issued that afternoon and executed at the Grant house. No arrests have been made. Tests were made and results are pending.

The media leave. Hackel decides on another search of Stony Creek in the morning, this time in the area of Werner's find. He tells King he's going to head it up. They start making the calls, telling officers scheduled to be off duty to come in, getting hold of reserves, asking Stony Creek officials for their help, getting the state police on board.

Darga's been on the job since 8 A.M. So, too, have a lot of the cops in the house. They're going to be there a while, she's got a diabetic tech she's worried about, so she tells everyone she's going to go to McDonald's, pick up a shitload of burgers and fries and be back soon.

Her mom has been calling her endlessly on her cell phone. She calls her husband, Kevin, tells him she's gonna be a while, please call my mother and tell her to stop calling. Turns out her mother heard that Grant has fled, she's picturing her daughter running down the street or through the woods after him. Worried.

Kevin tells her: "Grant's attorney's on TV. He said he's going to shove that search warrant where the sun don't shine."

You don't say, thinks Darga. You might want to rethink that, counselor.

At 10:30 P.M. now, Wickersham and Koz meet at Roger's Roost, a popular tavern at 15 Mile and Schoenherr. They want to go over the day's events, get organized for tomorrow, put together a checklist of what needs to be done by whom.

They're still there at 11:45; Koz gets a text message from

Bill Cataldo, the assistant prosecutor. He's heard uncon-
firmed reports they found a torso at Grant's. Their lid was still
officially on the night's find, keeping the media frenzy at
bay—shit, media was already in a frenzy, had been for weeks,
what word would you use to describe what was going to hit
the fan once they knew Tara's torso was what had been in
the Rubbermaid bin they'd seen being carried out?

Hackel had made it clear to everyone: not a word. Except
you can't keep a torso in a Rubbermaid bin a secret. Someone was going to tell a girlfriend or a wife or another cop, or
someone in the Prosecutor's Office. Besides the courtesy
they needed to afford the Standerfers, it would be better for
everyone, especially Hackel, at the top of the chain of command, if they got Grant back in custody before anyone knew
they'd let him walk off with his dog while they were standing chatting a few feet away from Tara's torso.

"Here," said Koz, handing the phone with the message
showing to his boss. Let him decide what to do.

They know Grant has fled. He's clearly capable of violence
and irrational behavior. They know he owns a gun. They know
he's been arrested before for carrying a concealed weapon
without a permit in his car. Hackel knows the bad blood between Grant and the Standerfers has been simmering. He's
worried Grant might be heading their way. He's got to be
pissed at the ex-girlfriend who told them about his salacious
e-mails. He might be heading her way, too. Guy'll cut up his
wife into pieces, pretty much will do anything to anyone.

Wickersham calls his ex-girlfriend in Lansing, tells her
she might want to find someplace else to sleep tonight. She
packs up some stuff and goes to stay with Tom Gromak, the
Detroit News staffer who had convinced her to go public
with her tale of the e-mails.

At 11:30, Hackel calls Erik Standerfer, wakes him up. He
wants them out of their house, and he needs to break the
news, but he isn't going to do it over the phone. He tells Eric

they've come into information that leads them to suspect foul play. Can he do him a favor and gather up the family, right now, and come to Detroit? He'll explain it to him when he gets here.

Erik doesn't press him about what's happened. From his tone and the lack of any questions, Hackel assumes Erik assumes the worst, that they've found Tara, or somehow know she's dead. Says they'll come with Alicia's parents, too.

The sheriff looks up the phone number for the nearby Best Western ConCorde Inn in Clinton Township, calls and asks the clerk to put two rooms on his credit card. The clerk tells him it's against company policy to do that over the phone. He'll have to come in in person.

What! You gotta be shitting me, Hackel thinks. Expresses it a bit more politely.

"You cannot take credit card information over the phone?"

"No."

"Look, this is Sheriff Mark Hackel. I'm in the middle of a murder investigation, I need to get two rooms for people who are driving in from Ohio. I've reserved rooms at hotels all over the country on my credit card."

"I'm sorry, sir. It's company policy."

"I can't believe this."

Jesus Christ! Like I don't have better things to do, he says to himself. He runs to his car, drives over to the motel, runs in, gives his credit card to the clerk, and gives him his business card, too. "Can you have your manager call me in the morning," he says sternly, seriously pissed.

He calls Erik and tells him he got them two rooms, asks him to call him when they get close and he'll give him directions, then returns to his office. The place is still abuzz, forget the time, cops hanging around, the media swarming outside, TV crews at the ready, none of them leaving, afraid they'll miss out on the next piece of news if they do. News of the torso has yet to leak, amazingly.

Hackel's been up for forty-eight hours. His head's swimming. He can smell the stress leaking out of his pores.

He needs a shower. He tells everyone he'll be back in an hour or so and heads home. The night is about to take an even weirder turn. There's no rest for the righteous.

On his way, he approaches an intersection. There's a car stopped right in the middle of it, under the stoplight, driver slumped over the wheel. Hackel slows down, approaches the side of the car slowly, his headlights shining in. He can see it's a woman, who suddenly straightens up and drives off. Hackel turns to follow her instead of going straight, last thing he needs is this. Woman's car is weaving from curb to curb and accelerating away from him.

"I hadn't seen one of those in a long time," he'd say later. "You gotta be kidding me. I'm in the middle of the biggest case of my life and I gotta deal with a drunk driver?" Hackel turns on his flashers, used so infrequently these days, and calls for backup.

The car in front of him makes a wide swerve, bumps up over the curb, and comes to rest on a front lawn. Just as Hackel's getting out of his car, a patrol car pulls up, and Hackel turns it over to them.

The Stenderfers get into town at 5:30 A.M. Alicia calls Hackel, gets directions to the motel, drops off her parents, and drives to the station. They know by now how to get to the employee-only parking lot under the building, avoid the madness that seems to be growing exponentially outside. Someone brings the Standerfers into his office. He's waiting with Wickersham.

He motions for them to sit. They stare at him silently, knowing what's coming. Yet, having no idea what's coming.

"You probably already know why I asked you to come. We have reason to believe that Tara was killed, and we think Stephen was the one who killed her," he begins.

Erik and Alicia stare at him, reacting almost imperceptibly, reflexive shudders like they've been pricked with something sharp. Trying to be stoic, awaiting more words.

"What I'm about to tell you is very bad news. We don't know conclusively that it's Tara, and there's a reason why." And then he told them the reason why.

Alicia lost it, of course. Erik grabbed her and held her. Hackel lost it, too, unable to keep from crying, too, and not interested in trying. Many months later, he'd still find it impossible to recount that night without having to stop in mid-sentence, look toward the ceiling in the small sitting room off his office and gather his composure, his eyes glistening.

"We found her torso in the garage." Has any sibling ever heard seven worse words strung together? Any brother-in-law? Hackel could only wonder what they were thinking. How they could hear such a thing and ever go on from it.

"It was like your worst nightmare come to life," Alicia would later tell the press. "It was just the worst possible scenario. It's something you never would have imagined."

"It's the worst thing you can do as a police officer, telling someone a family member is dead," said Hackel. "I'd gotten to know Alicia and Erik so well, which made it even worse. And then to have to tell them Tara had been dismembered?"

The good news was, in fact, that Stephen had fled. Had he stayed at the scene, it might actually have presented problems without corroborating forensic evidence. Yes, she was dead and her torso was there, but how to prove she didn't have an angry lover, or that someone wanted desperately to pin it on her innocent husband? But his flight before anything was found would be persuasive when and if it got to a jury.

Hackel told them they expected to have Grant in custody soon, and that they thought, this time, they knew where the rest of her body was buried. Soon after the approaching daybreak, they'd be out en masse to get her.

Back at the house, the techs worked the Grant house till three in the morning. They found no more body parts. They found plenty of interest, including a loaded CZ75 nine-millimeter

Ruger with two loaded magazines in a black case in the master bedroom, where they also found a roll of duct tape—interesting find in a bedroom whose occupant had gone missing—and a red photo journal. Verena's journal, filled with photos of her and her friends.

They found three caches of currency, $1,507, $389, and $106. Eventually, to Stephen Grant's chagrin, the money and his Hewlett Packard Pavilion 6745c computer would be turned over, not to his sister, but to Tara's.

Police found something else: Grant's peephole.

Koz had told the techs about the closet in the master bedroom, and the Ukranian au pair's conviction Grant had been spying on her. They had pulled out the closet organizer and all Tara's clothes. At the back of the closet, against the wall, was a small footstool. Up by the ceiling was a small rectangular patch of what seemed to be fairly new plaster. The rectangle aligned perfectly with the cold-air return in the au pair's bedroom. The bastard had been turning out the lights in his room, worming his way through the stuff in his closet, and standing on the stool to get an unimpeded look at his secret treasures.

About the time they were wrapping up at the house, David Griem called Wickersham. He'd just talked to Stephen, who had called him from a pay phone in a hotel lobby somewhere up north. Griem didn't know where. His client was drugged or intoxicated, he was depressed, rambling, nearly incoherent. Griem feared the worst.

"If you find the vehicle, you'll find Steve," he said, meaning: his body.

ON THE LAM

Friday night, Stephen Grant puts the leash on Bentley, walks down the street, into the wind and snow, can't believe they're just letting him walk off. He calls Mike, hides his panic, borrows his truck, and, shit, he's pulled it off!

He stops at a pay phone to call his sister, Kelly. He has the cell turned off, doesn't want to use it, knows they can track him with it somehow. His sister's at her church fish fry. He asks if he can stop by the church, borrow her keys, drop his dog off at her house and get something to drink. What I can really use, he thinks, is their .38. End this thing now.

He picks up the key, tells her the cops have been harassing him and are searching his house and he needs to switch cell phones with her so they can't bug him any more. He goes to her house, drops the dog off, can't find the .38. He finds a bottle of Ambien, but it's empty. Then he finds her husband Chris's Vicodins and takes those. His sister gets migraines. Grant finds some other bottles of pills, figures if they're for migraines, they must be strong. So he grabs those, too. One is something called Toprodeck. Finds some sleeping pills, some Benadryl, some Adderall, too, a stimulant to treat ADD, in case he needs to stay focused.

He calls his sister.

"I'm going to be arrested."

"For what?" Her reaction seems genuine. Grant is surprised she hasn't put two and two together.

"Griem told me if they find even a single drop of blood, they're going to arrest me."

Grant calls his voice mail a couple of times, from his sister's cell and from a pay phone, to see if there's anything more from the cops or Griem. Nothing.

Bad with a plan, Grant drives around aimlessly, this way and that. Where to go? What to do? Pops a couple of Vicodins, not necessarily good for working things out, but makes you feel better about the lack of progress.

Then he remembers: first trip he and Tara ever took was to Wilderness State Park, up north, tip of the mitten. They stayed at this cabin just off Lake Michigan, could see the Mackinac Bridge looming off to the right, the Upper Peninsula straight ahead. Had a romantic time there, boy. Great place to hide out in the winter. Good place to close the loop and kill himself, too.

Fastest way to get there is straight up I-75, and he starts out that way, but just a few miles on, he pulls off at the Lapeer Road exit, the exit for those going to the Pistons' basketball games at the big pink box they lamely named the Palace. I-75 veers a little to the northwest there, and Lapeer Road goes straight north. Grant had got off the freeway there one time while heading north and swore it was faster taking the side roads, and anyway, he's looking for a place to eat.

There's something going on at the Palace, a cop standing there at the edge of the road waving people this way and that. The cop looks at him and Grant is sure he'll be recognized and shot. But the cop just waves him on.

He's been keeping his sister's phone off, not wanting the cops tracking him. He turns it on to check messages. There's one from Captain Wickersham, wants to know where the key is to the wine cellar. Innocent question. Or supposed to be. Grant figures, shit, why would they care about the cellar now that they've found a bagful of torso in the garage? Or, maybe it never dawned on them to open the Rubbermaid. There's another message, telling him they're wrapping up, he should come back and lock up. Bullshit. He's not that dumb.

He stops at a party store and buys a pint of Jack Daniel's. Sees a second store, picks up a fifth of Baileys. If he decides to kill himself, he can always chug the booze. Booze and sleeping pills. That's how they do it on TV. That's how the rock stars do it. Eat the pills, chug the booze, fall asleep and freeze to death.

He calls his sister, tells her he's headed to the Waugoshance Cabin. Good place to end it, he thinks. Calls his dad. He gets to Lapeer, sees a cop parked to the side of the road. The cop doesn't pull out behind him so at least they aren't looking for him in a yellow truck. Not yet, anyway.

He runs into I-69, takes it west. Any sense of direction, he'd take a right when it intersects I-75 at Flint, but he's got fond memories of Lansing, lived there a few years as a kid, partied there at MSU. He can take US-27 north out of Lansing.

He checks the cell phone near Lansing. It's dead. He pulls off at a Rite Aid drugstore, nearly ten at night now, just a few minutes before they close. He buys a phone, and an Energizer charger for the dead one. It doesn't fit his phone, though, he's not thinking that straight and it didn't dawn on him to check. So he sticks the phone in his pocket and hopes maybe his body warmth will help the battery revive. That works sometimes.

He drives down the freeway, pulls into a rest stop, uses the pay phone there to call the 800 number he needs to get the new phone activated. What sense does that make? You wouldn't buy a phone unless you needed one, then you gotta make a phone call to get the phone to work? And when he gets done entering in a bunch of numbers, a computer voice congratulates him on his purchase and tells him it'll take twenty-four to forty-eight hours for the phone to work.

He continues on, sees a Meijer's department store. He goes in, thinks about possible tools for suicide, picks up a box of razor blades and some over-the-counter sleeping pills. Gets to the checkout counter. Expects to be asked what he has in mind. Disappointed when he isn't. Why else would someone buy blades and sleeping pills at the same time? What kind of coldhearted people are these? Or dumb asses, can't put two and two together. Nobody even cares if he's gonna kill himself.

He heads down the road, has another idea. Sees another Meijer's, goes in and buys a red plastic cap gun and a black Sharpie. Uses the Sharpie to make the gun black. If he changes his mind about the blades and pills, he can aim the gun at a cop and trick him into shooting him.

He gets on US-27 and drives north, finally making some time, goes through Clare, a crossroad town that bills itself as the Gateway to the North, better than St. John, which he just went through, St. John being the Mint Capital, not as cool as Kalkaska, home of the National Trout Festival. From Lansing on up, every town prides itself on something.

He pulled off in Mt. Pleasant, once known mostly as the home of Central Michigan University, now a destination of tour buses filled with gray hairs heading for the Soaring Eagle Casino and Resort, Indians finally getting the last laugh.

He stops at a cheap chain joint first, all booked up. They send him on to the casino, biggest thing for miles. No room there, some country-and-western act in town everyone apparently dying to see, bigger than Jesus, no room at the inn. But they got a pay phone in the lobby, pay phones a dying breed, it's got to where you feel like you hit the jackpot if you find one, probably why they have one in the casino. Can't hit a real jackpot?

Calls Griem. Thinking better than he's talking. Fucked up, man. Depressed, thinking about suicide, he says. Think about your kids, you got two reasons to live, Griem says. Shit like that. Doesn't sound like Griem knows there is, or was, a torso in his garage. Nothing about Tara. Bye.

Back to the car, the booze and the Vicodin kicking in bigtime.

Kicking in enough, he ends up off US-27, heading east, somehow. Winds up in West Branch on I-75, where he'd have been hours ago if he'd just headed up the freeway when he first got to it instead of meandering all over central Michigan, wondering why he'd had the bad luck to be on the run in a bright yellow truck. Except, shit, he keeps seeing yellow trucks. Can't believe it. Never noticed how popular they were till he's driving one. Might as well keep this one, then.

Couple of times he's thought about ditching the truck, get another vehicle somehow, not that he has the least clue how to do that. Doesn't know how to steal a car, wasn't going to buy one middle of the night, could always, you know, strangle someone, but things weren't working out so well from the last time he'd done that.

So he ends up in West Branch, late enough, or early enough, depending on how you looked at it, the early edition of the newspapers from Detroit, the *Free Press* and the *News,* are on the stands. Six A.M., maybe. Looking for a motel room there, he stops at a gas station and picks up both papers. COPS SEARCH THE GRANT HOME screams the headline on one, nothing on the other one, hell to pay in the newsroom Monday for missing *that* story.

He tries to catch WWJ 95 AM on the radio, an all-news station out of Detroit, but it's just static, probably blaring out "Grant on the run" every two minutes except when they do the weather on the eights and the sports at quarter after and quarter till.

He pulls over, parking lot somewhere, nods out, who knows how long, gets back on I-75, heading north, thirty-nine miles to the Four Mile Exit south of Grayling. He gets off there, heads west trying to find US-27. Dumbass. US-27 ran into 75 a couple of miles back. He's heading to Wilderness Park, he just needs to keep driving north. But west he goes. Grayling's a big town. Probably a state police post there, better to steer clear.

He ends up on a two-track in the middle of some kind of oil or gas field near Camp Grayling, a sprawling National

Guard base west of the city. Bunch of two-story-high insect-looking things, made of steel, bobbing their heads up and down, pushing and pulling and up and down, trying to get something out of the earth, wells, but nothing resembling the towers you see in the movies.

He worries about getting stuck, two feet of snow, ground under it a rutted mess from winter freezes, thaws and re-freezes. He pops the truck into four-wheel drive and ends up on a dirt road that seems to go nowhere. He keeps coming to right turns.

Until a sign flashes into view in front of him: DO NOT GO ANY FURTHER, UNEXPLODED ORDNANCE.

Shit! He's got himself onto the base. Now he's got MPs to worry about.

He turns around, back in the oil field, now. Workers have arrived at the wells and he stops and they tell him how to get out. Does he want to go to Grayling? No. They send him the other way, west. Come to an intersection, you can go left into Cadillac. Go right, takes you to Kalkaska. From Kalkaska, he thinks he knows how to get to Petoskey. From there, it's a straight shot along Lake Michigan to where he's going.

From Grayling to Wilderness Park by way of Kalkaska is odd navigating, but he's always got to the park by driving up the Lake Michigan shoreline, up past the rich summer get-away towns of Charlevoix and Harbor Springs, through the little town of Cross Village and, almost at the end of the drive, he remembers it wistfully, a spectacular stretch of road called the Tunnel of Trees.

First trip they ever took, Tara and he had been blown away, and they'd driven it many times over the years, never quite capturing the feel of the first time, what maybe was the happiest they'd ever been.

Next thing Grant knows, though, he's in Gaylord, epicenter of Michigan's downhill ski resorts. He's missed a turn. It's a blizzard, now. Snow's not coming down, it's blowing straight sideways. Can't see for shit. He's been hitting on the Baileys and the Jack and there's not enough left to kill himself, so he tosses them. Doesn't want a cop pulling him over and finding the booze, though by now any cop pulls him over, alcohol in the car is probably going to be the least of his worries.

Finally, there he is, at the southwest entrance to the park, sun up now, not that you can see it through the snow. He pulls off the road and parks. He starts to write a note to his kids, but he's so loopy from the Vicodins he can't figure out what to say or how to start and gives up. He's decides it's back to plan A: kill himself.

But for that he needs more booze, so he drives back to a little store in Cross Village. Forty-five minutes later he's back at the entrance to a park. He slides to a stop, seems like maybe he didn't do it right, truck's kinda leaning. A cross-country skier goes by, waves at him. He waves back. Calls his sister, tells her to call the sheriff on Sunday and tell him where to find his body.

He takes out his notepad of lined paper, three holes punched on the left side of each sheet, and writes in a crimped hand a letter they will never see, short of filing a freedom of information request.

Lindsey and Ian

I know that you two don't understand, yet, what has happened to mom and I. When you get a little older, Aunt Kelly can explain better.

For now, though, just know that I love you both more than anything in the world. Because I don't want to put anyone through MORE suffering, I have decided to end my life. I know that it hurts to lose me, now, after mom got taken from you, but it is BETTER. Now, no one has to go through what happened between mom and I over the past few years. Things kept getting worse and worse between us, ending up with a physical fight where I hit mom and she end [sic] up hurt very badly. I was afraid of losing you two so I ended mom's life in a panic. I am sorry.

He tears the page out, then mad at himself for not getting his thoughts right, he crumples it up and tosses it on the front floorboard. It's about 2:30 Saturday afternoon, seems like he's been gone a week. There are a couple of hours of daylight left. If he hurries he can make it. He gets out and starts running into the snowstorm.

A CALL FROM THE AU PAIR

Kalm, Wickersham, and the rest of the detectives met at 4 A.M. Saturday to plan the morning's events for those not taking part in the upcoming search.

At seven, knowing it was a long shot, deputies started searching area motels—and there were dozens of them in a wide area around Mt. Clemens, though Lake St. Clair formed a close boundary to the east.

About eight, Kozlowski met with Erik Smith and his staff for the formality of getting an arrest warrant on an open charge of murder. They could worry about the degree later; now they just wanted the paperwork done for a legal arrest.

Early in the morning, Hackel held another press conference. For the first time, he would officially name Grant as a suspect. That wasn't the news, though. He told the stunned gathering of media representatives—many of whom have a studiously practiced habit of never being stunned at anything, except getting scooped by a rival, or hearing the latest lame-ass feature idea by some assistant city editor in way over his head—what they'd found.

"The search for a missing person has ended with a very tragic result," he began. "A torso was discovered in the garage at the Grant residence. We believe the body to be that of Tara Grant."

He added an understatement: "By no means did we expect to recover what we did."

Grant, he said, "is the number one and, at this time, the only suspect in the murder of Tara Lynn Grant." He told them Grant was believed to be driving a white truck. He was still going by what Kelly had told them the night before. Someone on his staff gave him the update and he corrected himself. It was a yellow truck.

Grant is considered armed and dangerous, he said.

Soon, he finished, another search will be conducted in a different part of Stony Creek. They had reason to believe they would be looking in the right place, and that the search would reveal more of Tara's body parts.

Reporters began frantically calling their editors. Those from the dailies began filing Web updates. Those from radio stations went out into the hallway or into a corner to find a tiny bit of space to wing live updates. Whatever had been decided on for Sunday's papers, or already laid out, was as dead as last year's news. Reporters at home for the weekend were summoned back to duty by e-mail or cell phone. Sidebars were assigned. Charts of timelines had to be organized. The adrenaline would be cranking all day and into the night for reporters and cops alike.

Early in the morning, Koz ran into an unexpected complication with the truck. It was a popular brand and color, more so than you'd think for as eyeball-assaulting as that shade of yellow was, and there were a lot of them in the area. Unfortunately, Zanlungo couldn't remember his license plate number, and his registration was in the glove box. It had, he said, been leased through Manicotti Dodge on Van Dyke, near 19 Mile Road, a few miles south of Stony Creek.

Normally, Koz would have run a simple check with the secretary of state's office, but the registration wasn't in Zanlungo's name, it was in the name of a company that ran the leases through Manicotti, and Zanlungo couldn't remember that name, either.

Luckily, Manicotti was one of the few dealerships in the area open on Saturday. Koz called, asked for the manager, told him he needed him to look in their computer files and pull the information he needed. The manager told him that was confidential information, he couldn't just give it out to someone over the phone.

Koz was *not* in the mood. Hey, he said, you can get me that number right now or I'm gonna be out there with a shit-load of Macomb County Sheriff's Departments cops and cop cars, and we'll surround your new-car lot and your used-car lot. See what kind of publicity that works out to. See how many cars you sell today.

He got the numbers in about eight seconds and put them out on the LEIN network.

At some point, Koz had the TV on in the office, Griem back on, still the aggrieved counselor. He had yet to see a copy of the search warrant, didn't know what they had or why they were harassing his client.

"Bullshit!" said Koz to himself. He'd faxed a copy of the warrant over to Griem's office first thing.

A little later, Koz got another surprise, It was Verena, calling from Germany, a call Koz had been trying to arrange for a while. He wouldn't be able to get her extradited as a material witness, but her cooperation was, if not crucial, at least important.

He needed to know more about what exactly had been her relationship with Grant. Had it provided motive for killing Tara? Did she know what had happened? Out of the blue, his phone rang, he looked at caller ID and saw it was an international call. Could it be? Yep.

She told Koz Steve had called her about 2 A.M. her time, about 8 P.M. Friday night Detroit time, and then again two hours later. The first call was to tell her the police were searching his home and would she please call his kids, the second time to tell her he was sorry and good-bye, a good-bye she took to mean he might be going to kill himself. Steve had admitted to her that he'd killed Tara, she said, but that it had been an accident.

Koz told her he needed to set up his taping equipment, if that was all right with her. It was.

"Okay, go ahead," said Koz.

"He said that night that Tara came back, they argued, and she smacked him and she was yelling at him," said Verena in a flurry, words pouring out in an excited stream, "and he said she didn't stop yelling at him, and she smacked him, so he pushed her back and she fell and she was dead. That was what he said."

"Did he say where that happened?"

"No. I don't know." She sounded like she was about to hyperventilate. Or cry. Or both.

"That's okay. Take your time. I've got all the time in the world," said Koz, talking slowly, trying to calm her.

"He said he's sorry for what he told me. You know, what I told you, that Tara left. I didn't know what happened. I believed everything that he said. I believed everything. And he said he wanted me to call the kids, to tell them that he loved them and he's sorry for what he did. So, I don't know where he was, but it was like a good-bye."

"How did he say that to you?"

"He was crying." Her voice was breaking up, hard to get it out.

"Take your time, Verena."

"It was everything he said. I don't know. I don't think he wanted to go to prison. I think he killed himself, too."

"Did he say he was going to kill himself? Did he say anything, how or where he was or anything like that?"

"No. I asked but he didn't. He said, 'I'm somewhere where I feel comfortable,' but I don't know where it is. He didn't give me an answer."

"Okay."

"He said, 'Call my sister. The kids are at my sister's house. Tell them that I love them. Tell them they got to be strong, tell them they got to be good, and tell them I'm sorry for everything that I did.' "

"How did he end the conversation with you?"

" 'Good-bye.' "

"Why do you think he called you, Verena?"

"I don't know. I have no idea."

"You have no idea why he'd call you?"

"He got me into this. I mean, everything he said was a lie. Everything. And I believed everything."

"It's not your fault. None of it is your fault. It would have helped me a lot if I would have known a few more things from you. Is there anything you want to tell me about your relationship with Steve?"

"Nothing."

"You're absolutely sure about that, Verena?"

"Yes."

"Are you sure?"

"Yes."

"In the process of my investigation, you know, I've talked to a lot of people that you've talked to. So you know, when people are afraid of things, or they don't understand things, they pretty much will tell you everything. At this point, you know, you don't have anyone to protect, including Steve."

"I don't?"

"I don't believe that you're telling me everything. I don't believe you had anything to do with Tara. That's not what I mean." Koz paused. "I believe your relationship with Steve was a lot more than you just being his au pair."

"It was."

"Okay. It was what?"

"It was never physical."

"Your relationship with him was never physical?"

"Never."

"What would you call your relationship with him?"

"We liked each other. We liked each other a lot more than we should. And it started about four weeks ago. Three weeks ago. No, it was four weeks ago."

"Okay. What happened?"

"We started to like each other. But it was never physical. Never. On that I swear."

"Well, don't swear, because I don't want you to," said Koz, joking with her good-naturedly to get her more at ease. "Do you have a caller ID type thing there that would have where the call came from, or anything?"

"No. But from the display, it was in the morning. I was in bed. I was sleeping. And the first three numbers were 989. The rest of it I don't remember."

Koz had her go over the sequence of events on February 9. She was out with friends having a few drinks, Grant kept texting her. She asked him to stop, afraid her friends would be suspicious. She got home about 11:30 P.M.

"What happened when you got home?" Koz asked.

"Steve came running down the stairs. He said, 'What the fuck are you still doing here.'" I didn't know what happened. He apologized and asked if Tara was still out there. I said, 'No, where is she? She's not out there.' And he started crying and he told me what happened. He said that they got home. They were arguing, she unpacked her bag, she was talking to someone, saying she would be out there in a couple of minutes, and then she left. That's what he told me."

"After he told you, what did the two of you do?"

"Separately, we went to bed. Really. It was maybe one."

"After Steve talked to you, did you go to your room and sleep?"

"I did."

"Did you hear Steve at all?"

"No."

"When you woke up the next morning, did you get up early with the kids?"

"No. I woke up like ten maybe. Maybe it was even a little

later. Ten-thirty, eleven. But the kids were up early, maybe at eight, eight-thirty."

"How did you wake up? Did Steve wake you up?"

"Yes, 'cause he had to leave. That's why he woke me up. He said I had to watch the kids, but I didn't set my alarm clock, so he went into my room and woke me up."

"Did he say where he was going?"

"He said to the post office and something else. I forgot what it was."

"Up until the time you met me and Sergeant McLean, did Steve act strange or did he do anything funny? Out of the ordinary?"

"No."

"Nothing at all?"

"No. He was just worried. Because Tara left. That is what I was thinking. But the whole time he knew what was going on."

"Now, Verena, I've talked with Carolina and I've talked with Rebecca. We've actually talked to them quite a bit. Both of them are pretty scared right now. So, knowing that I've talked to both of them, and me asking you about your relationship with Steve, anything you think I should know about, or something you want to explain to me?"

"What do you mean? I don't understand what you mean?"

"Because I know. I mean, I spoke with both of them. And I asked both of them what they thought was out of the ordinary between you and Steve or your relationship or things that you had told them. And we were able to obtain all the e-mails that you have sent and e-mails that Rebecca sent and e-mails from Carolina, so . . ."

"There was nothing going on. There was nothing going on. I mean, we kissed, but that's all. And I told Rebecca that."

"I'm not saying you did anything wrong or criminal, do you understand that?"

"Yes."

"Okay. The questions I'm asking go to what Steve was thinking and why he may have done certain things."

"I know."

"You started by saying that you had no relationship with Steve other than being an au pair for the children, and then you said it was a little bit more of a relationship. And now you're saying the two of you kissed. I'm not asking you to give me the details of everything that happened. We're looking for Steve right now and we're trying to get an idea of what he's thinking in his mind. When you are saying he called to say good-bye, now he's not calling to say good-bye because you were the au pair for his children. Or is he saying good-bye to you because he loved you?"

"I would say he's saying good-bye because he liked me."

"Because he liked you?"

"Yes."

"Okay. Rebecca told me the relationship was more than being an au pair, actually. And she was quite upset about it. Not upset about telling me. And she said that your relationship with Steve was physical."

"It was not. I never had sex with him. Never."

"I know this is kind of a difficult question, and I'm not going to keep beating up on it. But what is your definition of 'having sex?' Or 'not having sex'?" A question that could have been asked of a certain recent U.S. president.

"Um. Ah . . ." Pause.

"I'll put it to you this way," said Koz, getting exasperated but not wanting to push too hard and lose her, understanding, too, why this was so tough for her. "Rebecca said she knew from talking to you that you and Steve had oral sex. I would consider that to be different than actual sexual intercourse, but not that it's that big of a point. I'm trying to establish what kind of relationship he had with you because you may in fact have been the last person that Steve called. Do you understand that?"

"Yes, I do."

"I need your help, Verena. That's what I'm asking for. I'm

not trying to cast judgment on you or make you at fault for any of this. I think that probably you were a kind of victim. But I have to establish an exact idea of what Steve's thinking was. Not only going back to February ninth, or four weeks ago, but, you know, even today. Because I'm trying to find him for his own safety. And you may be the only person who has any idea what he's thinking because of your relationship with him."

"Okay. I do. Okay. Rebecca was right. But it was just one time. It was one time and it was before that happened to Tara. It was before February ninth. Two days before. And just that one time."

"Was it mutual oral sex or was it just him?"

"It was just him."

"You know we searched the home, right?"

"Yes."

"Now, this is kind of an important question. We searched the home last night. The night that Tara disappeared, did you have sex with Steve?"

"No."

"Two days before Tara got home, you and Steve were involved in some type of sexual act. I'm not asking you to give me the details, but I'm trying, I want— I guess I've kind of beat you up a little bit. I want to be honest with you, Verena. Going from the beginning, as I've talked to you today, you've kind of changed your story as we went. What I want is to stop, and quit bothering you. To make it the easiest, I want one time for you to give me the entire truth."

"Well . . ." Long pause.

Koz had a feeling the au pair and Grant had slept together, and consummated their relationship, the night Tara went missing. *That,* a guy fresh off strangling his wife in his bedroom and hiding her in the garage is capable of fucking a nineteen-year-old in his wife's bed a few minutes later, is a picture he'd love to plant in a jury's mind.

But her pause tells him she's not going to fess up to it, not yet.

"I believe Steve killed Tara," said Koz, "meaning *killed* her, not just she fell and didn't get up and turned out she was dead. Like some sort of accident."

"He did," she said, so faintly he couldn't hear the words.

"What's that?"

"He did. He confessed. He told me. He told me this morning. It was an accident. He said it was an accident. He said, 'She smacked me, and she yelled at me. And I pushed her back and she banged her head and she was dead.'"

"Did he say where she banged her head?"

"No. I know that on Saturday morning, after he came back, he cleaned the floor by the kitchen. He cleaned it really good. I don't know if that has something to do with it."

"Inside the house, or inside the garage?"

"Inside the house."

"He's called you since you've been back in Germany, correct?"

"Yes."

"How many times did he call you?"

"Once a day. I don't know if it was every day."

"And what would you guys talk about?"

"I was always asking if there was anything new about Tara. And then we were talking about me coming back, because I wanted to come back. And not just because I wanted to come back because of him, I wanted to come back because of the kids and because of my friends there. And he always told me what was going on with the police and what he did, and I'd talk to the kids."

"Where would he be when he would call you and you would talk to the kids?"

"He was in the kitchen or the family room, but when we talked by ourselves, I think he was in the car."

Koz needed to get going, but wasn't sure he was done with her, yet.

"Verena, do you mind if I try to call you back? I know it's later there and it may not be until tomorrow. It may not be until next week."

"Why?"

"I don't know, specifically. But I might have another question for you. We may have somebody in Germany talk to you just as a follow-up. We may not. I want to be honest with you. I don't think you did anything wrong, and I appreciate you telling me this, but I kind of wish you would have told me a while ago. But I guess I understand the situation you were in."

"I believed everything he said. I believed it. He always said the thing between Tara and him was kind of all done." Meaning the marriage. "I didn't know anything. I was not even thinking that he could have done anything. And not just because we like each other. Even if that wouldn't have happened, I still would have believed him. Just everything he said was so . . . I don't know. I can't explain it. Everybody believed it. All his friends believed him. Nobody could have imagined he could have done something like that."

"Anything else that you can remember?"

"No. That's it."

Koz asked her about the first call from Grant. "It was a little bit after two in the morning. It might have been two-fifteen, and he said the police are searching in his house. He told me, 'I'm just driving around.' And he said, 'If you want to talk to the kids, they're at my sister's house.' And that was it."

"Did he end this conversation by saying he loves you?"

"No."

"His last conversation?"

"This morning?"

"Yes."

"Yes."

"How exactly did he end the conversation with you?"

"Good-bye."

"Sorry you had to go through this, Verena."

"Thank you."

"If you have any questions, you have my number, and you got my e-mail address. Just get in touch with me. Okay?"

"Okay."

"All right. Good-bye."

"Bye."

He got another call. They needed him at Stony Creek. They were finding body parts fast.

A GOOD DAY FOR DOGS

Sergeant Larry King, like many who'd worked the case so hard and long, was a lifer with the sheriff's department. A funny, witty, self-deprecating guy, he didn't strike people at first meeting as necessarily a leader, or a top cop, but he was both.

A local, he graduated from Lakeview High School in St. Clair Shores, in the southeast end of the county, in 1978. It didn't have a view of Lake St. Clair but was only a couple of miles inland, so that was good enough.

King spent a year at Macomb College. He saw an ad for a jailer for the sheriff's department in the *Macomb Daily*, applied and was hired. He did that a few years, applied to the police academy, and became a full-fledged cop in 1989.

He liked road duty, liked marine patrol even better, that being about the best job any cop ever had, in his estimation. What wasn't there to like? You cruised around Lake St. Clair all day, only you didn't have to pay for the boat or the gas. Only thing missing was getting to fish. He busted drunk drivers, checked boats to see if they had the requisite number of life vests, wrote tickets for boats that didn't have their marine licenses, broke up wild parties anchored off the islands at the north end of the lake, wrote up girls for going topless, flashing their boobs to the chants of drunken men.

Hard work but somebody had to do it.

And yet, although his fellow cops on road duty might disagree, it was work.

His second year on the lake, 1990, another marine cop, Lieutenant Don Bezenah, called for backup while chasing a suspected drunken boater. As King got close, he had a clear view of the drunken driver's boat careening into Bezenah's. King pulled up to the boats, which were wrecks, but still floating. Bezenah's broken, bleeding body was in the bottom of the boat. He was dead.

Until the Grant case, that would remain King's most memorable. He worked four years on the lake, then road patrol on one shift or another until 2001, when he was promoted to sergeant and named midnight shift commander. Then, a few months later, he was transferred to the detective bureau.

The search at Stony Creek began just after Hackel's press conference, about 9:30. Hackel arrived at the command center a little later. On short notice, they'd rounded up eighty, maybe ninety searchers. They'd all be on foot. They had three cadaver dogs and two tracking dogs, too. King had spent a lot of time in the park as a kid and later as an adult and knew the trails well, but they were heading out on off-perimeter roads, not the interior roads with trailheads and parking lots from which most of the hikers, runners, and bikers set out. King wasn't familiar with these trails. There were trees all around, but it wasn't deep woods.

It had been bitter cold overnight, a clear sky replacing the snow as the cold front moved through, all the surface heat escaping into the sky. It was a beautiful morning, sunny, great visibility. About perfect for what needed to be done. They strung police tape between trees to block public access to the trails and parked cop cars sideways to block off the roads leading into the search area.

Deputy Scott Lasky made the first find, about an hour and half in, maybe a thousand feet west of Mt. Vernon road,

150 feet west of a park trail. There was something pink on top of a mound, sharply defined against the previous night's pure white snow sparkling in the sunlight. It was one of Tara's thighs. King looked at it. The cut was clean. Something very sharp had been at work.

The news was called into the mobile command center. "You could cut the tension with a knife when we got the first report that they had found a body part," said Hackel afterward.

A little later, Conrad Maday II, a reserve, saw what looked to be fresh sand on an old uprooted tree stump. Didn't look right. He went closer. There was sand in its roots, too. Maday got down and looked into the exposed root structure. He needed a better view and lay down to peer in.

He got his better view. He could see hair. Looked human. He shined his flashlight into the hole under the stump and saw: a human head. King ran over. He and Maday shoveled snow and debris away from the stump. King could see plainly, more easily than you'd think, that it was Tara. He'd been looking for her for weeks and now he was staring into her face, a face he'd got to know so well, against a backdrop of the prettiest day of late winter. How to process that? "The features were all there," he'd say later. Except for the smile.

King secured the area and called the Medical Examiner's Office, said they needed to send someone out, gave directions. Called Koz, too. Twenty minutes later, two technicians arrived, took pictures of the thigh and the head where it was cradled. King put the head in the bag with the thigh and had the odd chore of carrying the bag around during the rest of the search.

They let the dogs loose then, having let them smell the first two parts they'd found. The dogs ran back and forth, excited at the work, at being useful, at *finding* stuff. The dogs would find a hand here, a foot there. Cops were digging up parts. "Parts were coming from everywhere," said King later. "It was like a *Halloween* movie."

A large bone, likely a femur, was found fully exposed on

top of the snow, forty-five feet from where they found the head. Animals, coyotes likely, had dug it up and picked it clean. It went into the bag. Her right hand was found behind a bush and went into the bag. The fingers were curled, partially closed, the nails on the pinky and ring fingers broken, just a partial nail of each remaining attached.

Kozlowski showed up. He told the techs to make sure they marked every spot they found something and to take plenty of pictures. He wanted to be able to walk a jury through here one day soon and point out what they found where.

Every time one of the dogs brought him a body part, his handler tossed a tennis ball for the dog to fetch. His reward. Keep throwing a ball for him, he'd work all day long. Every place they found a body part, they stuck an orange flag. The tree nearest each thing they found was marked with paint and evidence tape. They found a lower arm stuffed into a hole in a fallen tree trunk. They chain-sawed the trunk open to see if there were any more parts stuffed inside. There weren't.

They kept finding more of Tara, stuffed into squirrel holes in fallen trees, packed into pockets of snow, in hollow logs, out in the open where animals had left them after digging them up. A big chunk of lower leg. A foot. Smaller unidentifiable chunks. They went into the bag. Each time King opened it, Tara's face stared at him.

This is fucked up, he thought.

By now, radio and TV copters were circling overhead, a miracle none of them had rotared into another, creating more body parts to be dealt with.

King's cell phone rang. He looked at the number on the screen. It was his wife. He flipped it open and said hi.

"You're on TV," she said.

"No, I'm not." Thinking she's kidding. Hoping she's kidding.

She told him to touch his face, she'd tell him when he was.

He waited. Touched it.

"You're touching it now."

Motherfuckers! he thought. His wife was sitting at home watching his every move, along with tens of thousands of viewers. Maybe Grant, too. They're watching us dig up body parts and stuffing them in a bag? This is *seriously* fucked up.

King said good-bye, called John Cwikla back at the office.

"Get the choppers the fuck out of here," he yelled. Cwikla didn't take offense. "They're all over us."

Nothing Cwikla could do, King knew that. But if you'd been carrying around what King had been carrying around all day, you'd be yelling at someone, too.

There wasn't any thought to stopping. There was no need from the point of view of building a case to keep on looking for parts, but King thought if it were his loved one he'd rest a little easier knowing all the pieces had been gathered up.

Cops, being cops, cracked wise, only way they knew to make the horror less real, for the moment. Plenty of time later for reality. The rest of their lives.

"She must have been an alcoholic," one said.

"Why?" said another, the straight man.

"'Cause she's half in the bag."

As the sun set behind the leafless trees and the light started to fade, King called a halt. They had covered almost a square mile. The dogs were done in. So were his troops. The bag in his hand was heavy beyond its weight. Sherry Huntley, an assistant medical examiner, took the bag from King. One deputy was assigned to pull guard duty, keep the area secured until they could come back in the morning.

"We're confident that most of the remains that were available have been recovered," Sheriff Hackel told a press conference early in the evening. It was crazy in the conference room. Hackel was sick of it all, by now.

The search resumed Sunday at 9 A.M., fewer in number, the dogs at least glad to be back, working in the snow. What they'd been up to, life didn't get much better than that. The searchers found a few more body parts as the swarms of helicopters once again circled overhead. They found another femur, chewed clean by coyotes, and pieces of saw blades, bits of flesh stuck to the teeth.

When the pieces were catalogued, best anyone could guess was two pieces remained missing. They were never found, at least not by any humans. Coyotes had probably already found them and eaten them, bones and all.

At least a warming sun giving hints of spring made the task less bleak than it could have been. By 2:30, police removed the crime-scene tape, got back into their cars and left.

Aerial view of the Grant house, center.

Macomb County Sheriff's Department

Stephen Grant in jailhouse garb.

Macomb County Sheriff's Department

Tara, the April before she was murdered.
Courtesy of Alicia Standerfer

Tara with her sister at Alicia's baby shower for her son Alex.
Courtesy of Alicia Standerfer

Alicia, right, on her way to her senior prom, stopped to visit Tara, dressed for success at her first sales job at Manning's Shoe Store, while a sophomore at Bay de Noc Community College in Escanaba.
Courtesy of Alicia Standerfer

Whiteboard:

Feb 9

11:00 Steve calls Tara cell (1 min)
11:24 Tara calls Steve cell (5 min)
11:32 Steve calls Tara cell (3 min)
12:00 Steve calls Tara cell (6 min)
12:47 Tara checks V.M. in 53 P.M.
13:00 Tara Flight 476 Cont leaves S.T.R.
16:20 Approx time flight lands Newark
16:21 Tara checks V.M.
16:27 Tara calls Steve cell (20 min)
16:29 Tara checks V.M.
16:34 Steve calls Tara (6 min)
17:11 Tara call Steve (3 min)
17:55 Tara call Alicia cell (42 min) Newark - ALL OK
18:03 Steve calls Sue Morasky (15 min) - Steve cancels au pair dinner
18:36 Tara checks V.M.
18:38 Tara calls Steve (1 min)
18:41 Tara calls Home (7 min)
21:08 Steve calls Verena cell (1 min)
21:10 Tara checks V.M. (DTW)
21:10 Tara calls Home (1 min)
21:29 Steve calls Verena cell (51 sec)
21:32 Tara pans parking w/Amex - No video McNamara Terminal (will Isuzu produce)
21:32 Steve calls Verena cell (45 min) - Rebecca Vargas call + text
21:44 House phone call Tara cell (1 min)
21:47 Steve calls Tara cell (18 min) Last call from Tara cell
22:07 House phone call Verena cell (2 sec)

Verena states Steve gone to Post Office (09:30 - 15:30)

Verena states Steve @ work 11:30 - 15:30

Feb 10

01:34 Steve calls Bryan Rellinger 3 times - each 10 sec
02:17 Steves cell calls Taras cell (recorded) 2 calls
09:05 Bryan calls Steves cell
09:28 Home calls Tara (blocked)
11:56 Steve calls Tara
12:54 Steve calls Home (850)
18:02 Home calls Tara
23:10 Home calls Tara
23:11 Home calls Tara

Feb 11

13:42 Steve calls Tara

Feb 12

08:53 Steve calls Lou (STPE)
15:39 Steve calls Tara
19:44 Steve calls Lou (STPE)
19:48 Steve calls Tara
— Verified that Tara didn't board return flight to STPE

Feb 13

10:14 Steve calls Alicia - 2x @ Home
10:15 Steve calls Taras Mom (26 min)

Feb 14

07:53 Steve calls Lou 3x
10:14 Steve calls Taras Mom x2
11:49 Missing person report made at MCSO

A white board at police headquarters used to track Grant's calls.
Macomb County Sheriff's Department

A green Rubbermaid tub with a tarp on top caught Det. Kozlowski's eye. The tub contained a large garbage bag. Inside was a find that made even veteran homicide cops gasp.
Macomb County Sheriff's Department

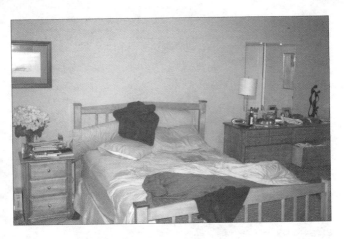

Grant slept naked with the au pair in this bed, soon after he killed his wife and buried her in the garage.

Macomb County Sheriff's Department

The empty space in his dad's shop is where Grant cleared room to dismember his wife. Grant would tell friends that his father owned a major auto supplier, rather than this messy, small shop.　　Macomb County Sheriff's Department

The woods at Stony Creek Metropark would reveal a ghastly secret. Police unearthed Ian and Lindsey's sled, which Grant used to drag their mother's body parts into the park.

Macomb County Sheriff's Department

Dogs from the K-9 unit, their tracks visible, unearthed this shoe, worn by Grant when he dismembered his wife. He discarded it when he was done.

Macomb County Sheriff's Department

A search for body parts turned up the bloody, broken pieces of saw blades used to dismember Tara.

Macomb County Sheriff's Department

Police chain-sawed into this bloody tree limb looking for more body parts, but came up empty.

Macomb County Sheriff's Department

Sheriff Hackel, in front of photos of Tara he used as props at his frequent news conferences.

Macomb County Sheriff's Department

Lt. Elizabeth Darga, left, and Sgt. Pam McLean, right, stand in front of the BP station where Stephen Grant bought newspapers every day to follow developments in Tara's disappearance. The big building in the background is the sheriff's department and county jail.
Tom Henderson

Sheriff Hackel, left, with Alicia and Erik Standerfer and their baby, Payton, at the finish line of a 2009 5K run in Tara's honor at Stony Creek Metropark, where she loved to work out and where her body parts were scattered in the snow.   Macomb County Sheriff's Department

CAGE FIGHT

Saturday had been a day of pandemonium, one thing after another. There'd been a big checklist of things to do, and it had only gotten crazier as the day went on. The FBI had showed up, which was just another intrusion into what the Macomb County deputies needed to do. The media were in a frenzy and seemingly multiplying like Jesus' loaves and fish. By then, there was a fleet of satellite TV trucks surrounding the building, aiming their masts skyward.

The neighbor across the street from the Grants' got so tired of reporters knocking on the door, looking for a quote, he printed out a statement and affixed it just below the knocker:

> NO COMMENT
> **RE: Grant**
> **Disappearance.**

Couldn't use him for a comment, use him another way. A photographer took a picture of the notice and the *Detroit News* ran it.

There were conflicts up and down the chain of command, little ego battles over who would take control of what. There was the usual second-guessing by cops who hadn't been at the Grant house the night before but who had been enlisted into Grant duty today: "How the hell could they just let that fucker walk away?"

The good news was they were tracking Grant's movements in rough snapshot fashion through his calls to Kelly. He was on a meandering route north, getting there by about the least direct route you could draw up on a map. Whether by design it not, it made it more difficult to intercept him. Had he been on a beeline up I-75, they'd have caught him by now. As it was, he'd been heading into the thumb area of eastern Michigan, then west through Flint to Lansing, then right turn north to Mt. Pleasant, a swing back east, then north again. Highways and two-lanes and dirt roads and two-tracks, they'd later found out, all of them had been silent witnesses to the bright yellow Dakota pickup going by.

The forensic exam and autopsy of Tara's body stretched out over three days, beginning about 11:15 A.M. Saturday. The medical examiner, Dr. Daniel Spitz, headed things up, assisted by several of his staff and three forensic nurses. He tore the garbage bags off the torso and they took off her clothing and catalogued it.

Spitz was the son of a legendary medical examiner, in state and national circles, Dr. Werner Spitz, the former medical examiner in Detroit's Wayne County and Daniel's predecessor in Macomb County. Spitz was a pioneer of sorts in the lucrative career of professional witnesses, both for prosecution and defense teams, and the range of his cases spanned the John F. Kennedy assassination to the Jon Benet Ramsey murder. His career had come to a sudden halt years earlier when he had joked in a magazine profile that he would dance naked on a table for money. It made him eminently impeachable on cross-examination.

Daniel had little of his dad's flamboyance but the same reputation for competence.

The forensic nurses used a rape kit to collect possible trace evidence, and Spitz examined the torso, concluding at least two different saws had been used in the dismemberment, one finer toothed. He wanted the torso X-rayed before he took the bone saw to it for the autopsy.

And he wanted to hold off and await developments of the day's search at Stony Creek, in case more body parts were found.

Sergeant Pam McLean and her mom had planned a day of shopping, Pam's heart not into it now, not after her short night's sleep and all the drama. On the way to Ikea, they stopped in at the station to see what was up.

At Ikea, her mom shopped, she followed along, cell phone to her ear, keeping abreast of developments, or lack thereof, with Darga and Koz and Wickersham.

Her mom would ask what she thought about this or that and her distracted daughter would say "fine," "looks good," phone to her ear, lost in thought or conversation.

She apologized to her mom. "That's okay. It's actually interesting," her mom said.

As the day dragged on, Kozlowski looked more and more forward to the only thing that could properly end it, other than Grant's capture—the big, world-title Ultimate Fighting Championship cage match on pay-per-view between Randy Couture and Tim Silvi.

I gotta get this fight in the office, thought Koz, not sure if it was doable, if he'd be able to order up the fight on the department's TV system. Things were about to work out so he wouldn't have to find out.

About 4:15, his cell rang. It was a cop calling from a car they had on Grant's sister's house, in case Grant showed up there or she left to go meet him. The unmarked sheriff's Tauruses might as well have been marked, as obvious as they were, all black, no frills, guy sitting in the car for hours on end.

Grant's sister had came out to the car, knew who was in it. "Steve just called. He said he's up north."

The cop in the car punched in Koz's number on his cell and handed it to her, told her to tell the story.

He's up north, she told Koz. Heading to some cabin he'd been to with Tara. "Wawgashance Cabins," she said. At least that's what it sounded like to Koz. He asked her to say it, again.

"Wawgashance." Accent on the "waw."

Koz got off the phone, got on the Internet, started Googling phonetic combinations.

Almost immediately up popped Waugoshance Cabin, in Wilderness State Park, far north as you could go in the Lower Peninsula. A couple of clicks and he even found a map. The cabin was near the west end of the huge state park, looked to be right on Lake Michigan.

"Gotcha," he thought. He told Darga what he'd found. She called the Emmet County Sheriff's Office to alert them that Grant was in their neck of the woods and should be considered armed and dangerous.

Emmet County has just 31,000 residents, though that swells much higher in the summer with tourists flocking north to motels and campgrounds, clogging the freeways north on Fridays along with those from Chicago or Detroit who have stately summer homes in Petoskey or Harbor Springs, and those with more modest cabins in the woods or on the inland lakes that cover some ten thousand acres.

It is beautiful land, deeply wooded rolling terrain that ends at the west and north in sixty-eight miles of Lake Michigan beaches. Vast Lake Michigan dominates the local climate. In the summer, breezes off the water act as a natural air-conditioning. In the fall, the warm waters of the lake mean an extended color season and another spurt of tourism. In the winter, lake-effect snow pounds the coastline on an almost daily basis, and a third tourist season of downhill and cross-country skiers and snowmobilers once again fills the highways and the motels.

The winds off Lake Michigan were pounding inland, carrying their load of giant snowflakes sideways. Emmet County has few residents but the police force is modern and with plenty of resources of its own or readily available to it. Sergeant Timothy Rodwell, who had seen the Law Enforcement Intelligence Network bulletin on Grant earlier in the day, took Darga's call. He was a native of southeastern Michigan who had gone north to avoid the congestion and hassle of the big city. The county hadn't had a homicide in four years. But that didn't mean its police didn't know how to react to one.

The Grant case had dominated Detroit's headlines and become something of a fixture on the national cable channels. But in the consciousness of those living in northern Michigan, Detroit news is about as far removed as, say, the headlines in Mobile, Alabama. Rodwell hadn't heard of Stephen Grant or his missing wife.

Rodwell ordered available county deputies to search the perimeter around Wilderness Park for Grant, to see if they could see any glints of yellow shining through the snow.

State police went door to door alerting residents near the park and advising them they might want to leave temporarily. They checked on cabins that were dark or had been closed for the winter to see if there were any signs of forced entry.

Wilderness State Park attracts plenty of visitors in the winter who come to see if it lives up to its name. They snowshoe in or ski in on cross-country skis to camp at the several bare-bones cabins deep in the interior of the huge park. A huge-wheeled truck from the state's Department of Natural Resources capable of riding over or through the snow went in and evacuated the registered campers. It was a voluntary evacuation but got full compliance, a bunch of cops in full battle array on your porch tending to act as all the incentive you need to listen up. Within two hours the park was, as far as they could tell, empty of humans, except maybe for one.

About 8:45 P.M., Emmet County Sheriff Peter Wallin called Kozlowski. A local resident, who'd learned on the TV news that police were searching for a yellow Dodge truck he'd seen earlier, had called the sheriff's department. Wallin had some men on it now. When they got there, it was empty, unfortunately, parked at the intersection of the aptly named West Lakeview Road and North Lake Shore Drive, near Sturgeon Bay at the southwest corner of the park. The truck had slid into deep snow on the shoulder and blocked the narrow intersection. A few yards away was a large brown sign proclaiming ENTERING WILDERNESS STATE PARK. Buried in the snow was the parking lot for the trailhead, the trail leading straight into the park.

The find was more dramatic than Wallin described it. Warned that Grant could be armed and dangerous, marksmen had surrounded the truck and taken aim while another officer slowly approached it. The cab was empty, and seconds later they saw remnants of Grant's footsteps heading into the woods, widely spaced, a runner's trail. They had called for a tracking dog and notified the various officers at the staging area at the park headquarters, and those out looking for the truck, to round up. Then they let all the air out of the tires just to make sure Grant couldn't use it to make his escape, in case he was still nearby.

Wallin said it was a blizzard out. Winds were up to thirty-five miles an hour now. It was fourteen degrees, wind chill way below zero, snow deep on the ground and getting deeper. Grant had gone in on foot. Snow was piling up on the roads. That would mean deep drifts in the park's pastures and swamps if they had to go in on foot.

Trackers would later find out that Grant, in superb shape, had continued to run for three miles in the snow, before he'd broken into a walk and his footsteps had grown closer together, and he'd started to meander. Off and on, the distance between his footprints would show he'd resumed running repeatedly.

"I can't tell you how jealous I am," said Koz. Explaining to Wallin what he meant. God, he'd love a chance like that, to hunt a man, a wanted killer, through the woods and snow.

This was a manhunt. But with that weather, it was a search-and-rescue, too. Get him before he dies in a drift.

With the finding of the truck, Sergeant Rodwell activated the Northern Michigan Mutual Aid Emergency Response Team, a forty-member unit which included representatives from Emmet County, the Mackinaw City Police Department, the Crawford County Sheriff's Department, the Montmorency County Sheriff's Department, the Petoskey Police Department, the Charlevoix Police Department, police from the Little Traverse Bay Band of Native Americans, snowmobiles and a canine unit. Joining them were several officers from the Michigan State Police and a member of the FBI named Joel Postema who had been in the area on holiday and showed up in his blue Ford Explorer armed with his hunting rifle—by then there were federal warrants out for Grant's arrest, too, as an interstate flight risk.

The Coast Guard in Petoskey was alerted and the commander there said they'd muster a flight crew and have a helicopter join in shortly.

The team used an old general store that supplied campers at the park with beer and ice in the summer, beer and firewood in the winter, as one staging area. Others gathered at the command post set up in the small cabin that served as park headquarters. At 9:55 P.M., the K-9 team arrived. At 10, word came that all cabins had been evacuated. At 10:17, the Coast Guard helicopter went airborne for the short flight north, a sheriff's deputy on board with night-vision goggles to try to spot Grant from overhead and serve as the eyes in the sky for the trackers on the ground.

By 11:45, all members of the response team had arrived, the helicopter was in place, the perimeter of the park had been secured, roads around the park closed, all the residents in the area notified. After a final briefing, about a dozen members of the response team headed down the West Sturgeon Bay trail from the trailhead, following Grant's tracks into the storm.

Koz needed two guys up there ASAP, to take control of Grant as soon as he's found. Mark Berger, a former Detroit cop Koz liked and trusted, was pulling road patrol, ending an overtime shift, when he got the call, in the middle of an arrest in the parking lot of a Marathon gas station, a routine stop having revealed an outstanding warrant. Drop what you're doing, said Koz, explaining they'd found Grant's truck and he needed cops there *now*. Berger tossed the driver his license back, he's hit the lotto, he's not going to jail, after all. Berger left him sitting in the parking lot stunned and peeled off for the cop shop to pick up different wheels.

Koz called Sergeant Jeff Budzynowski, too. Bud was normally assigned to a three-county task force tracking down parole violators but had been pulling some Grant duty, including sitting on Grant's house the night he'd reported Tara missing. A little later, he and Berger were racing north through the snow at eighty-five miles an hour.

Okay, now that they knew where Grant was, Koz could go home, await further developments there, and watch the frickin' fight.

During the preliminary fights, Koz watched with one eye as he worked on a yellow legal pad, timelining events of the past few weeks. Every five minutes the phone rang, most of the calls inconsequential, from fellow cops. "What's up?" "Hear anything?"

But for the championship fight itself, for the half hour or so it took for the fight to play out, five five-minute rounds of roiling action, Koz was totally transfixed. For the first time since he spotted Grant in the lobby at headquarters, there was no Tara or Steve.

There was just Couture and Silva, and it was a classic. Couture, a legend in mixed martial arts, was a huge underdog at 225 pounds to Silva, a hurting machine at 285 pounds who had inflicted unrelenting punishment on all his previous rivals.

Until this match. Couture took him apart. "Dominated him!" said Koz to himself when the verdict was announced at 12:35 Sunday morning, thrilled at being immersed in *this* kind of legal pain and suffering for a change.

Koz went to bed. Despite the adrenaline of the day, the adrenaline of the fight, he slept the sleep of the dead.

Berger and Bud get their shit together in a hurry, are off in a Taurus about 9 P.M., speed-limit signs flashing by irrelevantly as they fly up I-75. They get off at the exit that takes them west to Petoskey about 1:30 A.M.. They're geeked, been yakking at each other about the case, eager to be in on the hunt, if just peripherally, and . . . fuck! Car's about out of gas, needle below E, nothing open, no cars on the road. This baby runs out of gas and they're stuck in the middle of frickin' nowhere on the biggest case of their career? Koz can't do much with Bud, he's a sergeant, but Berger's just a patrolman, just two years with the department, there will be hell to pay.

Somehow, the needle keeps sinking lower. Somehow the pistons keep pumping. They finally see a lit gas station and pull in. "We had to be coasting, I mean there was just fumes left," said Berger later.

"Where are we?" he asks the attendant.

"Petoskey."

Thank God. They check in at the police station, get directions to where the yellow Dodge was found and head right out. The blizzard is over. Cold front has barreled through and driven all the heat way south, and the winds are dying and a full moon is staring down through the trees. *Man, that's pretty,* thinks Berger. They're on a narrow two-lane road rimmed with pines, the branches bowing down, heavy with new white snow. It's about the prettiest shot of winter you'd ever see, impossible to capture with a camera.

They pull up to the truck, resting on its rims. It's 2:30, now. Rodwell's waiting for them. The search team, he tells them, is about a mile and half into the woods north of them, making slow progress. Task force members have gone through the truck; Berger is pissed off they left the doors open, wind and snow've been flying through one door, out the other. Bites his tongue, though. No sense pissing off the locals. But they could've maybe figured someone else might want to have a go at the truck, too. Berger searches it, anyway. In the back, stuck to some snow, are receipts from Meijer's, for a Sharpie and some razor blades, a receipt from the bank, and a receipt from McDonald's. And a piece of eight-and-a-half-by-eleven-inch lined note paper balled up on the floor in the front. Berger reads it. It's a note to Grant's kids. Looks like maybe Grant is going to do them all a favor, kill his worthless self.

Berger and Bud—sounds like a lunch option—and Rodwell hang around for an hour, listening to his radio crackling updates on the search for Grant. It's clear by then that Grant's not doubling back, though he is going in large circles, according to his trackers. They don't feel the need to stand watch on the truck and head over to the command post in the park, to see what the rest of the night brings.

LIVING UP TO ITS NAME

Grant runs through the wind and the falling snow and the deep snow on the ground and it doesn't matter all the booze and pills he's taken and the lack of sleep, he's running. And he keeps running. He's not dressed correctly for this, like he would be back at Stony Creek. He doesn't have lightweight synthetic fibers next to his skin, wicking his sweat to the next layer, to keep him dry and warm. He doesn't have his running shoes. But he's a runner, and he runs and he runs and he runs. For miles, it seems.

No matches, he thinks. How am I going to light a fire when I find the cabin? Fine, just another reason to get it over with. Another way to get it over with. Get there and freeze to death.

It's maybe five miles or so to the cabin, north and then northwest along the bending shore that forms Sturgeon Bay. In the summer, you hike in on well-groomed trails. Winter, depending on how recently it's snowed and whether or not there have been cross-country skiers and snowshoers out, walking in can be relatively easy. But it's been snowing hard and not many people have been out and there's no path for him to follow, no crust of snow to stand upon, and finally he stops running. And he starts a long looping walk interspersed with bursts of running.

Come to a place, it's impossible really, all the lake-effect snow built up over the winter covers a relentless maze of dead and fallen saplings and broken tree limbs that have been rotting below the forest canopy for years. He climbs and trips and falls and slips and slides over unseen wood at weird angles.

He sees Lake Michigan to his left and heads there, makes it there eventually, frozen to the bone now, and makes much better time walking on the ice. Still has knee-deep snow bogging him down but no saplings and limbs to trip him up. He keeps thinking he sees someone far ahead of him, and when he looks back, someone behind him, too. Are they moving with him, or is it just trees at the edge of the forest? They seem to be moving with him.

He sees a sign to the right, heads off the ice and across snow-covered beach. He's looking for a sign that says WAUGOSHANCE CABIN. The cabin is on the north side of the park, a few hundred yards inland, south of the wide stretch of sand and grass called Waugoshance Beach, and he thinks for a minute that's what the sign says, but when he gets closer, it says BIRD NESTING AREA. KEEP OFF GRASS.

He keeps walking inland, across wide, rolling sand dunes, and now he's back in deep woods and he's tripping again, over the fallen trees and limbs. Now he's down in a deep valley, snow blows in here and doesn't blow out, and it builds up deeper and deeper all winter and he's at the end of winter and not getting anywhere, like in a dream.

More trees are looking like people now. Or is it people looking like trees? He talks to them to keep awake. He sees his sister-in-law, Alicia, and her husband, Eric, and they're sitting there in judgment of him. He talks to them, but they won't answer.

His hands are in excruciating pain. So are his feet. He remembers that Waugoshance is one of four cabins to what he thinks is the northeast. He's right. He thinks he remembers a fifth cabin, to the south of the other four. He's right, again. He thinks that one must be closer. He has to be near it by now, and he keeps pushing on, wind howling. He's tired of falling. So when he falls again, he just sits there. And goes to sleep.

"Get down, motherfucker," he thinks he hears someone say. He thinks he sees someone, with a machine gun. He thinks he is down. He thinks he hears helicopters, too. But he thought he heard them before but they weren't there. Or were they? Are they?

And two guys, really big guys, are picking him up out of the snow under a tree and telling him something.

"You have to get up. You have to walk," one of them is saying. But he can't. He vaguely remembers that somewhere along the way, as he fought through hidden tree limbs, the snow had sucked off his shoes—not shoes really, but black Solomon clogs, fashionable, popular, but beyond worthless in the snow—and he hadn't bothered trying to find them and get them back on. He lost his jacket at some point, too. How did that happen? He can barely limp on his frostbitten feet, so they half carry him.

They get him out of the woods, put him on a sled, and tow him by snowmobile to the edge of the lake, where a helicopter is hovering. And then he's in a basket, like an Easter basket, he thinks, and the basket is floating, rocking and floating and rising toward insanely loud whirring. And he recognizes the whirring. It's a Coast Guard helicopter. His dad's shop is on a flight path and the Coast Guard flies over it all the time, and the copters have turbines that make a markedly different noise than a regular helicopter, and so he knows, now, who's found him. The authorities. Cops and Coast Guard. He knows that they've got him. And that he isn't going to die, after all. Another thing he's fucked up.

Next thing he knows, it's Sunday morning and he's in a hospital bed, and someone's looking at his feet. He thinks they're there to cut them off. "No! No!" he says. But they aren't listening to him and they're going to amputate his feet.

And he wakes up later and he's still got his feet. There are two cops there from the Macomb County Sheriff's Department, and they end up talking hockey, it being hockey season.

"GET THE LARGE FROSTIE"

About 6:45 Sunday morning, Koz's phone rang with the news. Minutes earlier, they'd got Grant. He'd meandered through drifts and deep forest for twelve hours before giving up and sitting down, death at hand. But they'd found him alive, under a tree in the park, suffering from hypothermia and frostbite. They'd airlifted him to Northern Michigan Hospital in Petoskey, but, amazingly enough, he was basically okay, saved by his fitness as a long-distance runner and mountain biker.

The full moon had been the key near the end. The Alberta Clipper that had been driving the big flakes of snow sideways in from Lake Michigan took the clouds and some of the wind with it as it went through, and the crew in the chopper spent the last part of the night looking down at woods and snow lit up to something approximating daylight.

Sheriff's deputy Scott Ford had hunted the park for most of his life, was the obvious choice to ride above the forest, night-vision goggles helping pierce where the moon's rays had trouble. "The visibility was fantastic," he would say later. "We could clearly see his tracks and we were guiding the team." With Grant possibly armed and in desperate enough state that he had headed off on foot into the wilderness, they were worried about taking fire from the ground, so the chopper would follow the trail a bit, turn and accelerate away, come back, follow the trail a few seconds, peel off again, limiting its exposure as a target.

It wasn't as easy as Ford made it sound. The trail would disappear into the woods, or there'd be patches where it was covered with snow, only to reappear farther on. And even with guidance from the air, the troops on the ground still had to make their way through the same bogs and over the same logs and limbs as Grant. At 1:30 A.M., the helicopter left the chase to refuel at the Pellston airport nearby, returning an hour later.

A little after 4 A.M., the ground crew found Grant's Timex Ironman wristwatch on top of the snow. A sign of hypothermia? The cold sensors on those getting close to death from the cold go haywire. They can misperceive cold as hot, and a common reaction sufferers have is to start peeling things off.

At 6:37, Grant was spotted, sitting in the snow under a tree, half a mile east of Lake Michigan. Michael Parker of the Petoskey Public Safety Department shouted at him to put his hands up. As Grant slowly moved his hands toward his midsection instead, James Pettis of the Charlevoix Police Department charged him and flipped him over onto his belly. He was cuffed, read his Miranda rights, and told he was under arrest. His feet and arms were sickly white. He didn't have any headgear, either. His arms and hands were covered with scratches and dried blood.

They needed to get to the beach, where the helicopter was hovering, waiting to airlift him to the hospital. Grant couldn't stand on his own, so they half carried him, half dragged him through the snow. Put him on a sled, towed him by snowmobile the rest of the way. At 6:55, the helicopter lowered its basket to the ground, Grant was lifted into it, and he was on his way.

Grant was conscious, sort of. Eyes were open. Told someone just before they put him in the basket that he was in Lansing. He didn't say a word during the flight.

At the hospital, Grant got the best treatment possible. Literally. Dr. John Bedner, the hospital's medical director and chief of staff, treated his frostbite after a team of doctors had worked to warm up his extremities. When Grant got there, his body temperature was 87.8 degrees. The team put warm towels on his head, wrapped more warm towels around his hands, and stretched a full-length warmer over his bed that blew a 104-degree breeze down on him.

By the time Berger and Bud got to the hospital, 8:05, Grant had been stabilized and was in a bed in the ER. Grant was awake and talking with the nurses, three Emmet County deputies on guard. Bud talked to an attending physician, who told him Grant wouldn't need and wouldn't be given any medication that would impair his judgment or make him drowsy, and then he and Berger met with various hospital officials to figure out the protocol for the day or two ahead.

At 10:30, Grant was wheeled out of the ER and into a private room in the intensive care unit, at the end of a hall. Soon after, Bud and Berger formally relieved the Emmet County deputies. The two cops and Grant hit it off. "He was Mr. Cordial," said Berger.

Dr. Spitz and his crew began part two of the examination of Tara Grant at 10:45 Sunday morning, examining the parts that had been found Saturday and cataloguing what they had and what was missing, which by now was just the right arm from shoulder to wrist, lower left leg, and right foot.

Spitz examined the torso some more and noticed that the sternum had been fractured, with signs of internal bleeding. The injury had come, he concluded, before death. He wanted to wait another day, see if searchers found any more parts Sunday, before doing the autopsy proper.

Sunday morning, David Griem surprised reporters by announcing he was stepping down as Grant's attorney. After weeks of highly publicized maneuvering on behalf of Stephen Grant, he was, to the surprise of many, jumping ship. He didn't exactly have to summon the media to a press conference. They'd been hounding his every step since Saturday morning, had even followed him to his son's hockey game. So they were handy when he chose to make the announcement.

Griem said he couldn't elaborate about why he was stepping down as Grant's attorney at such a critical juncture because of attorney-client confidentiality. He did acknowledge that the case had worn him out like no other in his long career, and that while the decision might seem sudden, it wasn't.

"It was a series of events over the last week that made it no longer possible to give him my everything as an attorney," he said. It was, he said, "erosion rather than one sharp event. And I don't blame Mr. Grant. If I can't give a client everything I have—my blood, my sweat, and my tears—it's time for that client to get a new attorney, and it's time for me to move on down the road."

He was not, he stressed, abandoning his former client. He'd meet with Grant's new attorneys to go over the case when the time came, he said. Later, he would say the public resignation was the best way he knew to get the word to Grant that he no longer had an attorney

Counsel of record or not, Griem still spoke up sharply on behalf of Grant, strongly accusing Hackel of grandstanding and his police of misconduct.

"The police have unfortunately chosen to try this case in the media," Griem told reporters. "It hurts the proper administration of justice when law enforcement states opinion as being fact." His ex-client, he said, "just can't get a fair trial."

Griem said he doubted the warrant to search Grant's home, or its fruits, would be upheld upon judicial review. For days, the sheriff was saying, time after time whenever asked, that he didn't have probable cause for a search warrant, said Griem. "Then all of a sudden, it changed. What happened?"

What happened, of course, was Sheila Werner's bloody

find at the edge of Stony Creek on February 28, although neither Griem nor the press knew that yet. That find, Hackel argued when seeking the warrant, and would argue later, constituted all the probable cause in the world.

Griem's comments rankled Hackel. "It's obviously posturing by a defense attorney."

Hackel said that both the prosecutor and the judge had reviewed the request and agreed there was probable cause to justify it. He said he'd like to elaborate on why he asked for the warrant after weeks of refusing to seek one, and why it was approved, but there was a court order in place sealing the issue from public scrutiny for now, and precluding him from specifics.

"We were so methodical in this case every step of the way," he said. "I don't recall any [search warrant] case we've lost in recent years, because we understand individuals' rights."

And then, perhaps to provoke Griem over his charge that the sheriff was trying the case in the media, Hackel tried it in the media. "For Mr. Grant, the best thing he could do right now is plead guilty," he said. "When people find out what we know and how we got to this point, they are going to understand that Mr. Griem's criticisms were really misplaced."

Eric Smith reacted to the news about Griem and his shots at Hackel. "I think Dave was maybe conned like a lot of people," he said, referring to the various press conferences and interviews where Grant had wept over his missing wife. "Where you see those crocodile tears, where he claims or professes his innocence."

Darga had grabbed a few hours' sleep, was up at 6 and in the office about 7. She had the TV on and caught Griem's performance. She called assistant prosecutor Tobin. "Did you see Griem on TV?"

"Yeah."

"Does that mean that if Griem's not on the case, Grant is free to talk to us if he wants to? We still Mirandize him, but we have the right to talk to him?"

"Absolutely."

She found Koz. "Get home, pack your bags, get McLean, and get on the road," she told him.

It was a little after noon. She called McLean, who was cooking a big family dinner for her parents. She'd just put the asparagus wrapped in prosciutto in the oven when the phone rang. "I'll be there in an hour," she said.

"Enjoy dinner," McClean told her family. She quickly packed an overnight bag and left for the station to meet Koz.

Darga carried out one of the weirdest and saddest tasks of her career Sunday. She and Sergeant Mark Grammatico took a photo of the head that had been found Saturday to the Concorde Inn, where the Standerfers were staying. Alicia, her heart breaking—broken—looked at it and identified it as her sister's. It was Tara.

Sergeant Rodwell inventoried the stuff the search team had found in the snow as it tracked Grant down. He'd turn it over to Berger and Bud later as possible evidence.

Along the way, resembling a bizarre take on Hansel and Gretel leaving bread crumbs in the snow, Grant had dropped, or discarded: his wallet, a pen, a key, his watch, a cap gun, a notebook, an empty Jack Daniel's bottle, a candy bar, a pair of pliers, and a shopping bag.

Koz called Budzynowski about 2 P.M. Despite the circumstances, Grant was being, well, Grant: chatty. They were talking Red Wings hockey, always a topic of conversation in Michigan in March as playoffs approached. Big matinee game against the hated Colorado Rockies going to come on the tube a little later. Grant was pissed off how much hockey players made, thought it ridiculous.

Talked about the scenery in Petoskey some, too. Grant loved it, nothing Bud could dispute there.

At one point Grant asked if he could watch the news on TV. Might not be a good idea, said Budzynowski. Bud also told him not to bring up the case, he didn't want to trample on his rights, hear anything he shouldn't, that Kozlowski should be the one he said anything to about what had happened.

Not that he needed to, but Koz told Bud not to let Grant talk to the press. Don't let him talk to any other cops, either, in case the state police or Petoskey PD asks. He, too, was being extra careful to avoid any charges later that Grant's rights had been violated. And see if you can find out anything about how soon we can get him released and on the road home, Koz asked Bud.

"Let Steve know his attorney of record has quit, and ask him if he's interested in talking to us," said Koz. As he explained later: "This was my loophole, the loophole we never get to live in. The bad guys and the defense attorneys always get the loopholes."

An attorney of record who has strongly made it clear no one can talk to his client without him being present is no longer on the case? Grant has become fair game? A rare gift, indeed, and Koz hoped to take full advantage of it. Bud said he'd ask him and call him back.

After he got off the phone, Budzynowski told Grant what had happened, that Griem had gone on TV and said he'd quit the case. Grant would have to get himself a new attorney. He was free, if he wanted, to talk to Koz.

Grant wanted to know, would he get a deal if he talked? Bud told him he couldn't give him any legal advice and couldn't make any promises or deals.

"Do you think I meant to kill her?" Grant asked. "This was not premeditated. I was—"

Bud cut him off. "You need to speak to Detective Kozlowski directly if you want to discuss the case."

Grant nodded.

They turned on the Red Wing game. Wings were up, 1–0, end of the first period. During intermission, Grant turned to Berger. "Call Koz. I'm ready to tell him everything that happened."

Don't fuck with him, said Bud, telling him, if you're going to do it, do it. Don't waste his time driving five hours up here and then you lawyer up on him. Grant promised he wouldn't.

Berger picked the phone book off the table. "Look, you want a lawyer, we'll get you a lawyer. We'll get you one out of the phone book," he said. Nailing it down, in case anyone was looking for an angle on appeal later.

"I don't want a lawyer," said Grant.

Bud called Koz back. "He wants to talk, but only to you," he said.

Grant got on the line. "Come on up," he said.

Bingo, thought Koz.

A couple of times later, Grant started talking about the case.

"Stop," said Berger. "We're not talking about anything related to your case. You wait till Koz gets here, tell him."

"I can draw you a map."

"Stop."

There was a newspaper in the room.

"Can I see the front page?" said Grant. There were headlines about him on page 1.

"No," said Berger. "You can have the sports section or anything else, but nothing pertaining to you."

Grant told them he was worried about what might happen to him back at the Macomb County jail. Was he going to get beat up?

"Dude, if you did what we think you did, you're going to have superstar status," said Berger. "They'll take care of you."

The Wings won. Berger and Bud were hungry.

"Steve, you want anything from Wendy's?" asked Berger.

"Sure. A single cheeseburger and a medium Frostie."

"Dude, where you're going, this might be your last chance for fast food. You might think about the value meal," said Berger. "Even if you get second degree, you'll be gone a long time." Long pause. "Get the large Frostie."

It was a hoot outside the hospital. Media started showing up early Sunday, intercepting radio reports Grant had been found, kept arriving at the hospital all day, like a big tide pushed ashore by a nor'easter, nothing's going to stop it. They just kept gathering out front of the hospital, lucky there wasn't any sand for them to suck out, cause any damage.

When Berger went to Wendy's, to get Grant his last Frostie, a bunch of them had run to their cars, all riled up, sure they were in on the shit coming down, no one pulling anything on them, Berger probably off to some side exit to spirit his prized hostage away. No fucking way. So they raced to their cars and were on his ass pulling out of the parking lot, and on his ass as he made his turn, and on his ass all the way to Wendy's. And back.

False alarm.

SETTING THE STAGE

Kozlowski drove to headquarters to pick up some taping equipment and get McLean. He'd work with a tape recorder only. He didn't want to use video. He needed Grant as cooperative and talkative as possible. There was a chance if he got Chatty Cathy on a roll, they could blow the case wide open. Grant liked to dominate conversations. Fine, he thought, let the frickin' sociopath dominate this one.

A camera was just too much of an intrusion, too much of a risk. Koz had done enough interrogations, he knew the best thing you could hope for was to get a guy talking like you were a pal, spilling his guts, and cameras are a constant reminder of who's talking to you and why.

Hackel told him to be very, very clear when he read Grant his rights, and to make sure the tape recorder was working and captured Grant giving his willing approval to an interview. With Griem off the case, whoever replaced him wouldn't need to have graduated at the top of his class to know that the interview, given the circumstances, was the place to attack, especially if, as they hoped, he gave a full confession.

This was a crucial tactical juncture. Should they get him back to Detroit and wait until he had an attorney to question him? That would certainly stand up to legal scrutiny. Or should they take advantage of being able to talk to him hundreds of miles from any future legal representation, take advantage of the guy who didn't seem capable of shutting up?

Hackel was rolling the dice. McLean was one die. Koz was the other.

Meanwhile, Hackel knew that Grant's defense would certainly focus on two issues—the search warrant of his house and the impending interview at Northern Michigan Hospital. Had there been probable for the former? Hackel didn't think he had much to worry about there, though you never know. Even the president of the Criminal Defense Attorneys of Michigan, Jill Price, had told reporters it was "extraordinarily rare" for warrants and their results to be suppressed. "I would say it's a very, very small percentage. We see them in the media when they are granted, but the vast majority are not," she'd said.

But the interview McLean and Kozlowski would soon be racing to? Given the circumstances—a man high on drugs and booze is found in a snowbank, suffering from frostbite and hypothermia, likely near death, and is interviewed the same day for hours without an attorney being present—how sound of mind and judgment could he be? Sound enough for the interview to be legal? Hackel was less sure on that count. They were questions certain to be litigated in the weeks or months ahead.

But with Griem out of the picture, and Grant telling Koz to come on up and talk to him, well, Hackel wasn't going to interfere, to call it off. This was no time for the timid. Get Grant talking, you could have this whole thing wrapped in a bow today.

Griem had already starting framing the arguments when he met with reporters to tell them he'd quit the case. He lashed out at the search, unaware of what precipitated it. He hadn't known at the time that his ex-client was about to ask Kozlowski to come interview him. But his words to reporters would serve as a starting point for the court-appointed attorneys who would replace him.

He'd told of talking to Grant on the phone in the early hours of Saturday morning, after he'd fled. Grant had, he said, been "increasingly emotionally distraught. He had a hard time getting sentences out coherently. He was rambling," he had said.

Well, they'd tape his interview and see how coherent he sounded. It was Koz's and McLean's job to talk to Grant. It'd be some judge's job to decide if whatever they came up with could be used in court.

Sunday night, as Koz and McLean were about to arrive at Northern Michigan Hospital—despite the weather, the drive had flown by as they talked strategy and kept checking in with Bud to make sure Grant hadn't changed his mind—Alicia Standerfer, a rock throughout the last few weeks, stoic, polite, gracious with the ever-present (too present) media, held a press conference at the sheriff's department, her husband, Erik, at her side.

The press conferences had long ago outgrown the conference room on the fourth floor across the hall from the sheriff's office. They were now being held in a large training room that had been given over to the press and the conferences.

To either side of Alicia and Erik were two larger-than-life-size photos of Tara. The one to Alicia's right showed Tara in three-quarter profile, head turned to the right, looking past the camera's left, her huge smile a stark contrast to Alicia's lip-pursed grimace at the microphone as everyone took their place.

"My family and I would like to take this opportunity to express how deeply saddened we are at the loss of Tara, a genuinely beautiful mother, daughter, sister, and wife, whose life was needlessly and abruptly ended the night of February ninth," she began, reading from a prepared statement.

"As Tara's only sibling, I feel passionately about maintaining my sister's voice, since it's become impossible for her to speak for herself. Tara loved her children, her two beautiful children, with all her heart and did everything in her power to provide for her family. Those truly close to Tara remained confident throughout this whole ordeal that she would never desert her children or her employer. While this outcome represents the worst possible scenario imaginable to anyone, we take comfort in the fact that Tara is now in a better place. Our memories of Tara and our faith in God will be our cornerstone in providing us strength to endure.

"We are filled with grief and horrified by the manner in which Tara's life was needlessly taken and are filled with many, many unanswered questions. We hope and believe that Tara's kiiler will ultimately be brought to justice," she continued, her words coming out with more and more difficulty, her voice cracking with emotion, some finding it difficult to watch her, wondering, perhaps, how in the world *they* could ever manage such a thing, so soon upon the horrific news and grisly finds of Friday and Saturday.

"Tara's death leaves behind two beautiful children, whose lives are going to be forever affected by this gruesome act. Her children will certainly need your continued support," she finished, having never mentioned Stephen by name.

Erik's sister, Jeannie, stepped up to the mike. "I just want to thank everyone for being so supportive and vigilant in looking for Tara and then Stephen," she said. "It's a blessing he was caught and that she was found, in that we can begin to move on."

As for the Grant children, they were now in the care of Stephen's sister. "They're safe and that's the most important thing."

Alicia had kept the tears at bay, but as she turned and hugged Sheriff Hackel at the end of the conference, her body convulsed and the tears started to flow, from both her and the sheriff.

* * *

All day Sunday and into the night, TV, radio, and print reporters arrived at the Utykanskis' house in Sterling Heights. They were greeted by a note on the front door: *"Do not knock on the door or ring doorbell. Children sleeping."*

A CHAT WITH STEVE

Kozlowski and McLean hit the road in a black Ford Taurus about 3:45 P.M. for the 280-mile drive up I-75 to northern Michigan, bucking strong headwinds under a gloomy, dark gray sky to get to Grant as quickly as possible. Get to him before he could change his mind about talking.

They made good time despite the white-knuckle weather, heading against the grain of Sunday traffic returning to the Detroit area after a weekend up north, the southbound lanes filled with SUVs and trucks carrying ski gear or hauling trailered snowmobiles, the same thick snow that trapped Grant a boon for motel, bar, and restaurant owners.

Spring was just around the corner and any weekend that promised snow meant crowded roads, the snowmobilers not wanting to miss what might be the last good weekend of the season.

Koz didn't bother putting the flasher on the roof. He drove like the roads were dry and clear, eighty to eighty-five the whole way. The farther north they got the faster the snow was flying, coming at the windshield horizontally as they flew into it. *Thank God this baby has front-wheel drive,* he thought.

On the way, Koz asked McLean if he could lead the interview. There wouldn't be any good cop, bad bop. No need for it. Plan was, keep the questions to a minimum, get him talking and let him talk. The reason Koz wanted to lead the interview was that he was worried Grant might be inhibited, reluctant to be candid about the injuries he'd inflicted on a woman, if he had to speak to another woman.

Koz told her to take notes, jot down follow-up questions. He wasn't going to take any notes himself, be easier that way to keep up the illusion of a conversation.

They pulled into the hospital parking lot about 7:15, had to be a record considering the conditions, three hours and fifteen minutes start to finish. "I cooked," Koz said later.

Grant was sitting up in his bed in the middle of a private room, a big corner room, some food on the table next to him. Koz sat on the left side of the bed and put his tape recorder on the table. Pam sat on the right side. Shit, thought Koz, pretty comfortable setting for an interrogation, subject propped up on pillows. Much better than sitting around a table on hard chairs with a harsh overhead light.

McLean turned on the tape recorder and she, Kozlowski, and Grant spoke their names in turn. There weren't any hospital employees present. Periodically a nurse would walk in to look at a monitor attached to Grant, but that was about it.

Kozlowski asked Grant to say his Social Security number.

"Three six four, nine six, one oh two nine," he said.

Kozlowski asked him if he was waiving his right to have an attorney present and was speaking voluntarily to him and McLean.

"Yes."

He asked him if he knew what day and date it was.

"March fourth, 2007. Sunday."

"How do you feel right now? Tired? Exhausted?"

"I'm a little tired, but that's okay."

"Do you think you're of sound mind to talk to us?"

"Yeah."

Koz read Grant his Miranda rights, then gave him a form to read and sign. It had five statements, each followed by the question "Do you understand?" And a box to circle either the word "yes" or the word "no."

The statements were: "You have the right to remain silent; anything you say can and will be used against you in a Court of Law; You have the right to talk to a lawyer for advice before we ask you any questions and to have him with you during the questioning; If you cannot afford a lawyer, one will be appointed for you before any questioning, if you wish; If you decide to answer questions, now, without a lawyer present, you still have the right to stop answering at any time until you talk to a lawyer."

Underneath those statements, in larger type, were two questions: "Do you understand each of those rights I have explained to you?" and, "Having those rights in mind, do you wish to talk to us now?" Each of those offered yes and no choices.

Grant circled "yes" seven times and initialed each circle. Koz printed the time at the top of the form: 7:46 P.M.

"I said I'll let you ask a couple of questions first and then we'll just start. We're in no rush," said Kozlowski.

"We got all night," said McLean.

"We've got all night. We're actually staying up here for the night. No press is going to be coming in here and bugging you, and I appreciate you talking to us for a lot of reasons," said Kozlowski. "Obviously, uh, you know, we met under, uh, unfortunate circumstances but, you know, I'm not here to judge you. I'm just doing my job . . ."

Koz was doing what he had to do. Right now, that was tough work. Grant was lying there in front of him, shrinking into himself, looking and acting like the poor little scared, put-upon guy who'd had it so rough. He'd been lost in the snow, and cold, and almost lost his feet and everything was happening to him at once, and his voice was shrinking in on itself, too, becoming childlike, wanting sympathy.

And there was Koz, providing it. Doing what he needed to do. "What I wanted to do was take his IV line and wrap it around his neck and choke him with it," he said a day later.

Instead: "I'm not here to judge . . ."

"I know," said Grant.

"I don't tell you I'm here to help you in a lot of ways, but I'm gonna do what I can to give you direct and honest answers. And I know Sergeant McLean feels the same way. So, you got any questions you want to start with?"

"I don't even know where to start with questions, so why don't you guys start?" said Grant.

"Okay," said Kozlowski.

"If questions come up while we're talking, just let us know," said McLean.

"You do in fact understand that you are in fact under arrest right now?" asked Kozlowski.

"Right."

"For the murder of your wife, Tara?"

"Yeah."

"Okay. You do understand that?"

"I do have a question," said Grant. "Tonight, I asked the deputies earlier and they said they couldn't answer. What is the difference between the level of murder? First-degree murder—isn't that where you plan it out ahead of time. Is that what it means?"

Kozlowski told him the warrant they arrested him on was for an open charge of murder, and that later it would be determined whether to charge him with first-degree murder, second-degree murder, or manslaughter, and that the differences between them could get complicated.

Grant told them he knew first degree mean life without parole.

"How do you know this?" asked McLean.

"I know. Watching TV."

Kozlowski told him there was a second charge, of mutilation of a body, which carried a ten-year sentence. He asked him if he wanted to read the warrant.

"No, I don't need to see it."

And with the preliminaries out of the way—Kozlowski stopped the tape, rewound it a bit, and started it to make sure the machine was recording, and was set at a proper volume—they got down to the business at hand. Periodically, trying not to be too obvious, Koz would lean over and make sure the tape was still turning. Nothing worse than being in the middle of some confession and you realize the batteries died some time ago.

"Why don't we go back and let's just start it from February ninth?" asked Kozlowski. "Which was Friday. I'm not here to try to play tricks on you. I'm not going to be mean, and Pam's not gonna be nice or anything like that."

"We're not playing good cop, bad cop," said McLean.

Grant told them that the day before, he was thinking it might be best for everyone if he just died, but now he thought maybe it would be best if the truth did come out, good for his kids, too.

"I actually started to write things down yesterday," said Grant. "It's almost like therapy, writing things down."

"Okay, go into February ninth, Friday," said Kozlowski.

Grant told him it actually started that Thursday, the eighth. Tara was in Puerto Rico. He'd called her, told her he was going out to the Hamlin Pub in Rochester to see a friend named Ken play. She said she'd just be hanging around, didn't have any plans.

"Ken McCauley?" asked McLean.

"You talked to him, too?"

"I told you, we talked to everyone in your life, man," she said, establishing dominance, not that it needed establishing. "It's okay, go ahead."

But, said Grant, when he checked Ken's Web site, he found out he'd been mistaken, he wasn't playing at Hamlin that night. So he called Tara to tell her he'd be at home, instead. To his surprise, ticking him off, she wasn't at her place in Puerto Rico, she was at a bar. Not like her, going out to bars. She had met an older couple, she said, was talking to them.

Friday, maybe about noon, she left a message on his cell. She was stuck on a layover in Newark and was going to be late. They talked two or three times later that day.

"Arguing?" asked McLean.

"No," said Grant. "I mean, there was a little bit of back and forth. The weekend before, we had talked about, uh, the fact that she travels too much. And she told me then that, that she was gonna try to get things so they weren't traveling so much. And then on Friday night, when she got home, um, what time? I don't really remember the time, but when Tara got home, we started talking, and we were back and forth about the travel schedule," he said.

"Uh-huh," said McLean, using the short interjection as a way to let him know they were letting him keep the floor.

Grant kept the floor, all right. For three hours. It was the most surreal thing McLean ever sat through in her life. A butchered wife, a torso in a bin, body parts in snowbanks, and hearing all about it in a calm, matter-of-fact, chatty tone. When she listened to the tape later, it had the tenor, as she would describe it, "of you and I sitting in a bar telling stories."

It struck her as odd, too, the lack of remorse. Not just lack of remorse for killing his wife, but lack of remorse for anything. "I've sat through hundreds of confessions. All of them had some remorse, even if it's 'Shit, I got caught.' But he showed no remorse at all. None. You just don't think you'll run into a monster like that in real life."

But you had to hand it to him. He could tell a story. He told them one, now.

"LIKE WATERMELON ON CEMENT"

Things go bad from the start. He's upstairs, getting ready for bed, and he hears her coming in the house. He hollers down to her but doesn't hear anything back. So he walks down and there she is wearing her iPod, listening to music, pissing him off already, can't even come in the house without something to distract her from him. It more than pisses him off, it disgusts him.

But he bites his tongue. He doesn't say anything, and the rest of the night begins mundanely. He helps her carry her stuff upstairs and they exchange polite how-are-yous. She starts unpacking her bags, unfolding clothes, putting toiletries away in the bathroom. He's already undressed for bed, meaning nude, the way he sleeps.

In the middle of unpacking, she goes downstairs for something, comes back up, stands in the bedroom doorway, and mundane comes to an end. She tells him she's thinking of leaving again Sunday, going back to Puerto Rico.

But saying she's "thinking" in a way that he takes to mean she's already decided. It's not a maybe. She's going back. It's set, no thinking needed.

"No, not okay," he says.

"Well, I need to go on Sunday," she responds, coming

into the bedroom. Her boss, Lou, is going down Sunday, and she needs to go down, too. It's important.

"No, you don't need to go down there with Lou. You spend too much time with him, already, and you don't spend enough time with us. You're only going down there 'cause Lou's going." And they went back and forth about Lou and why does she travel so much with him and how come she can't spend more time with the family. It's ground they've gone over many times before, always fruitlessly. He thinks he's fighting for family, she always acts like he's whining.

"Fuck off," she says. "I've got to do what I have to do in my job, and it's none of your business."

"You're not going anywhere," he says, meaning Sunday.

"I'm not talking to you anymore," says Tara. She turns and starts to leave. Grant grabs her by the wrist. They are just inside the bedroom, in front of the double doors to the bathroom.

"Are you fucking him?" he says.

"Fuck off!" she says and slaps him with her free hand.

Grant hits her back, connecting with the side of her neck, can't remember later if it's with his fist or an open hand, but it's hard enough that she falls back and bangs her head against the floor, in front of the bedroom TV.

She's dazed for a second, "knocked for a loop" is how he describes it.

"That's it!" she screams. "I'm going to take the kids. You're gonna be fucking homeless. You're a piece of shit."

She's sitting up, screaming that it's over, she's taking the kids, he's hit her and that's it.

"You hit me first," says Grant.

"It doesn't matter," says Tara. "I'm calling the police. I can ruin your life! It's over!"

She's yelling that if a man hits a woman, he goes to jail and she gets the kids and the house and everything. "Screw you, you'll never see the kids again!" Her mouth is going a mile a minute. "You're done! You're through!" Blah-blah-blah.

She's still sitting. Grant falls to his knees, thinking she's gotta shut the fuck up, he's gotta shut her up, and he locks his hands around her slender neck and begins choking her. She doesn't fight back at first, shocked, maybe, that this is happening.

And now he thinks, I'm going to go to prison for choking her. She's gonna tell the police I choked her. *So he has to keep choking her, keep her from talking. She grabs his hands, scratches the back of one of them. Grant knows he can't stop, and he chokes her until she stops moving. His words later?* "I just kept squeezing, squeezing, squeezing and wouldn't let go."

And yet, he says he let go long enough at some point to cover her face with a gray T-shirt or gray underpants, something gray lying there that was handy, and covered her head so he wouldn't have to look into her face while he kept on choking her.

Finally, her body relaxes. He lets go, walks downstairs and starts crying.

Grant grabs his cell phone and texts Verena to not come home. She's out with some friends at Mr. B's, a bar and restaurant in Royal Oak. They'd been texting back and forth to each other all day, and the last text she sent had told him what time she figured to be there. And that wasn't gonna work out, not if he was going to do what he needed to do, now.

So he texts her and comes up with some lame excuse why she should wait a while before she comes home.

And then he goes back upstairs to move the body. Get it someplace better than where it is now.

Kozlowski's cell phone rang.

"We're going to stop the tape. I'm gonna let you take a break, okay?" he said.

"Okay."

It was 8:13. Two minutes later, they resumed.

"We're going back to February ninth. You're upstairs. Tara's come home. You guys have fought," said Kozlowski.

"I know I'd hurt her bad," said Grant.

Back upstairs from texting Verena, knowing he needs to move Tara and knowing he needs help, he grabs his brown leather belt and wraps it around her neck. Black skirt, silver shirt, he notices her wearing. Funny what you notice and when. She isn't moving when he gets back up, she doesn't move when he puts the belt around her neck and cinches it tight. She isn't breathing. Dead. Has to be dead, right? No going back.

Naked, ready for sleep at one point but no sleeping now, not bothering to dress, he tugs on the belt and leans back, awkwardly hoisting her body up so only her feet drag as he pulls, his elbows high and bent outward, her feet thump-thump-thumping on each step down.

And then he's dragging her out the side door and into the garage.

He races back upstairs to check on the kids, makes sure they're sleeping, that they haven't been awakened by the screaming or the thump-thumping. They both have their eyes closed, lie motionless as he opens the door and looks in. They're sound asleep. He goes down the hall, gets a piece of paper, writes a note and leaves it on Verena's pillow.

"You owe me a kiss," it reads.

He runs back to the garage.

He drags Tara over to her white Isuzu Trooper, not much room between it and the big garage door, barely enough for the rear of the Trooper to fall down when he tugs it open. He yanks her up off the ground, straining to get her high enough to wrestle her into the cargo area, but before he can get her in, the belt snaps in half and her body falls, the back of her head slamming into the concrete.

* * *

"It was the most disgusting, like, it sounded like dropping a watermelon on cement," Grant told Kozlowski and McKean. "There was no movement. There was nothing. I knew then that I had killed her. I didn't know what to do. The only thing I could think to do was to hide her."

GOTTA MAKE HER SMALLER

Grant manages to get Tara into the back of the Trooper, getting her in on her side, one leg pulled up. Verena will be back soon. If she pulls her Mazda into the garage, Tara, with that silver blouse, will be all too visible. What to hide the body with? He looks around the garage. He's taken the liner out of his black 2006 Jeep Commander to wash and it's sitting there to the side, on top of a storage bin.

Grant grabs it and wedges it in on top of Tara's body and closes the door. It looks okay. The body is hidden. He turns out the light and goes back into the house.

Just seconds later, Grant hears the click of the garage door system engaging and the hum of the door opening. It's an old system and takes its time getting the door all the way open. He runs upstairs, puts some pajamas on, and runs back down, a plan having formed.

"What the fuck are you still doing here? Go! Just go!" he yells.

"What? What do you mean?" asks Verena.

"Oh, nothing. I thought you were Tara, come back." He apologizes.

Grant tells her he and Tara had a fight over her frequent trips, and in a huff she'd left, for the airport, he thought.

She'd called someone and said to meet her outside and had left. When he heard her, Verena, he thought she was Tara, was glad it wasn't.

"I was thinking as fast as I could. My brain was going a mile a minute," he told the two cops. "I kept thinking, 'We've got a body in the garage. What in the hell do I do with a body?'"

He goes upstairs with Verena, talking small talk in the family room. Verena asks him about a scratch on his nose, a nick Tara had inflicted while he was killing her.

"Tara slapped me," he explains. He'd called his wife a whore, he says, and she'd popped him.

Verena goes to bed. Grant sure hopes she'd bought his story. He needs her as part of his alibi. He'll need to convince people that Tara has left in anger.

Grant calls a buddy named Brian, gets his voice mail, calls him back a few minutes later and leaves a message: "The shit's hit the fan."

Grant sleeps fitfully, visions of strangulation and violence jolting him out of REM sleep. The next morning, in a daze, he heads out to do errands in his Jeep, going to the bank and the post office while Tara waits in the trunk of the Trooper.

The plan is, he'll get up late Saturday night and go hide the body.

Except it's cold Saturday night. Too cold. He'll figure something out Sunday.

Hide the body? Or hide parts of it? Which would be easier in the cold Michigan winter, ground everywhere frozen hard as concrete?

Sunday morning, Grant tells Verena he has to go to the shop, his dad's shop, and do some work. He calls his dad first, to make sure he isn't going in to do some work, too. He isn't. Has plans.

He loads up a big green Rubbermaid storage bin and

some garbage bags and a big sheet of plastic. The Rubbermaid bin is marked on the top: "Boy's Clothes." They're clothes Ian has grown out of. Tara has been saving them for her sister, Alicia. There's another Rubbermaid bin marked "Girl's Clothes," Lindsey's outgrown stuff for Alicia's daughter. He grabs that one.

Steve thinks about buying more plastic tarps but is worried someone will see him buying big sheets of plastic and know he is up to something bad.

He needs to get her smaller than she is with her leg and arm jutting out in opposite directions, so he loads up his big bow saw, too, and drives the few miles to the shop. He opens a bay door and backs the Trooper in. There's too much stuff on the floor of the shop to get the job done properly, so he pushes it all to one side.

Then he spreads the tarp on the floor and starts wrestling Tara out of the back of the SUV. It's like a scene in some black comedy, her body frozen from rigor mortis and the cold, one arm jutting out one way, a leg jutting out the other, awkward as hell, impossible to get a good, balanced grip as he leans into the vehicle.

Grabbing, pulling, feet slipping, body slipping out of his grip, fighting him harder now than it had in life. And finally he has her out of the truck and down on the tarp.

He pulls the truck out of the shop to give him some more room and closes the bay door.

He grabs some pieces of steel and weighs down the four corners of the tarp, gets down on his knees with the bow saw and starts cutting on her wrist, trying to cut something small to see how it works. And it doesn't. She's so hard, it's like trying to saw through steel. The bow saw is good for saplings but not this. He starts to panic. He stops, washes his hands, goes to the Trooper and grabs a pint of booze he'd brought from home. He gulps down a few swallows.

There's other work he can do. If his story is going to be that she was going back to Puerto Rico, then he has to make all her stuff disappear, too, not just her body.

He gets her briefcase and runs all the paper inside, including documents and business cards, through the shop's paper shredder and pours the pieces into a large paper bag. That calms him down. Now, I can do the dirty work, he thinks. He goes back to the body, stares down. No, I can't.

He takes her laptop over to one of the band saws in the shop and cuts it into pieces. Something—the disk drive?—shatters into a million pieces that hurl themselves around the shop, and now he has to clean all that up, too.

A sliver of steel pokes him in the finger and when he pulls it out with a tweezer, his finger starts bleeding. Ohmigod! *he thinks.* There's blood here now! *As if a body on the floor isn't more than enough to worry about. He panics.* I killed my wife! I killed my wife! I killed my wife. What the hell do I do now?

Grant takes the shredded computer parts and dumps them into a large cardboard box.

He needs a better tool. He's looking for a hacksaw, something small but tough, and sharp. And then he sees the band saw and thinks how that would work just fine, but then: "No, you can't use the band saw. It's gonna be too much of a mess."

He'd seen a band saw flinging wood chips and metal chips all around, last thing he needs to see now is what it would be flinging around as it cuts through her body.

He remembers his dad making a make-do hacksaw out of pieces of a broken band saw. The band saw blades are carbon steel, with ten teeth an inch, wonderful cutting tools. So he takes an old, used saw and breaks it in two, then snaps another piece off, wraps the end of it in a blue towel to give him a grip and starts sawing away.

He cuts off one of her hands, no problem, and starts hacking on the other wrist, but the saw piece is already dull.

So Grant gets a new blade and breaks it into pieces and that works a lot better. After both hands are off, he takes off her forearms, then moves up to her shoulders, laying the body parts on the tarp as he works.

It surprises him, the lack of blood. Makes it not so bad. Doesn't keep him from throwing up, though. He drinks some whiskey to clear the taste of the vomit from his mouth.

"Look," he tells himself, "if you don't do this, you're going to prison for the rest of your life."

He can't get her pants off, so he rips the pant legs up to the waistband and starts in on her legs. As he works his way up high, the cloth keeps getting caught in the teeth of the blade.

By now, he has a collection of body parts on the tarp. He puts some of them in one of the plastic bags he's brought from home, but they're cheap ones, too thin for the task. He looks around the shop and finds some industrial bags, with a much thicker ply, and he puts parts into several of them. And stuffs the bags into the big Rubbermaid bin, marked "girls' clothes."

All that is left on the tarp, now, is Tara's torso. There hasn't been much blood during the dismembering of her arms and legs, but there is a lot of blood that has congealed in the torso, thick like syrup, he thinks, and he throws newspapers on the blood and wraps the torso and the blood and the papers in the tarp, and it fits into the Rubbermaid, on top of the other stuff.

The job has, after the slow start, gone surprisingly well. There isn't much mess to clean up. He's only poked a couple of holes in the tarp during all his cutting, and only a bit of blood has leaked through to the floor, and he wipes it up with some rags. There is enough room on top of the torso for the dirty rags and all the blade parts, the bits of blade he's used and extra bits he hasn't needed.

Grant opens the bay door, backs the Trooper into the shop, and puts the Rubbermaid bin in the back. He tosses in the shredded documents and the shredded computer parts and her shredded purse on the front seat so he'll be able to throw them out quickly.

Then, it's genius, it really is, he calls Tara's cell phone, leaves a message. "Tara, pick up the phone! It's fucked up that you won't call me or your kids. CALL YOUR KIDS!"

Back to the plan, which is, throw the box and bag in a Dumpster, over near where he grew up on Riverland Drive in the nearby suburb of Sterling Heights. There is an apartment complex with Dumpsters out back, but when he gets there, there's too much Sunday traffic and people and he is paranoid someone who lives there might get mad at a visitor using the Dumpster and write down his license plate, or confront him.

The bin, he's going to bury. Thought of putting it in a Dumpster, too, but man, he could just see some guy emptying the Dumpster and the bin rolls out and the lid comes off and out come body parts. No, gotta bury it.

So he chickens out on the whole Dumpster thing and drives home, leaves the Rubbermaid bin in Tara's car, jams a red sled in on top of the bin to hide it, puts the other stuff in his Jeep, and spends the rest of the day in the house. Sled'd come in handy later.

It is bitter cold. With Tara gone to Puerto Rico, no need to worry about her car being left outside and not being able to start in the morning. But he can't very well leave her car out in plain sight. And he can't leave Verena's outside, she'd wonder why it wasn't in the garage in this cold, Tara gone, who cares about her car? So he leaves his Jeep in the driveway and Verena's car parked next to Tara's, giving him another thing to worry about. Would she notice anything he's missed if she has to get in her car and go somewhere?

Grant considers himself a natural flirt. It isn't work for him. Usually. He needs to make everything seem as normal as possible, and since he is always flirting with his au pair, he starts in again as soon as he walks in the house. Flirts up a storm with the young, hot thing, who flirts back, easy and natural.

"I kept thinking, 'What am I dragging her into?' " he told Kozlowski and McKean. Then confided, "If I was fifteen years younger . . ." Meaning the big age difference between him and the girl. As if that was all it'd take, being fifteen years younger. He'd need to be younger *and* need to be somewhere other than right here admitting to cops he'd cut his wife into pieces with bits of a band saw and put them in a green bin.

"I had fallen in love with Verena. Easily. Because she was a sweet girl, and she was nice and she was kind. And this whole time she's thinking that Tara's left me. So she's trying to be comforting and . . ."

A DAY AT THE PARK

Grant gets up early on Monday, 3 A.M. or so, Verena and kids still asleep, of course.

He heads in the dark to Stony Creek Metropark, where he used to run with Tara. It's huge, acres of deep forest, miles of trails, and at this time of night it will be deserted. The official entrances are closed, but you can easily access the park by a number of roads that run by it or dead-end into it. Mt. Vernon Road near the Nature Center is perfect. It's a dirt road, no houses nearby, a big open field just off the road, a field with a hunting blind out in the middle, to show you how out in the boonies it was.

He pulls over, snow deep enough that while he was driving here, he thought he might be getting stuck a couple of times. He gets the sled out, puts the geen bin on it, gets it balanced, and heads out down a track in the road a ways before turning into the woods.

Goes a little ways and starts down a big hill, loses his balance, lets go of the sled just for a second, and—like that!—the sled's sliding down the hill, picking up speed, thank God for the snow so there's enough light he can see to run off after it.

"It was like the Keystone Kops," he told Kozlowski and

McKean. "The sled took off and now I'm chasing after the sled with Tara's remains and cut-up body in it down a hill."

And so he's chasing it down the hill and at the bottom the bin hits a log. It tips over as a chunk of green plastic breaks off, the lid pops off, and body parts go flying out all over the place. He freaks out, turns tail and runs up the hill and out of the woods and back to the Trooper, and he drives home.

He parks the Trooper in the garage, gets a bottle of Simple Green from a shelf and sprays the mat in the cargo area, then walks in, sits down on the couch, hits the remote to watch the local news. He sits there in a daze until eventually he hears Verena and the kids moving around in their rooms.

She comes out. "You were up early," she says.

"What do you mean?"

"I heard you rustling around. Were you out?"

"No. I've been here the whole time," he says, freaking again. Is she suspicious?

A few minutes go by. Enough time so he can say matter-of-factly he's gotta go. Says good-bye to her and the kids and this time leaves in his truck, no worries with the Jeep about getting stuck in snow, and drives as fast as he can back to Stony Creek, and drives off the road and into the woods.

He pulls on a pair of vinyl gloves he'd brought from home, too small, looking like O.J. trying to pull them on, they were Tara's for when she dyed her hair. He pulls them on at last and he grabs Tara's torso and buries it in the snow. He gathers up pieces of saw blade and starts flinging them one at a time into the trees, in various directions. Then the bow saw. Then the rags.

He piles the rest of the body parts on the sled and he buries the sled in a mound of snow, two piles sitting there now, the torso in the other pile, two mounds of snow about as obtrusive as two piles of snow can be; the only thing missing is a sign that says BODY PARTS BURIED HERE. He walks back to his Jeep in a daze, carrying the Rubbermaid bin and the broken-off piece, and drives off.

First stop is a few miles south, at Twenty-Two Mile Road

and Shelby Road, an apartment complex on a lake where he and Tara used to live. He throws the bin in a Dumpster there, heads by his dad's house, sees a Dumpster at the Peachtree tennis club, gets his nerve up and tosses in the box of computer stuff. He drives over to Riverland Drive and throws in the bag of Tara's other stuff. Then he goes to work at the shop, trying to do his work thinking all the while about the other work he'd done there. Just yesterday?

He spends the rest of the day thinking what a fuckup he is. What an absolute dickweed. How when it comes to covering up a crime, ain't nobody worse than him, best he can do after two whacks at it is two big-ass piles of snow in the woods. She was right. He is a loser. He worries about those piles the rest of the day and late into the afternoon; when he gets off work, he's figured out that he has to go back again on Tuesday and make it right.

He calls Verena on the way to Stony Creek and tells her he's going to be late getting home, he's going to go for a run, a pretty normal thing for him to do.

He parks at the Nature Center at Stony Creek this time, changing his routine, and heads out on an eight-mile route he often runs that will get him close to where he needs to be. He's got to run past a shooting range and there's a guy there with a dog, dog starts to chase him, the guy hollering out it's a nice dog, don't worry, the way guys always yell when their dog is chasing your ass down some dirt road.

And Grant's not worried about the dog so much as: "That guy saw me!"

Like if he's running down a road in a park, it must mean he's on his way to his wife's body parts.

Grant doesn't know it, but the guy is the club's caretaker, Nicholas Amicone, lives on the gun club property, is out fetching mail from the mailbox. Amicone thinks, *Boy, that's some dedicated jogger, nasty and cold as it is. Good for him.*

He gets the torso and body parts out and puts them back on the sled and heads out toward a trail he knows will be

*easy sledding because cross-country skiers use it and pack
the snow hard. He goes down the trail till he sees a house,
just outside the park boundary, lights lit up in the dusk, and
not wanting to get any closer, he pulls the sled into the
woods, a low spot with lots of fallen trees, probably a swamp
in the summer.*

*It's a good place to hide stuff. He empties the plastic
bags of their body parts and one by one digs little holes in
the snow under the limbs of the fallen trees and puts a body
part in each hole and covers it up. His hands freeze about
solid in the gloves, vinyl not exactly insulating like wool,
but he keeps digging holes and burying parts.*

Grant seemed to be enjoying center stage. Wanted to fill them
in on every detail. The gloves, for instance. Wasn't enough to
have them, had to tell them how he came to have them.

"On my way home is when I bought the razor blades and
the rubber gloves. And then I bought coffee filters, too. And
you're thinking, why did I buy coffee filters? Because I told
the lady I was making a project making flowers and we were
gong to dye them and that's why I need the rubber gloves.
But then I thought about it and went, 'Oh, great, now I look
like a crystal meth manufacturer.'"

McLean laughed, comic relief.

"Well, that's what they always say on the news," said
Grant, referring to reports about meth labs. "They're always
buying coffee filters and rubber gloves. I'm thinking, 'Oh,
great, now they're calling the police, telling 'em that I'm
manufacturing."

"You didn't make any crystal meth, did you?" asked
McLean, joking.

"I didn't make any crystal meth, I promise."

"We didn't find a crystal meth lab in your house, so that
shouldn't be a problem," said McLean, into it.

"So," said Koz, getting them back on track, "you're back
out there. You're hiding the body parts under the trees."

* * *

He finishes burying body parts, gathers up the bags the parts had been in and stuffs them into a gallon Ziploc bag. He doesn't want to run holding a razor blade, so he puts it under his hat and runs to his truck. At a river near the Nature Center, Grant takes off his hat, puts his gloves inside it, and throws them into the river. He hides the Ziploc bag behind a big tree.

At the truck, he peels off his fleece top, two pairs of tights, and an old pair of Asics shoes and throws everything in a garbage bag, and on his way home, he tosses it into another Dumpster at the Charter Oaks condos behind the Peachtree tennis club.

Before he goes home, he swings by Clinton Township, to pay off $900 in parking tickets and see about paying off a couple of speeding tickets. He's ready, now, to report Tara missing and he wants a clean record when they run his name. It's February 13. He'll go to the sheriff's department on Wednesday. Valentine's Day.

"I'M SCREWED"

After the flurry of the fourteenth and the fifteenth—filing the report, Koz and McLean showing up at his house and asking for a polygraph, hiring an attorney, getting arrested on an outstanding warrant—nothing. Expecting to get arrested, or have the house searched, and nothing.

Just about the time he was calming down, thinking he might get away with it after all, Hackel announced on Thursday he was organizing a search of Stony Creek for Saturday, February twenty-fourth.

I'm screwed, thought Grant.

He sets the alarm for 3:30 Friday morning, planning to go back to the park and try to make it right, collect the body parts. Do something, not quite sure what. But either the alarm doesn't go off or he sleeps through it, and when he wakes up it's broad daylight, too late to be out in the park doing that kind of business.

So he sets the alarm for 3:30 A.M. Saturday. His mom is staying at the house. He can't risk her hearing him drive off, asking him later where he'd gone in the middle of the night, so he gets on his running gear and runs over to Stony Creek to carry out what amounts to nothing of a plan.

He runs to the park and up the Nature Center trail, worried they'll see his footprints, the snow all crunchy and his shoes leaving fresh imprints. On his way in to where the torso is buried, he's following snowshoe tracks, clear as can be. And the tracks go right up to the mound of snow that had covered the torso, except in the eleven days it's been there, there have been a few warm days, and the snow has half melted and the torso is sticking out. There's blood on the snow, and bloody newspapers, but the snowshoe tracks go right past the mess, just a couple of feet away.

Grant claws at the rigid torso with his hands, digging it and the plastic sheeting it's stuck to out of the snow, the sheeting hard to pull because it's frozen to the snow and ground. He lifts the torso up, no easy way to do it, it's so awkward, finally hefts it up onto his shoulder and carries it a mile or two, seemed longer, out to the edge of the park, at Inwood and Mt. Vernon roads.

And tucks it behind a tree and runs home. Sneaks in the house, finds his mom, says he's going to get her a cup of coffee, and heads off in Tara's truck with two large black garbage bags, panicked that it's 7 now and gonna get light soon. The search is gonna get started and there's bound to be people showing up.

He stuffs the torso in one of the bags and stuffs that bag in the second bag and stuffs that bag in the back of the truck and races off to Caribou Coffee at Twenty-Six Mile and Van Dyke just outside the park boundary. But the Caribou is jammed and he's too freaked out now to stand in a damn line, so he goes into the Speedway gas station next door and gets a newspaper and forgets that they serve fresh-brewed coffee, too. He races home and tells his mom he couldn't get her coffee 'cause it was too busy. Leaves it at that, let her get her own coffee, and goes back to the truck.

About noon, Grant tells his mom he's going to get a haircut and drives over to his dad's shop in Tara's truck. He stuffs the bags with the torso into two more plastic bags, worried it's going to thaw out and start leaking where he puts it, up on the roof of the office that's built inside the shop.

He drives home. Waits to hear news on the radio they found the other body parts. Expects to hear cop cars squealing into the driveway, come to arrest him. Hears nothing on the news. Hears no cop cars. Finally hears they searched the park but found nothing.

I got away with it! *he thinks.* I'm shocked. Wow! I can't believe I got away with it!

He leaves Tara's torso in the shop till Thursday, March 1, now. Everything quiet. Nothing further from the cops. No one showing up with any search warrants. But he can't leave her there forever. The power goes out in his neighborhood, so with nothing else to do anyway, he drives over to the shop Thursday night, props a big orange ladder at an angle against the office roof, climbs up with a green plastic Rubbermaid container he's brought from home, puts the torso in the container and, leaning out over the roof, slides it down the ladder, puts it back in Tara's Trooper and drives it back home. Takes it out of the Trooper and leaves it on the ground.

Friday morning, Grant clears out some space behind his truck and sets the container there, a few feet over from where it had been. Not much of a plan, but all he had. It could sit there while the plan evolved.

George Hunter of the News *stops by. Good guy. He likes George. George likes him. He drives to work a little while at the shop. Comes home. Hank Winchester's coming. Finds a search in progress, borrows his neighbor's yellow truck and books.*

The story continued to tumble out. Koz kept checking to make sure the batteries hadn't died, that the tape was still spinning. Grant told them as best he could recall through the hazy, booze-and-Vicodin memories about his crazy, meandering trip north.

The words came out in a tumbling jumble, Grant getting into that high register of his, eyes apoppin', hardly could tell where one sentence stopped and another started. He seemed to particularly enjoy himself when he got to the Meijer's store in Lansing, where he got offended no one seemed interested in saving his life when he bought the razor blades and sleeping pills, not thinking, apparently, that someone might shave before going to bed.

Grant looked at McLean. "Wouldn't you have said something?" he asked, meaning if she were the cashier.

"You would think," she said, humoring him.

"Well . . ." said Koz. "Well, they aren't as observant as you think, you know?"

McLean laughed.

"You know them scanner people, they just scan it," said Koz.

"No, I went to self-scan," said Grant. "But people still saw me buying stuff. And I'm thinking to myself, how is somebody not going 'Hey, you have new razor blades and sleeping pills. No! No! No! Do you need to talk to a crisis person or something?' "

Self-absorbed schmuck, thought Koz. Like people give a rat's ass about him picking a couple of things up at the store. And if you're going to slit your wrists, what the fuck you need sleeping pills for?

Grant explained he paid cash, having stopped a little earlier at a gas station with a LaSalle Bank ATM. That's his bank. He stopped there so he wouldn't have to pay a service fee on the $500 he withdrew.

"You find a LaSalle Bank so you don't get charged a service charge?" asked Koz.

"But you're intending on committing suicide," said McLean.

"Yep," said Grant.

"You're all right in my book, Steve," said Koz.

"Keep going, this is getting good," said McLean.

"WHAT PIECES ARE THEY LOOKING FOR?"

Grant filled them in on the rest of it, as best he could remember, trying and failing to get a room at the Indian casino in Mt. Pleasant, nearly getting stuck in a field with live ordnance at the National Guard base in Grayling, eventually finding his way to Wilderness State Park and the hallucinatory hours spent trudging through the snow before he was pulled out of a snowbank and flown to the hospital.

"Okay, that puts us to right now, then," said Koz. It was about 10.

"Can I ask what they found? Like what pieces they're still looking for? Maybe I could help," said Grant, meaning Tara's missing pieces.

"Sure, they found, obviously, her torso," said Koz. "Found Tara's head, we found both her hands, one of her arms. Um, basically what we are missing is a foot, from the knee down, and one of her arms."

"It's all under the trees, like if they look in the same area, I didn't walk but maybe twenty-five yards in any direction to find a tree. Did they find the sled?"

"No," said McLean.

"That's right there somewhere. It's like right by the edge of the woods, where the power lines start."

"Was the sled buried?" asked Koz.

"I kinda tossed some snow over it, but it was a bright red sled. I didn't want it to be so visible that you could see it, but I didn't take it out of there. Maybe someone took it who was walking the trail. Like 'Hey, I found a free sled.' But it's got blood all over it."

"It does?" asks Koz.

"I would assume it does."

"So, when you went back to move her torso, you did not remove some or any other parts?" asked McLean.

"I didn't know where they were. It was that morning of the search, and I figured that stuff was hidden well enough because I had put it up under trees and stuff. I figured, unless they bring dogs in there that know how to smell for that kind of stuff, then there's no way."

"Now, when it wasn't found that first day, and we still weren't coming to your house, you were thinking you got away with it, correct?" said McLean.

"That's exactly what I thought. And I kept asking David, 'Why don't they search the house? Why don't they search the house?' But there was nothing at the house."

Grant told them something that pissed both of them off, about his polygraph examination with the former Oakland County sheriff's deputy. According to Grant, the result of the test, arranged by Griem, had been inconclusive. The ex-cop told him he knew more about what happened to her the night she went missing.

" 'I'm not saying you killed her, 'cause that question's kind of in the air,' " said Grant, quoting the ex-cop.

Grant claimed the ex-cop told him that based on his answers, he knew Stephen had hurt Tara that night.

"I started crying," said Grant. "He said, 'That's okay. I'm not going to push.' 'There's so much I want to tell you.' And he was like, 'Well, you can't.' "

I'm not going to push you? thought Koz. *Are you fucking kidding me?* If what Grant was telling him was true, and the ex-cop had pushed him, he probably would have confessed.

And the ex-cop would have told Griem, and Griem might have done something to cut through all the intervening bullshit and wasted time and effort.

"Going back to Friday night now, you know, two nights ago—I'm having a hard time with days, too, now 'cause they're all running together," Koz began, "so, Friday night when you're driving up here, you stopped and called Verena. What was your relationship with Verena? What would you call your relationship with Verena before February ninth?"

"We were friends. We became close friends. We kissed one night," he said. Well, depends on your definition of "kissed."

Grant told them about how his crush on the au pair grew. Seemed like months ago, years ago, it all happened. How in mid-January, he'd got up the nerve to tell her he'd like to see her playing with Michelle, the family friend, and instead of being mad, Verena thought it funny.

How a week later he'd built up the nerve to tell her he wanted to kiss her, and sneaking kisses had led to her, to his delighted surprise, giving him a blow job almost out of the blue.

"Did you do anything more?" asked McLean.

"Before February ninth? No."

"What happened after February ninth," she asked.

"She thought Tara had left. She thought we could do whatever we wanted. A lot of nights I slept in her room. I needed someone to hang on to."

"It's understandable," said Koz, not understanding at all.

Grant told him about a mutual friend of theirs, a German woman who was an acupuncturist, telling him at one point that Verena was in love with him, and what was he going to do about it?

"Verena knew nothing about it? That you had killed Tara?"

"She had no clue."

"And then you guys are sleeping with each other days after. Your relationship was sexual," said Koz.

"We never actually had sex. We never had intercourse."

"Did you exchange oral sex with her?" asked Koz.

"I did."

"Did she have any plans of staying?" asked Koz. "I know from talking to her that she wanted to stay here. I don't think she really wanted to go back to Germany."

"She didn't. She didn't want to go back to Germany. The kids loved Verena."

"How are the kids doing?" asked McLean.

"I don't know."

"The last time you talked to them they were okay?" she asked.

"They're fine."

There was one last thing.

"Steve, it's getting kind of late," said Koz. "I just want it on tape that you're willing to make a written statement, correct?"

"Yes," said Grant.

"We're not going to bug you anymore while you're at the hospital. Okay? We'll let you rest up here. When you get back to the jail."

"Yes."

"Okay. The time is now 10:56 on the fourth. This concludes the actual interview with Mr. Steven Grant," said Koz into the tape recorder. "Anything else you want to say before I turn it off?"

"No."

"Anything you can tell us that we didn't ask?" asked McLean.

"I think I've told you everything. I mean, as much as I can remember. It might be out of order."

"Thanks, Steve," said Koz.

"Thanks, Steve," said McLean.

"No problem."

Koz handed Grant several copies of a lined form called

the Macomb County Sheriff's Office Witness Statement and a pen, and Grant began printing in a crimped sloppy hand an abbreviated account of the events he'd just described. It ran to two and a half pages, forty-eight lines that seemed woefully few for all the drama and horror. (Two days later, back in Mt. Clemens, Grant would be asked to sign another consent form and to sketch out a map of the area where he'd dispersed Tara's body parts; it looked like the doodling a four-year-old might make, a line at the bottom, two parallel squiggly lines coming off it, a large oval, a small oval, nothing you could make of it or from it, just a banal collection of marks that conveyed so little of their real meaning.)

Koz picked up the recorder, and they walked out of the room.

SERVED UP ON A PLATTER

The interview had gone far better than Kozlowski or McLean could have dreamed of. Grant had served himself up on a platter. How was any defense attorney going to rebut *that*, sort of getting it all tossed out somehow, claiming it had been coerced, or that Grant had been in no condition to give his willing approval.

Koz should have been satisfied. He wasn't. He was pissed. He felt manipulated by Grant. Grant had, he felt, given himself up, sure, but on his terms. He'd put himself in as good a light as he could, given he had confessed to cutting his wife into pieces and spreading her body parts by sled through a public park.

But what Grant had confessed to, you could argue, was second-degree murder, something that might get him back on the street at some point. Grant had told a tale of an argument gone bad, of an unpremeditated response to his wife's first slap. Koz didn't buy it. Neither did McLean. "When the first words out of his mouth when we walk in are 'What's the difference between first degree and second degree,' you know he's been thinking about it," she'd say later.

"You can't tell me he didn't preplan it," Koz would say. "He wanted to swap Verena for her and that was how to do it. He was waiting for her in the house and he attacked her when she got home."

Koz has choked people to unconsciousness during arrests turned violent, after, for example, foot chases that ended up down blind alleys when the subject had turned and the chase turned into "okay, you're gonna have to fight to keep me." And Koz had been choked out himself. He knows how tough it is even for a 250-pounder with bulging biceps to choke someone who is fighting back until they pass out. You don't do it and come out of it with nothing more than a scratch.

"He waited for her at home and knew what he was going to do and he ambushed her. And how could he put something over her eyes while he was choking her, and he only gets a scratch?"

Invariably, choking victims end up with flesh under their fingernails from their attacker. Scratching wildly is a universal and instinctive response to getting choked. Why hadn't the forensic exam revealed any skin under Tara's nails?

"This wasn't a one-on-one. She didn't know it was coming. He came up on her from behind and pounced on her like a true coward," said Koz

"I think it happened as soon as she walked in," said McLean. "It didn't happen upstairs. It wasn't a front-to-front confrontation. No way. He jumped her from behind."

Darga was of the same mind. If he had been choking her while facing her, she would have had two arms and hands free and would have inflicted significantly more damage to him than she had.

Darga thinks that during the series of long calls between Tara and Grant during the day of February that Tara went missing, Tara had had enough, said something to Grant along the lines of: "I'm done. I can't take this anymore. I'm not quitting my job. I'm not going to put up with your bullshit anymore. I'm getting an attorney and a divorce."

And control freak that he was, he stewed about it and stewed about, and decided to do something about it. "He didn't want to lose his meal ticket," she said. Her take on it was,

Grant was waiting for her in the kitchen. When she walked in from the garage, he pounced from behind, knocked her down, choked her out, and dragged her out to her car.

Koz and Darga wouldn't get to argue their theories at trial. Whoever would end up as Grant's attorney, on the other hand, would have Koz's own interview tapes to say: "See, this wasn't something planned. It was spur-of-the-moment. It was, you could argue, even Tara's own fault."

At the subsequent trial, Koz volunteered to Prosecutor Erik Smith to have someone choke him out in front of the jury, show them how tough it was, how long it took, let them wonder why Tara wouldn't have been flailing away with her hands and fingers for all she was worth. He was, of course, turned down.

Then there was the second-guessing of their surveillance tactics. If only they'd spent more time on him they could have put an end to it all the morning of the first search at Stony Creek. The department had put surveillance on Grant on a hit-or-miss basis almost from the time he'd walked into the station. Well, not quite hit-or-miss, but somewhat sporadic. The police got lucky with a vacant house across the street from the Grants' that they access to. They wanted to learn his habits, his comings and goings, see if he had a girl-friend coming over to spend the night, something to add up to a motive.

But the department didn't have the resources to have someone in the house, eyeball on his house, twenty-four hours a day. The days they were on him, they left at lights out, were back in the morning. After all, when they got news of Tara's disappearance, five days had already passed. No one ever dreamed that a full-time surveillance might catch him unburying Tara's body early on the twenty-fourth, just ahead of the first search effort. But, sure enough, crew's not on him, what happens? He's off on foot at 4 A.M. to do his dirty work, digging up the body, then off in the car a little later to fetch the torso.

Media would probably have a field day with that if they found out. You had a crew on the fucker but you're not following him when he goes out to dig up the body? Shit!

Dog-assed tired, he and McLean headed to the motel rooms hospital officials had arranged nearby. Koz turned on the TV to get his mind off Grant, if possible. Conan O'Brien was on.

Wrong time for comedy. It wasn't possible; Grant won't leave his mind. Koz thinking, *I've never known a bigger sociopath. A true sociopath. A pure narcissist. What a motherfucker!*

Wished he'd have wrapped the IV line around his neck and choked him out. See how *he* liked it.

His phone rang. It was Hackel, wanting to know how the interview had gone, wanting assurance they'd done it by the book, read him his rights, had a coherent, willing subject, that the thing was going to stand up to scrutiny.

"People are going to be all over it," Hackel said.

Koz told him they nailed it. Nailed Grant. He was toast.

Koz had asked for a wake-up call Monday morning. He didn't need it. He woke up wired, lay there staring at the clock until it was time to get up. They were on the road by 7.

Flying across M-32 on the way to I-75, only a few minutes out of Petoskey, a cop pulled him over for speeding. Koz flashed his badge. "Sorry, we're coming back from a homicide investigation."

"Okay. Be on your way."

They were back by 11.

Meanwhile, the Grants' home had been cordoned off by yellow crime-scene tape. But that didn't stop neighbors from coming by and paying their respects to Tara. Neighbor Audrey Brown, accompanied by her two small children, said a silent prayer for her and placed yellow and pink flowers at the base of the mailbox at the curb in front of the house.

The mailbox soon became a makeshift shrine. Someone placed a candle. Another placed a card that read: "Thinking of you."

A STATE TRANSFIXED

There hadn't been anything like this in decades, if ever. Given the stunning nature of what happened to Tara Grant— the circumstances in which her body had been found, in pieces, scattered, the torso in a Rubbermaid bin, the cross-state erratic flight of her husband and his bizarre and un-imaginable trek through the wilderness, shoeless in hip-deep snow—the entire state was transfixed. Even residents throughout the sparsely populated Upper Peninsula were following avidly, given Tara's roots.

A murder in the Detroit area normally wouldn't merit mention north of Flint. This was nonstop attention. It was top of the fold in all the state's daily newspapers. If the motto for TV and radio journalism is "If it bleeds, it leads," well, imagine how this one was playing out, with no end of breath-less updates.

The *Detroit Free Press* circulated statewide. From Monroe, down near Toledo, to Copper Harbor at the tip of the Keweenaw Peninsula, sticking out halfway into Lake Superior, its yellow and blue racks quickly sold out.

The headline Monday that blared across the top of page 1 read:

Tara Likely Strangled

Under it, a smaller headline:

We Are Filled With Grief

That atop a large color photo of Alicia Standerfer being hugged by Sheriff Mark Hackel, her eyes closed, her husband standing behind her, his lips pursed tightly, his eyes downcast. Behind him, and to his left, a larger-than-life-size photo of Tara smiling.

Reporter Amber Hunt's lead story ran down the right-hand column. Above it was this headline:

Torso Was
Wrapped In
Garbage Bags

Hunt's lead was that a preliminary examination Sunday showed that Tara had likely been strangled before her body had been dismembered, according to Medical Examiner Daniel Spitz. There were no visible injuries, not counting the cuts to her flesh, except for bruising around her neck. And no readily apparent signs of blunt-force trauma.

Because the torso had been kept in the cold, it was fairly well preserved, he said. The other parts, dug out of the snow, were, as well. The evidence was clear, he said, that she had died before being dismembered.

Spitz said he expected to issue his formal findings as to cause and manner of death on Monday. That the manner would be murder was not much in doubt.

"There are no gunshot wounds or stab wounds," he said. "We're not thinking it's a poisoning, though we'll run toxicology tests. That leaves trauma and strangulation." And since a preliminary exam of her body parts showed no signs of trauma, he said that left strangulation.

Although there was little doubt, he said, that the remains were Tara's, DNA tests would be conducted to make sure.

At 9 A.M. Monday, Hackel and Prosecutor Eric Smith held a joint press conference at the sheriff's department. The converted training room was filled with media, their gear and anticipation. They weren't disappointed. Hackel once again delivered a surprise: Grant was expected to be released from the hospital in Petoskey soon and would be in custody in the Macomb County jail before the day was over.

"Grant gave a very lengthy confession, laying out exactly what took place. I think he felt the need to get it off his chest. This was something he initiated," said Hackel, adding the last in case any defense attorneys were listening, Grant now in need of one. "He voiced interest in wanting to discuss this with our people. He said he wanted to clear his mind."

Hackel told them that Grant had been very detailed in describing what had happened, confirming the coroner's conclusion that Tara had been strangled. And he said that he had dismembered her at his father's machine shop.

Someone asked, were Ian and Lindsey in the house?

"The kids were at the house, but they were asleep," he said.

What about Verena Dierkes? Did she help? Had anyone talked to her?

Hackel said that the au pair had been interviewed at length on Saturday. "As we've indicated, Stephen is the only suspect," said Hackel. "The au pair has been very cooperative."

It was Smith's turn. Thin, good-looking, boyish like Hackel, he shared Hackel's local roots, and he shared an odd, scandal-plagued ascent to office, as well. His father, Robert Smith, had been the chief of police in nearby Clinton Township for twenty-four years. His brother, Robert Jr., was a fireman in the township and the fire marshal.

Smith had joined the prosecutor's office in 1993, and had made his reputation as a tough, aggressive prosecutor for eight years in the department's child-abuse unit.

Smith was elected to office in 2004 after an odd, to say the least, scandal embroiled his boss, Carl Marlinga. Marlinga was a well-liked, well-respected longtime prosecutor who became embroiled in federal bribery charges. Marlinga had pushed for a new trial for a man convicted of rape based on testimony by an expert witness that bite marks on the victim matched the suspect's teeth.

In subsequent cases, the so-called expert witness was revealed to be a charlatan, and his science bunk. Marlinga, doing the right thing, petitioned the court to set the conviction aside. However, the feds alleged he did the right thing only because of a donation of $34,000 to his campaign fund.

Marlinga was acquitted, but by then his political career was ended, or at least on a long hold. Coincidentally, charges were dropped against his two alleged co-conspirators, one of them a state senator, after pressure and good legal work by defense attorney David Griem.

Smith eked out a narrow victory, one in doubt throughout much of the night after the polls closed. His first day on the job, he announced he was banning plea bargains in felony cases with life sentences, particularly first-degree murder, and he appointed an old friend of his from law school, Therese Tobin, as chief trial attorney, which made her the highest-ranking female prosecutor in the history of the office.

Tobin is an imposing figure, a former college basketball star who is more than six feet tall, her aggression on the hardwood court a metaphor for her aggression in the courtroom. In 1988, she was captain of the St. John Fisher College team from Rochester, New York, which made it to the NCAA Division III championship finals, and is a member of the school's athletic hall of fame.

It was certainly no surprise when Smith announced that Tobin would be on the team prosecuting Grant, and no surprise that she would be joined by assistant prosecutor Bill Cataldo, the chief of the homicide unit who during his long stint as a defense attorney was most remembered for the case of the transsexual who killed his uncle to get the money to pay for his sex-change operation. Around the office, they called Cataldo "Shaggy," for his shoulder-length hair, befitting his status as an after-hours guitar player in a band called Hung Jury.

What did come as a surprise was that Smith announced he would head up the prosecution case himself.

"This case is probably the biggest case in the country right now. A lot of people have been glued to their TV sets," he said, helping fuel speculation that his participation, motivated no doubt by a demand for justice, was also motivated by a politician's attraction to and need for publicity.

Smith told the crowd that he had upped the original charge from an open charge of murder to first degree. Grant might have been angling toward manslaughter or second degree with his tale of an argument gone wrong, a slap, a slap back, and then, *snap*. He also had been charged with the disinterment and mutilation of a dead body.

Smith said that while it may have been a death that grew out of an unplanned series of events, the time it takes to kill someone that way, up to five minutes, has generally been accepted as evidence of intention to kill. In that amount of time, you can pull back, stop choking, reconsider. That you continue the act becomes premeditation.

Smith was asked, would Grant's confession stand up, given its circumstances?

"I'm sure his new attorney, whoever it is, will try to challenge it, but I doubt anything will come of it," said Smith. "The detectives interviewed this defendant at his request. It was all recorded on tape. He is recorded waiving his Miranda rights. This is pretty cut-and-dried."

And what about the search warrant that led to the discovery of the torso? Griem had said it wouldn't stand up to scrutiny. Would it? If the warrant was tainted so, too, would be its fruits.

"This was the most thorough search warrant I've ever

seen. Our chief of appellate was involved, along with seven or eight prosecutors. We made sure we not only met but exceeded the probable cause standard."

Finally, what about Verena Dierkes? Would she be a witness at the trial?

"The au pair is definitely someone we want to talk to," he said, "but it's a logistical nightmare. It's very difficult to subpoena someone who is a citizen of another country. She's not charged with a crime. We'd just like to talk to her and potentially call her as a witness. But that could take months of negotiating with the authorities in Germany. It's not an easy thing to do."

Smith would prove to be less than clairvoyant. The trial would have at least one major surprise.

The autopsy of Tara Lynn Grant began at 9:15 A.M., parts laid out on the medical examiner's stainless steel table, tools of the trade in place. Much of it was routine procedure, cutting off the top of the head to weigh the brain, cutting open the chest cavity to measure the organs there, ruling out all the things that allow you to determine the manner of death as homicide. Yet, how routine could *this* be?

One of the deputies on the scene took fingerprints of her right hand.

The thyroid cartilage in her neck had been broken, there was blunt force trauma to the back of her head and skull fractures at its base, a severe contusion on her left jaw with internal bleeding.

Spitz removed small samples from each body part for DNA analysis, to make sure for the record there was just one victim. Those samples as well as the heart and rib bone were placed on ice in a cooler. And Spitz collected the bone ends he had cut off for possible matches with tool or saw parts that might surface.

Spitz finished at 11:40. The manner of death, he con-

cluded anticlimactically, was homicide, and the cause of
death was strangulation.

At six Sunday night, Bill Mangan and Mike Vandenboom,
two Macomb deputies who had been sent north to relieve
Berger and Bud, had arrived at the hospital. Berger and Bud
in turn relieved them at 5 A.M. Monday. Grant woke up at
nine, was happy to see them.

Bud asked how things had gone with Koz.

"Fine. I feel better about things, now," said Grant. They
watched TV the rest of the morning, awaiting the okay from
the doctor in charge of the ICU for Grant's release. Word
was, it'd be early afternoon. Question now is, what about the
media? How can we sneak Grant out?

Fuck it, say Bud and Berger. They arrange some wooden
barricades at the main entrance, keep the media at least a
little at bay, wheel Grant out in his dumbass, zebra-striped
jail duds they've brought with them, wide black and white
stripes that make him look all the more ridiculous in the
next day's front-page photos, and let him stare bug-eyed at
the media while they snap their digital shots and holler out
their questions.

They get him into Mangan and Vandenboom's Ford Ex-
pedition, pull out at 1 P.M., head east to I-75, then a straight
shot south to Detroit. Berger and Budzynowski are leading
the miniprocession in their Taurus, Grant in the second car,
a Channel 4 on-air guy named Kevin Deitz trailing in the
third. Berger keeps it at eighty-five, to see how bad the TV
guy wants to keep up. At Pontiac, north of Detroit, the TV
helicopters join the procession, making it a 3-D affair. Just as
every porn director worth his or her salt knows *it* all revolves
around the money shot, every TV producer or director in
America has a need, a desire morphed through recent evolu-
tion into hard-wired genetic code: get the O.J. shot. Overhead
view, cops in procession. So, all the Detroit stations cut in

live, Bud and Berger in front, Mangin and Vandenboom in the middle, Dietz bringing up the rear, Grant, poor-ass substitute for O.J., but a wife killer nonetheless, down there somewhere, hidden under metal.

And the copters follow them, traveling close to the speed limit now, to the Macomb County Jail, the first two cars going under the building, Dietz stopping out front. Hidden from viewers at home, Grant is led to his cell. It's four-thirty, they've set some sort of land-speed record for Petoskey to Mt. Clemens, justice swift and sure for one afternoon, at least.

State social workers removed Ian and Lindsey from Kelly's custody on Monday and placed them with the Standerfers. "Whatever's best for the kids," said Kelly. "I'm not gonna make it a huge custody battle."

A third search of the park, this by just one Macomb County deputy and a dog named Trooper, was conducted Monday. A reconstruction at the ME's office had revealed three major pieces were still missing, Tara's lower right arm, her right foot, and her lower left leg. Another dog named Bullet, working with his handler, Deputy Philip Neumeyer, found a size 12 black shoe and a blue rag but no body parts. Other officers, one using a metal detector, soon found the matching shoe, with what appeared to be a piece of flesh stuck to the toe, a metal saw blade with what looked to be blood and bits of skin between the teeth, and a red plastic children's sled buried in the snow.

The missing body parts were never found.

Grant was arraigned at 1 P.M. Tuesday. Normally, the arraignment would have taken place in Romeo, at the district court for the area that included Washington Township. But for security reasons, the arraignment, to formally notify Grant of the charges against him, was held at the jail. Count one was a charge of first-degree, premeditated murder, which carried a sentence of life without parole; count two, disinterment and mutilation of a dead body, which carried a sentence of ten years and a fine of $5,000.

On Wednesday, news broke that police and prosecutors were looking harder at a possible sexual relationship between Grant and the au pair, Verena Dierkes. Local and national media staked out her family's house in Aulhausen, Germany. The *Detroit News's* automotive columnist, Christine Tierney, then on her way to Stuttgart about the possible sale of Chrysler by Daimler Benz, was told to detour to the Dierkes.' By the time she got there, TV crews had staked out their territory across the street from the house.

Dierkes' father, Ludger, would periodically come out of the house to chase off reporters who had come onto his property. No one got their scoop. Verena remained off-limits.

PART THREE

RETRIBUTION

A FUROR: GRANT CATCHES
A BREAK

On Thursday, Macomb Circuit Chief Judge Antonio Viviano created an uproar when he named Stephen Rabaut, a high-profile, top-dollar criminal defense attorney, to represent Grant. Standard procedure is for attorneys who are on an approved list of public defenders to get assigned cases as their name comes to the head of the line.

Azhar Sheikh, well down on the local lawyer food chain, was supposed to get the next assignment, and a plum one it would have been, lots of hours and plenty of media time to raise his profile and, if he came off well, his hourly rate to the private sector.

"This is very suspect," he said, biting his tongue.

Ben Liston, prosecutor Smith's chief of staff, wasn't so circumspect. "All the other murder defendants in the county have to line up in the cafeteria, while Grant gets breakfast in bed," he said, waxing metaphorically, living up to his moniker of the Professor.

"An outrage that reeks of special treatment," he continued, for those inclined to mixed metaphors.

Kozlowski had a cow. He'd had his fill of what he saw as kid-glove treatment for Grant. When Griem had been on the case, everyone seemed so leery of doing anything that might cause him discomfort. There had been such attention paid to Grant's rights and perceived slights to Griem's every wish. And now? Instead of getting the typical public defender jammed up trying to make a living on the county's meager wages, he gets Stephen Rabaut?

"Who's the best trial attorney you can get? I've testified at a lot of trials, and for my money it's Stephen Rabaut. And now Grant's getting him for free?" he asked. Pissed him off, system continuing to lean over backward for a scumbag who'd leave his wife in a Rubbermaid in the garage.

Viviano defended his decision. He granted it was rare, if not unprecedented, but so, too, had been the publicity in this case. The average public defender had no idea how to cope with that attention. The appointment was, he admitted, the first time he'd heard of such a move in his thirty years on the bench and had come only after consultation with his fellow judges. He thought it proper, and necessary, nonetheless. He wanted an experienced attorney who was going to make all the right decisions in the face of relentless scrutiny.

"The extraordinary nature of this case and the intense attention it has received requires a defense attorney with a proven ability to handle potential distractions while providing the best possible counsel for his client," Viviano said in a prepared statement.

Rabaut said: "I will represent Mr. Grant ethically, professionally, and protect his rights. Beyond that, I have no statement for the media."

No one disputed Rabaut's skills. He had a reputation as being particularly good on search-and-seizure issues, certain to be at the heart of the Grant case.

A small, silver-haired man, he was known for his high-profile defendants, including Susan Chrzanowski, a young, beautiful rising star of the local legal system who had been elected as a district judge in the big Detroit suburb of Warren in 1998.

One of her frequent public defenders was a strikingly handsome young attorney named Mick Fletcher, who in

1999 was accused of murdering his pregnant wife. The motive? The prosecution alleged it was so he could continue his affair with Judge Chrzanowski, which had come to light in the subsequent police investigation when police found compromising photos of the judge in Fletcher's home office.

What got her in legal trouble was that she had given the lion's share of her public defender work—fifty-six cases worth $17,000, more than that given to all her other public defenders combined—to Fletcher while she was sleeping with him.

(A book on that case, *A Deadly Affair,* was published by St. Martin's Press in 2001.)

Rabaut did her well. She got a slap on the wrist that surprised most observers, a six-month unpaid leave, after which she was allowed to resume her judicial duties.

Other high-profile or colorful defendants included government informant Youssef Hmimssa (CQ) in a federal terrorist trial in 2003 and Detroit drug boss Edward (Big Bill) Hanserd, who waged a long and bloody battle with Richard (Maserati Rick) Carter and other cocaine dealers in the 1980s. Rabaut once got a seventy-nine-year-old ex-con who had been charged with being a bag man in a gambling ring acquitted despite an eyewitness who saw his client pick up a package stuffed with hundred-dollar bills at a New Jersey Turnpike rest stop.

Critics of Rabaut's appointment got another reason to be riled when another high-profile attorney, Gail Pamukov, was named by Viviano to provide co-counsel, another highly unusual event.

Smith was unusually blunt later in criticizing that appointment. "I've never heard of a defendant in Macomb County getting two public defenders," he said. "Viviano's meddling has opened up a Pandora's box, because now we're starting to get other defendants asking for two court-appointed attorneys."

Pamukov made her reputation while serving on the Thomas M. Cooley Law School Innocence Project, proving that lab evidence in an old rape case had been tainted. Accused rapist Kenneth Wyniemko was released after nine years when new tests proved his innocence.

The stars were aligning for Stephen Grant.

Griem visited Grant in jail on Thursday the fifteenth. He told Grant that his confession to Kozlowski wouldn't hold up. It didn't matter, he said, that he had told the press that he had quit as Grant's attorney, he hadn't told Grant, and so the resignation had not yet become official when Kozlowski and McLean taped him.

On Friday, Koz went back to Stony Creek with a Topcon Electric Total Station, a piece of surveying equipment, to accurately detail what had been found where. And what would be found where, as it turned out. While there with him, using a metal detector, Sergeant Jeff Gornicki found three pieces of saw blades under five inches of snow. One, stamped "Made in China," was twenty-one inches long. The other two were about nineteen inches long. There were frozen bits of flesh stuck in the teeth of all three.

Saturday, evidence technician Adnan Durrani was back near the Nature Center with Sergeant Kevin Weldon, gathering and photographing more weird stuff that continued to be found—a left-handed glove with blue and red stripes with what looked like frozen blood on the thumb and skin tissue frozen to the fingers, a nineteen-inch piece of saw blade half buried in the snow, tissue from what looked to be a foot frozen to a tree root, two more pieces of skin tissue, and a three- or four-inch patch of dark hair.

On Monday, the twelfth, Koz and Weldon went back to the scene to look for more grisly bits and pieces of evidence and body, as the receding snow gave up its secrets. They found another piece of saw blade next to a fallen tree, the matching glove with red and blue stripes, two clear plastic gloves turned inside out, the silver handle of a bow saw, two pieces of bone now lying in plain view on the south side of a tree, a ball-peen hammer, and a five-inch knife with a wooden handle.

Koz and Weldon went back on Tuesday, the snow ninety-five percent melted now. They found another piece of saw blade nineteen inches long, but no more flesh.

On March 16, preliminary DNA results done at a private lab came back from tissue collected during the autopsy and forensic examination of the torso and body parts.

"The genetic profile from the unidentified torso is consistent with that of a female child of Mary and Gerald Destrampe," the report read. "The genetic data are 1,986,000,000 fold more likely if the torso is that of Tara Grant than if the remains were from a random female individual."

Results that came back March 23 from the state police crime lab were even more decisive. The odds against the body parts coming from a Caucasian woman who was *not* Tara Grant were 3.7 quadrillion to one, a thirty-seven followed by fourteen zeros.

A SISTER'S MESSAGE

On Sunday, March 25, twenty-three days after she learned her sister's fate, and the day of visitation services for Tara's family, friends, and coworkers in the Upper Peninsula city of Escanaba, the *Detroit Free Press* ran an emotional, heart-rending, lovely remembrance by Alicia on the front page of the Sunday paper. A big, bold black headline read I REMEMBER TARA, and in small print beneath it, "as only a sister could."

There was a photo above the fold, showing the sisters as toddlers, sitting on the grass, each cuddling kittens. You could tell it was the family farm; a pickup truck was parked in the distance, a ladder more in the foreground, leaning against a tree. Tara's hair was blond then, but with the same curls on the headshot of her that ran atop the boxed spread.

There was a smaller photo below the fold, Alicia and Tara posed at a forty-five-degree angle to the camera, looking to the camera's right, Alicia with a medium-sized smile, Tara flashing the same smile that had been beaming out at readers for weeks.

The story broke to page 10A, which was dominated by a large color photo of what looked to be twin girls, a bright late winter day, shadows from maple trees cutting across pure white snow, what looked to be curly-haired twins in ear muffs leaning against a tree trunk, taking a break from their chore of tapping the maple. Behind them, aluminum pails could be seen attached to other trunks, sap running, spring not far away.

The *Free Press,* in a fiercely competitive battle with the *Detroit News* over the story, billed Alicia's tale as: "An exclusive remembrance of Tara Lynn Grant." It began:

"As I write this, I have in mind a photo of Tara and me. Our mother took it years ago when we were kids. In the picture, Tara is clinging to one of our kittens with the biggest smile you would ever imagine. That was Tara, always a happy kid. Her grin and curly pigtails put a smile on the face of everyone who came in contact with her. She enjoyed every aspect of life. And she loved to talk. Even as an infant, she eagerly said 'hi' to everyone she encountered.

"In elementary school, teachers always noted on report cards: 'Talks too much.' She never had a problem striking up a conversation with a perfect stranger, a trait passed down by our father," wrote Alicia, who told how Tara's fourth-grade teacher got the chatterbox reined in by rewarding her with a piece of gum for each day she managed not to get in trouble for talking in class.

Alicia told about growing up on the hobby farm, her and her sister's love for the various animals, their chores, the 4-H club and its hiking trips throughout the UP, of Tara's crowning achievement of having her pig declared Grand Champion market hog at the UP state fair, of her love of scouting.

"Just the other night, I was going through Tara's childhood box and discovered her Girl Scout sash. It was filled with pins and patches signifying her interests and accomplishments," Alicia wrote.

"I recall spending weekends at our small school, roller skating in the gym—something that would not be allowed these days. We took long bike rides together and explored along the river a mile from our house, looking for crawfish. We were always so proud of our catch.

"Tara loved her Appaloosa, RJ's Broken Finger, the most. She spent hours brushing him and getting him ready to ride. We took riding lessons, even though Tara's horse was trained very well and was easygoing. Another of [her] passions was her involvement in shooting sports. Our father was determined to teach us everything he could about handling a firearm safely, and it didn't take long before Tara became an excellent markswoman," wrote Alicia, recounting Tara's skill on the 4-H BB gun team, as well as trap shooting with a shotgun and target shooting with a .22-caliber rifle.

"Every March it was a family tradition to make maple syrup. Tara and I would come home from school and get on our snow boots and snowshoes and head out to collect the sap that had flowed that day. It was a great bonding experience for us," wrote Alicia. "We loved yelling across the woods to find out how much each of us had collected."

It was quite a picture she was painting of Tara—champion farmhand, woodsman, hunter adept with all manner of weapons, horsewoman and snowshoer. And cheerleader. And musician.

"Tara's high school years were memorable for her. She loved cheerleading and was full of spirit," said Alicia. "She was active in the school band and played first-chair clarinet. Tara was also a skilled pianist, having taken many years of lessons. She and I played silly songs together on the piano. We were always able to laugh at each other, and with each other."

And quite the salesperson, too.

"Tara knew from the start that she wanted to study business. She was always a great businesswoman. One of her first jobs was working at a local shoe store. With her knack for sales, she could likely sell you the shoes you were wearing," wrote Alicia.

There was nothing Tara couldn't do. Nothing she *didn't* do. What Alicia had done, far better than any of the professional reporters who had been covering the case for six weeks, was really and truly show just how much had been lost when Stephen Grant went into his rage. How special this girl and then woman had been. What a love of life she had, and an unmatched skill in living it. This wasn't just a family loss. It was everyone's loss. How many Taras are there? How can you afford to lose them at age thirty-four?

Alicia briefly recounted Tara's college years and her steady rise through the ranks at the Washington Group, then concluded:

"Tara's loves in her life were her two children, Lindsey, 6, and Ian, 4. She made sure birthdays for them were just as special as our mom had made them for her. I recall many conversations with Tara as she excitedly planned their birthdays. One time, she had a cowgirl-cowboy party for them, complete with a horse.

"Christmas was another special time for Tara. She loved seeing the kids' faces when they opened their gifts. I think a part of her was more excited than they were. She was just a big kid in that sense.

"Tara was very proud of her beautiful children and lived for them. Her wonderful personality can be seen in their little lives, and her continued influence will be painfully missed. She enjoyed spending time with her family and was a very hardworking mother who did everything in her power to help provide for her family.

"I recall Tara's excitement when my husband and I announced that we were starting a family of our own. She said, 'Our kids will grow up together and be close, just like you and I were.'"

Little did Tara suspect her words might very well end up as literal. As Alicia wrote those words, her kids and Tara's stood a very good chance of soon being united by adoption, and growing up together.

"TARA'S SPIRIT WILL LIVE ON"

From as far as Texas, Tara's friends and family came to Escanaba for her visitation on Sunday at the Crawford Funeral Home, and for her funeral services in the nearby town of Gladstone on Monday.

Gladstone is a small town by most standards, pretty big for the UP, a little more than five thousand residents living along Little Bay de Noc, a deep, narrow bay at the northwest edge of Lake Michigan. Gladstone is on the edge of the sprawling Shingleton State Forest, a few miles north of Escanaba, the only real city in the area, near the Wisconsin border, boasting an actual cineplex and big-box chain retailers in shopping malls. Actor and playwright Jeff Daniels spoofed it lovingly in his play, *Escanaba in da Moonlight,* and in the movie of the same name.

Winter comes early and stays late in the UP. Hunting, fishing, and snowmobiling are major pastimes. Locals punctuate their sentences with "you betcha" and "don't you know?" As for the sound of their vowels, think Frances McDormand as the sheriff in *Fargo.*

People leave their cars and front doors unlocked. They remember their own, even those young ones who have left, as so many of them do, as Tara did, fleeing either the weather or the economy. They remembered Tara.

The marquee on a motel down the road from the funeral home read in big black letters:

IN MEMORY OF
TARA LYNN
DESTRAMPE GRANT
GOD BLESS YOUR FAMILY

It wasn't just family and old friends from high school who came. So did her bosses. Her supervisor, Lou Troendle, came from San Juan. Washington Group International's CEO and the rest of upper management came, too. The Upper Peninsula isn't an easy place to get to, not if you're driving, not if you have to deal with the weird and limited airplane connections. It would have been easy, and understandable, if the company had sent one representative and bought a splashy display of flowers and made a donation to the trust fund for the Grant children. But they all came.

At the funeral home, the old friends from the UP, her family, and her new friends from the Detroit area and work traded tales of the bright-eyed sparkplug with the big smile, who was just as happy trapshooting on the family farm as she was solving work problems on a tight deadline in Puerto Rico.

Melissa Hanson, Tara's best friend in high school, told of canoe trips and 4-H events—who, then, would have envisioned Tara as a high-powered executive with an office in the Caribbean and business to be negotiated in places like London, such an exotic thing not even the subjects of dreams—of chasing boys and being chased by them, in turn.

They'd more or less lost touch after Tara's graduation from Michigan State University, but never, not for a minute, had Hanson stopped thinking of her as a close friend.

Tara's kids, unaware of the darker nature of their mother's death, or so everyone thought, wandered among the easels bearing pictures of their mother in happier times, her visage beaming out at the sadder faces surrounding hers. The kids flashed smiles, good-natured, greeting and being greeted.

Ian was cute as could be in his tie, spending a good deal of time being held and passed around, a little big at age four but happy for the attention, and people happy to hold and hug him. Lindsey was the very image of her mom, same long, curly hair, same bright smile, wearing a pink dress over white tights.

Some had brought gifts for Ian and Lindsey, stuffed toys eventually filling a basket next to the casket. Inside the closed casket were handwritten notes from Alicia and from their mother, as well as drawings by the kids.

The photos of Tara? So touching. So sad. There, one of her on graduation day, mortarboard tilted on her head, Alicia next to her, both smiling at the camera. Tara, maybe four, sitting on a pony. And maybe twelve, thirteen, in a pink and blue outfit, holding a short rope attached to the muzzle of a bog cow. Alicia and Tara, looking like identical twins, same red and white cheerleader outfits for Mid Peninsula High, same big hair favored by the country-and-western singers of the day, chins resting on red and white gloved hands, same big smiles. The two of them and their fellow cheerleaders, during a time-out at a basketball game, out on the floor in mid-routine. On the beach at Lake Michigan. Kneeling, embracing a blondish sheep. Other farm shots with pigs and puppies. Another of Tara as a cheerleader, younger, smiling through braces.

Amid the flowers lining the walls, a sympathy card was affixed to a clear plastic holder. At the top, the letters imprinted on the card read: "With Deepest Sympathy." Under those words, written in a bold hand: "For Tara, I will not stop fighting for you."

It was signed, "Detective Kozlowski."

Sheriff Hackel was there, having made the drive up. He could have driven to Atlanta, Georgia, in less time. "We're here for the family," he told *Detroit News* reporter Ronald Hansen. "It's closure for them, and it's closure for us."

Michael Zanlungo, the neighbor who lent his yellow Dakota truck to Grant, was there, too. He and Hackel hadn't met yet, and Zanlungo was profusely apologetic. Hackel told him to forget about it, no one held it against him.

Two hundred attended visitation on Sunday. Two hundred and seventy—four times the population of Tara's nearby hometown of Perkins—crammed into the First Lutheran Church for the funeral services in the nearby town of Gladstone on Monday.

Her uncle Tim McLaughlin urged those gathered not to be ruled by grief or anger. "Certainly, it would be easy to be caught up in those emotions," he told them from the pulpit. "But for Tara's sake, we cannot let that happen."

The family would survive this tragedy, and so would Tara's spirit. "These children," he said, pointing to Ian and six-year-old Lindsey, "will be reflections of Tara's life and love. Tara's spirit will continue to live on."

Tara was remembered by other family members for her intelligence, her strength, her joy of life, the love she shared with them all. The specifics of Tara's death weren't mentioned. Ian looked quite the little man in a blue shirt and striped tie, and quite the little boy as he sucked his thumb, waving to someone as he was carried from the church.

After the seventy-five-minute service, a long line of cars drove to the Gardens of Rest Memorial Park and Mausoleum in nearby Wells, just outside Escanaba, where they released a flock of large purple balloons at her gravesite, purple the color chosen to help raise awareness for domestic violence and its victims.

The globes of purple stood out against the dark green of the nearby evergreen trees and the gray branches of the hardwoods a month away from their first buds of spring.

Fittingly—it seemed to match the spirit everyone said Tara possessed—a bright sun shone down.

Neither at the church, nor at the cemetery, did any of the speakers mention Stephen Grant by name. His sister, Kelly, and his father, Al, both attended the church and the graveside ceremonies. Al could be seen sobbing at one point. There were paroxysms of grief. Alicia, who had been a rock throughout, stoic, calm, and reasoned, cried. Lindsey, in a pink, flowery-print dress, cried, too.

Another of Tara's uncles, John Destrampe, began to read a poem about his niece, broke down in tears, tried to collect himself—"Oh God, where do I begin?" he asked.

The Reverend Jonathan Schmidt, First Lutheran's pastor, told the gathering that Tara wasn't dead. Her life in this flesh was done but she would live on in heaven.

"Death has done its worst. Death has failed," he said at the graveside service. "God will not abandon you."

Some mentioned an overpoweringly sad irony. As she had many early springs, Tara had been planning to return to the family farm just about now to help tap the maple trees, to collect what would be boiled down into the sweetest syrup anyone ever put on a pancake. Instead, she was to be buried in a coffin made of maple, next to her grandparents, nothing sweet about it.

After the long and emotionally draining weekend, Alicia got back into her SUV for the long, long drive back to Ohio, with her two kids and Ian and Lindsey. Several times she found herself lost in thought during the monotony of the leafless trees going by and the drone of rubber on blacktop, and she thought of something she needed to tell Tara. She'd pick up her cell phone, start to punch buttons, and realize there was no one on the other end to pick up.

And the tears would begin, anew. The drive home was never short. It had never been this long.

HITTING THE FAN

April the thirteenth was a lucky Friday for the Detroit media. Almost two months after Stephen Grant filed his missing person report, Eric Smith, to the surprise of the legal community, released 230 pages of reports on the case. Grant's attorneys had tried to block the release but were overruled by Romeo District Judge Denis LeDuc.

The result, as soon as reporters could begin sifting through their gold mine, was a media frenzy almost to match the aftermath of Grant's mad drive north and his mad dash through Wilderness State Park.

Radio and TV was filled with it, breathlessly reporting, then repeating, what they found. The reports, dry as they were in cop-ese, were filled with dynamite stuff.

Saturday, the *Detroit News* devoted nearly the full front page to the story, making room only for five paragraphs at the bottom for an update of radio legend Don Imus's latest troubles, over calling members of the Rutgers University women's basketball team "nappy-headed hos."

A red banner with white letters across the top of the page read: THE DEATH OF TARA GRANT—FOUR PAGES OF COVERAGE

The big, bold black headline under the banner read: GRANT'S CONFESSION

A six-inch photo of Grant in profile ran along the left side, above the fold. Also above the fold, a smaller, smiling photo of Tara. Six paragraphs break to page 8a. Under those few paragraphs, excerpts of Grant's written confession to Koz and McLean were reproduced.

"I found myself squeezing and choking her with my right hand."

"Once she was dead, I started to panic."

"I ended up cutting off everything."

"I wrapped the pieces in plastic bags."

Inside were stories about Grant's affair with the au pair, how detectives immediately started unraveling his story, details of how they found Tara's torso and their reaction, excerpts from Grant's confession, and, on page 10, after all the breathless coverage, a story questioning why Smith would release all of this now, and whether it could possibly jeopardize his case.

Prominent criminal lawyers around the region were critical of prosecutor Smith, wondering if it was smart tactics. Some questioned its legality. Would this jeopardize Grant's right to a fair trial? They said there was no case in memory where so much material was disclosed so prominently. Some suggested Smith, who didn't have much trial experience, had made a strategic blunder.

"Whatever his motivation, he guaranteed the potential jury pool will have prejudged Mr. Grant," said Margaret Sind Raben, the incoming president of the Criminal Defense Attorneys of Michigan. "The prosecutor seems hell bent on ensuring that a fair trial won't happen. Justice flourishes in the arena of the courtroom. What justice is he [Smith] talking about? Justice for whom?"

What struck her as particularly egregious was that Grant's preliminary exam was still a month off, and in advance of the prelim, mum is usually the word.

Larry Dubin, a law professor at the University of Detroit Mercy and a favorite go-to expert by media seeking legal commentary, sharp, quick to return a call or e-mail, and able to shape a quote, said: "On this issue, I would side with the defense. I'm not aware personally of the public disclosure of a file that could likely contain inadmissible evidence made available for public consumption."

He was referring, of course, to a certain defense challenge to the admissibility of Grant's hospital bed interview, and likely to the issue of whether the bag Sheila Werner found near her home was reasonable cause to search the Grant home.

Dubin said that the state's legal rules instruct attorneys not to release information that suggests guilt or someone's confession to a crime. While it was rare in Michigan to have a trial moved because of pretrial publicity, that might happen in this case, he said. If it wasn't moved, any assessment of damage done to the jury pool would need to wait until they tried to seat a jury.

All much ado about nothing, countered Smith. He'd merely responded to a slew of freedom of information requests from print, radio, and TV, for those weeks of police reports they hadn't been able to see. "The court order that I comply [with the FOI requests], and that's what I did today," he said.

Besides, he told the gathered reporters, it was Grant who had helped feed the media hunger for this case with his frequent calls and e-mails to reporters, his frequent interviews, and his appetite for the spotlight.

Smith and his staff, and all of the many sheriff's department deputies involved in the case, got a big kick out of it. Screw that asshole. Takes his wife apart with broken pieces of a saw, and people are worried about whether or not the police reports of the investigation are made public? They're worried about his rights?

Alicia Standerfer's reaction when she read the transcript of the confession? "The devil is what came to mind," she said. "It is nothing more than the devil's work."

PROCEEDINGS

Sparring over publicity and who was responsible continued.

On Wednesday, May 9, defense attorneys Gail Pamukov and Stephen Rabaut filed a motion protesting what they alleged were improper leaks to the press and the release of documents and videotapes to the media that were not given to the defense. They said Prosecutor Smith was guilty of a violation of the professional rules of conduct, asked Judge Dennis LeDuc of the 21-1 District Court in Romeo to hold him in contempt of court, and asked for a show cause hearing requiring the prosecution to prove that the recent release of materials to the press was proper.

They went on to claim Grant's right to a fair trial and due process had been compromised because of the releases of footage showing the Grant home and the family business. The jury pool was, they said, potentially contaminated.

They also protested a leak that led to media reports that a drywall patch in the closet wall of the master bedroom was used by Grant to sneak peeks into the bedroom of his beloved au pair. (In fact, the written report about the patch merely mentioned its existence. It was a local TV news reporter who had gone on the air with the titillating news that police he didn't name claimed Grant used the patch area to peer into Verena's bedroom.)

Finally, the motion protested that information provided the press on April 27, as a result of a freedom of information request, had not yet been provided to the defense.

Pamukov argued in person before about delays in getting autopsy photos from the prosecutor's office and forensic reports from the Macomb Area Computer Enforcement Team, which had examined the computers taken from Grant's home and from his father's business.

LeDuc disagreed with defense contentions. He refused the request for the show-case hearing, declined the motion for a contempt judgment. Just the opposite, in fact—he praised both the prosecution and defense for behaving in a professional manner. "Continue in the professional way that both sides are doing," he advised.

LeDuc did postpone Grant's preliminary exam, which had been scheduled for the next week, because Rabaut was in the middle of a murder trial in nearby St. Clair Shores.

LeDuc scheduled the exam for June 4, and set aside the fifth and sixth, if more time was needed. That would almost certainly not be the case, not because of the evidence in this case, but because of the pro forma nature of the exams in Michigan.

Preliminary exams are held in Michigan's local district courts, with the actual trials on felony counts moving on for disposition to circuit courts. The exams are held so prosecutors can present evidence that there is probable cause to believe a crime has been committed and that the person charged has done it. The evidence need not rise anywhere near the level necessary to convict and are basically rubber-stamp events, so much so that defense attorneys often waive their right to even have a hearing, preferring to save their time and words for the main event.

Outside the courtroom, Prosecutor Eric Smith was steaming, clearly angry. "This is ridiculous. I've never seen a motion filed like this in the prosecutor's office, maybe ever in the history of this office," he said, calling defense contentions a frivolous joke.

Maybe the charges were a smokescreen, he said, intended to deflect ongoing criticism that the defense attorneys had been appointed to the high-profile case despite not being on the selection list the court maintains when appointing attorneys to major cases.

If the prosecution was stalling, asked Smith, how to explain the 630 pages of documents and thirty computer disks that had already been handed over to the defense?

Smith said if there were any reports missing, they were from other agencies or departments, not his. "They have everything we have. We don't control the pace of when the [state police] crime lab or the Coast Guard completes reports. We're at the mercy of other departments," he said.

Later in the day, County Medical Examiner Daniel Spitz acknowledged his office had been slow getting photos into the hands of the defense, but there was nothing nefarious involved, no plot by the prosecution to hold the defense at bay.

The problem, he said, was the sheer volume of photos, necessitated by the various body parts that had to be shot. He said there were hundreds of autopsy photos and that his office didn't have the technology that allowed for them to be copied quickly. They would, he said, be ready any day.

On Wednesday, May 16, Grant lost both $50 million in a wrongful-death civil suit and all rights to his wife's estate. First Macomb County Probate Judge Pamela Gilbert-O'Sullivan—yes, Gilbert-O'Sullivan—revoked Grant's rights to control the estate, then moments later Circuit Judge Matthew Switalski entered a default judgment in the wrongful-death suit.

"We don't expect to see any of that money," Patrick Simasko, the Standerfers' lawyer, told reporters. "But what it will do is prevent him from profiting from a book deal in the future, or selling any pictures on the Internet. We stopped that."

Neither the outcome of the lawsuit nor of the petition aiming to strip him of his rights were in doubt. Still, there was drama involved, as there had been at every juncture. Simasko said that he and the Standerers had been going through the house, after a judge had ruled it was no longer a crime scene, and found a script on top of a microwave. He said Grant had written it before Tara's body had been discovered, and it was intended for his sister to use when responding to the media's questions about Tara.

Simasko discussed the typed script, in which Kelly said she should talk about how much Stephen was concerned about his wife's disappearance and how much he had wanted to participate in the first search at Stony Creek, but that the sheriff's department didn't want him there.

Kelly responded angrily. She said she and her husband, Chris, had prepared a sheet of talking points for a meeting they had with the media, "but Stephen never told us to say anything. I want to see the document. If it turns out to be the same thing we typed up, I'm going to file a lawsuit against Simasko for slander. I won't allow him to drag my name through the mud like that."

Kelly said she and her husband had spent the day in the Grant house after the search and probably left it there, then. She didn't explain why she'd been carrying around talking points from before Tara's body had been discovered and before her brother fled.

On Monday, June 18, Grant was arraigned before Macomb County Circuit Judge Diane Druzinski, who had been assigned the case by luck of the draw. She had a reputation as a fair but tough, no-nonsense judge.

Rabaut entered a plea of not guilty and told the judge he would be filing several motions soon, in addition to the request he'd filed the previous week that the county pay for Grant to get an independent psychiatric evaluation. It was the second time Rabaut had made the request. Earlier, he'd asked District 42-1 Judge Denis Leduc to approve an examination. Rabaut claimed the request was filed "ex parte," meaning it was supposed to be shielded from the public. LeDuc, though, made it public, resulting in local headlines and a blow-up by Rabaut, who accused LeDuc of bias and asked that he be removed from the early proceedings.

Chief District Judge Paul Cassidy had denied the request and the issue was left to circuit court to resolve.

Sure to be included in upcoming motions were efforts to have the trial moved out of the county and to toss out the search warrant of the Grants' house and his confession to police.

But, said Rabaut, none of this should be seen as delaying tactics. "We will file motions in quick order and in quick order we will be ready to go to trial," he told Jameson Cook of the *Macomb Daily*. "We are not looking to drag this out."

Druzinski set a beginning trial date of September 19.

Following an arraignment, it is common for negotiations on a plea deal to commence. Smith made it clear there would be no such talks this time.

As the Grant murder case worked its way through the criminal courts, Ian's and Lindsey's futures worked their way through the court system, too, as the two sides of their family waged a bitter battle for them. Alicia and Erik had been granted temporary custody and the kids were living in Ohio. Grant and his sister spent many hours of jailhouse visits and collect calls from jail plotting how Kelly could get custody. Grant even made a list of what he said were building-code violations for the Standerfers' house in Ohio so the court wouldn't send them there. He told Kelly he'd helped Erik Standerfer build a bedroom addition, which he personally knew was in violation of code.

It was all delusional, of course—what court was going to give Grant's sister, on her fourth marriage, though that was the least of it, custody of the kids when Tara's sister wanted them?

None, of course. But it didn't stop Grant and Kelly from plots and stratagems, including how they might recruit former au pairs to say how strict Tara was, and a bitch, apparently with the hope that the judge would be swayed by genetics, and instead of giving the kids to the sister of a bitch, would give them to the sister of a murderer who kept body parts in his garage.

In June 2007, tired of the public squabbling between Alicia and Kelly and all the press reports, Macomb County Circuit Judge John Foster issued a gag order barring comments about adoption proceedings to the media by either side.

On Friday, July 13, Grant's sister filed paperwork for something called a relative adoption, the latest in a series of filings by one party or another, and another chance for the media to trumpet the case.

On Monday, the seventeenth, Foster let everyone know he'd had enough. The two had been scheduled to be in court that day to discuss other matters, but Utykanski's filing before the weekend made that the topic of discussion. She told the judge that the Standerfers hadn't let her see her niece and nephew since before Easter.

Assistant Prosecutor Jodi Debbrecht, who was representing the Michigan Department of Human Services in the case, countered that officials in Ohio, where the children were living with the Standerfers, ordered that Utykanski not have access to the kids.

"DHS in Ohio stopped visitation with the paternal relatives," she said. "The two children are having behavioral issues at this time—"

The judge interrupted her. "Well, maybe part of it is, they aren't seeing the family members they like as well as the other family members," he said.

He ordered the Standerfers to let the Utykanskis see the children. "I'm not going to make a decision based on some caseworker in Ohio sending you a letter saying that they shouldn't see these children," he said. "The children have seen them their whole lives, and now they aren't good enough to see them? Why are the Standerfers good enough to see them?

"Am I going to have to order these children to come back to Michigan? Whatever you do should be in the best interests of the children," he said.

The judge said he would rule on Utykanski's petition on August 6. After the public portion of the hearing was done, the judge met with both sides in chambers and admonished them, again, not to talk to the media. And to work it out among themselves on a reasonable visition schedule.

The Standerfers left, seething. They were the ones being chastised? They'd see what could or could not be worked out with Kelly.

On the criminal-trial front, on July 10, defense attorneys Rabaut and Pamukov, in eight separate motions filed with the Macomb County Circuit Court, asked for a change of venue, saying a fair trial in Mt. Clemens was impossible, that the autopsy photos of Tara be suppressed, and that the search warrant that authorized the search of the Grant home be tossed out, and its fruits—namely the finding of the torso in the Rubbermaid bin and the finding of body parts in the subsequent search of Stony Creek—be tossed out, as well.

"The prosecution and law enforcement authorities were proceeding with said search warrants on mere speculation that there was some evidence of some crime to be found," read one of the motions.

The attorneys also asked for more money to fund their defense, including $3,500 for an independent autopsy and money to pay for a private investigator and for additional experts, consultants, and records.

* * *

The Standerfers and the Utykanskis all met again on August 6, but Foster wasn't ready, yet, with his ruling. But he did narrow Kelly's chances. He said Grant likely would have no say in who would get to adopt his children. Gathered in his courtroom were a bevy of attorneys, eight by actual count, representing Grant, his sister, the Michigan Department of Human Services, and the Standerfers.

Grant was in the courtroom, too. He'd put on weight in jail, looked fleshy, his chin much less sharply defined, the skin under his jaw running at a forty-five-degree angle from the tip of his chin to his throat. His hair was very tightly curled. A jailhouse perm?

"Mr. Grant, you have a choice," said the judge. "You can voluntarily terminate your parental rights to allow an adoption, but it will be an adoption you can't direct. If you don't, we'll hold a hearing to determine whether your parental rights should be terminated."

Grant nodded.

Utykanski's attorney, Melinda Deel, protested. "The law is clear," she said. "If Mr. Grant's rights have not been terminated, then he can consent to an adoption by his sister."

The Utykanskis, she said, "love and adore their niece and nephew. There's an important need for the children to have both sets of relatives in their lives, and [the Utykanskis] would be willing to sign an affidavit to ensure both sides of the family would get ample visitation."

The Standerfers' attorney, Michael Smith, also said the law was clear and gave prime emphasis on the children's best interests.

"It's not Mr. Grant who makes this decision, it's the court," said Smith.

Foster ordered all parties to refrain from badmouthing each other and adjourned the hearing.

It was clear that Tara's hopes that the sisters' children would "grow up together" were one step closer to reality. Grant wasn't going to be able to pick his sister; no one in the courtroom thought that anyone else would, either.

* * *

Stephen Grant's trial originally had been scheduled to begin on September 19 but was pushed back by repeated defense motions, for more money, for a change of venue, to toss out the search warrant and Grant's confession, and so forth.

On October 18, with the trial now scheduled to start on November 27, the defense threatened not only another delay but to quit the case. Rabaut and Pamukov filed a motion with Judge Druzinski asking to be removed from the case, blaming Prosecutor Eric Smith for inundating them with material in an untimely fashion.

On October 15, Smith gave the defense thirty hours of taped audio that had been made of Grant's various conversations, either with visitors to the jail or in collect telephone calls.

"There's no way we can go through all this material, and I'll tell you right now, I don't intend to go through this material," Rabaut feistily told Druzinski in a hearing on the motion to withdraw held on Monday, November 5. "It's not that I don't want to represent Mr. Grant, it's just that I can't be effective counsel if I don't have time to review the evidence. It's ridiculous. On Friday, five more CDs were dropped off to my office."

"Six weeks prior to the trial is not the eleventh hour," countered Smith. "Yes, we dropped off more tapes on Friday, but it's only because Mr. Grant won't stop talking about the case. It's not our responsibility to tell him to stop talking. That's the responsibility of his attorneys."

He was just warming up.

"I think this motion is the defense's opportunity to cover their reputations, because they failed to do the most basic thing an attorney should do: Which is to tell their client to stop talking about the case," he said. "With a straight face, they say they were not aware their client was being taped. Well, every attorney in this room knows people are taped in the jail. It's posted in three languages.

"The defendant certainly knew he was being taped, because several times in his conversations, he held up notes to his visitor so he wouldn't be heard. So, apparently everyone knew he was being taped except his attorney."

Druzinski ordered the defense attorneys to remain on the case—"Withdrawing is not a feasible option at this stage," she said—and said the defense could argue during the trial whether the tapes were admissible.

The lawyerly gamesmanship continued unabated. Druzinski had long since issued a gag order to keep the case from being litigated in the press. On Monday, November 19, with the trial just a week away, Smith charged Rabaut with violating the gag order during an interview broadcast on the local ABC affiliate Friday night.

Smith—certainly knowing there wasn't a chance in the world of prevailing, not at this point, but happy to stick it to someone he was developing real animosity toward—asked Druzinski to remove Rabaut as lead attorney and to hold him in contempt of court for "inciting a fresh round of media attention."

Thus, Smith ignited a fresh round of media attention, and top-of-the-fold headlines in Tuesday's dailies. Tuesday afternoon, Druzinski turned down Smith's request, ruling that Rabaut's comments had not been on specific details of the case but on defense work, in general.

During the interview, Rabaut said he was surprised when Alicia Standerfer came up to him and shook his hand during one of the early hearings and had told her he appreciated her gesture; that his job as a defense attorney was to protect the U.S. Constitution, which requires all defendants to have representation; and he admitted he had represented persons who had committed crimes "many times. I know they've committed them because they told me." But, he said, a defendant isn't guilty until "a judge or jury says so."

TRIAL

Officially, jury selection began on Monday, November 27, although they wouldn't actually begin interviewing would-be jurors until Tuesday. Monday was boring enough, attorneys going through the twenty-three-page, 130-question forms prosecution and defense attorneys had put together for prospective jurors to fill out.

The way the jury-selection process works normally is, county residents are summoned weeks in advance to show up on a Monday morning at the Mt. Clemens courthouse downtown for a week of possible duty. They start the day in a large waiting room, watching too-loud daytime TV or reading magazines and books. Names are called throughout the morning, and would-be jurors are told where to go. Those whose names aren't called are told about noon that they can go home for the day but to be back bright and early in the morning to start the process over.

They'll repeat the process day by day until their week is done. Some will finish the week having done nothing more than be captive and bored each morning. Some will get a two-hour trial over some minor infraction on Monday and be done for the week. Others might get a two-day trial about whether someone in possession of four ounces of high-grade marijuana is guilty of possession with intent to sell, or merely of possession, something requiring serious life-ruining jail time or a slap on the wrist?

The process was much different for the would-be Grant jurors. Court officials had culled about five hundred names from voter registration cards for the pool and they filled the courthouse to overflowing. So many of them had failed to fill out their questionnaires in advance that the day's agenda was thrown way out of whack. In-person questioning of prospective jurors started at 1:30, P.M. three hours behind schedule.

A new-look Grant was led into the courtroom, his hair cut short, dressed in a new black business suit, his hands free but his legs shackled. The new look went way beyond the hair and suit. His attorneys had had Grant practice a no-bug-eye look, which didn't come easy to him. Pamukov and Rabaut talked repeatedly with him about how his pop-eyed, crazy-man look alone, forget the evidence, would ruin him with any jury. So, after much practice, the wild-eyed Grant newspaper readers had come to love—his fellow jailhouse inmates loved it, too, constantly telling him to do the Stephen Grant eyes—was no more. The irony was that through much concentration, the accused murderer was able to look relaxed.

For some, it might have seemed lucky, finding yourself with the chance to serve at the heart of the weirdest murder case in memory, a chance to do something you'll remember the rest of your life. Maybe even—who knows?—get a book out of it. That group was mostly the elderly or unemployed, happy to get out of the house.

To most, a major life interruption suddenly loomed, just in time to mess up the holidays. What is usually a one-week commitment would instead likely be weeks. How's the boss going to feel about that? What if you're a stay-at-home mom? Or self-employed?

As for the questioning of pool members? Forget the drama of the case or the issues involved, it was brutally dull and tedious, the string of would-be jurors answering the same questions from prosecution, defense, and judge. The three hours of it Tuesday seemed like six.

Had they heard of the case? Could they set their prejudices aside? What did they do for a living? Did they know anyone involved in the case? Did they have any relatives who were attorneys or police officers? Over the coming days, some would claim to know Koz. Some he knew back. Some he didn't remember ever seeing before.

To Kozlowski, it was boring beyond belief, a tedious exercise, a version of *Groundhog Day* except you were stuck inside listening to lawyers all day. "It was the worst thing, it was just brutal," he said. Give him a duke-out with a B&E guy at the end of an alley any day. A choke hold would be an improvement.

The timing, at least, had worked out. For a while, it had looked like jury selection was going to coincide with duck season in October, and that would have presented a big, freakin' problem. Every year, Koz and his dad go duck hunting on Drummond Island, a big island off the eastern edge of the mainland of the Upper Peninsula, in Lake Huron.

Ducks are passing through on their migration south then, and for ten days to two weeks every year, the Kozlowskis are waiting for them to glide down out of the sky and alight on the water, attracted by decoys and the chance to rest. It is gorgeous on the island then, the still relatively warm waters of the great lake making for a late color season, and the Kozlowskis' backdrop is a landscape of sugar maples gone scarlet, birch shimmering in yellow, and the tamarack, the only pines to lose their needles each fall, in various shades of Day-Glo orange.

Koz had worried about the trial screwing up hunting season for months. "They're going to have to come get me," he'd tell his buddies, swearing nothing would keep him off the island come October, though of course they all knew it was just bitching, he'd be sitting in the courthouse, next to Erik Smith, whenever the trial started.

But one delay followed another, so there he'd been with

his dad, shooting ducks and enjoying the view. And here he was now, bored out of his mind. "It was brutal."

Sunday, he'd gone out for the last day of the duck season, a bunch of buddies in four small sixteen-foot boats in the St. Clair Flats, a large area along the Michigan shore at the northern edge of Lake St. Clair. It was a choice stopover for ducks, shallow water, tiny islands, wild grasses and cattails grown high, and a perfect place to hide a boat up in the grass and patiently wait.

A fog had rolled in, thicker than any Koz had ever seen, and by late in the day, sun gone, it was so thick you couldn't see more than a few feet ahead of you. *We're fine,* thought Koz. They had food, they had water, and they were properly dressed. They could just lie up on the bank and wait. And wait. But at some point, none of them wanting to sit out there all night and Koz having to be in court first thing Monday, they decided to head back to the nearby cottage one of them owned. The boats, which were scattered about, fired up and started to wend their way slowly through the dark, looking for the channel that would lead to the cottage.

Koz's boat made it back to the cottage. The other three didn't. A few minutes went by, a few more. A phone rang. It was one of their buddies calling. "We're lost. You gotta come get us."

The others with Koz started moving toward the boat. *No way,* thought Koz, *we head back out into that stuff, we'll have four lost boats.* "I'm not the best duck hunter or the best guy with a boat, but I'm the meanest guy here, so listen to me. We're staying here," he said.

He called the lost hunters back, told them they'd start hollering out from the shore in front of the cottage, and flash their flashlights. Look for the lights, listen for us. Soon, they were all back. Later that night, Coast Guard rescue crews had to go out looking for several boatloads of hunters who hadn't made it back through the fog.

* * *

Compared to that, jury selection was particularly boring. Compared to anything, jury selection was particularly boring.

The Detroit area has a wide variety of ethnic communities and has been a destination for generations of new arrivals to this country. It has the largest Muslim community outside the Middle East. Hispanics have built a thriving community in Southwest Detroit in recent decades, and having grown more affluent, they were fast spreading throughout the suburbs. In recent years, Russians and Albanians have carved out communities. There were Thai and Vietnamese, too.

One consequence? A lot of licensed drivers speak no English, which meant that a lot of the pool of five hundred jurors didn't, either. During the week, one Albanian woman who did speak English broke up the monotony. She had been a prosecutor back in Albania. "In my country, you kill someone, we kill you," she said. An eye for an eye. In fact, Albanians had made more than a few headlines in Detroit in recent years for their quick, and lethal, payback among themselves for slights real and imagined. She was excused

Twenty-one potential jurors were grilled Tuesday. Ten were excused for cause, eleven kept in the pool of potentials. The judge would want at least two alternate jurors to go with the twelve who would eventually vote guilty or not. Once a pool of fourteen had been picked, the prosecution and defense would each likely use their voir dires to excuse others without cause.

If any observers thought that because eleven would-be jurors had passed first muster, things would proceed quickly, they were mistaken. Of the eleven who had been kept, most had admitted to being biased against Grant. Juror number 7 went so far as to say Grant was guilty of killing his wife. "I have little kids at home," she said. "She [Tara] was a mother. The images in this case really bother me." Nonetheless, she passed first muster.

"In cases like this, I wish Michigan had the death penalty," said juror number 13. "Why wait for him to die in prison?"

Juror number 24, a lieutenant in the U.S. Naval Reserve,

had written on his questionnaire that he thought Grant had killed his wife with premeditation. "I believe I would be able to listen to the judge's orders," he told defense attorney Rabaut. "If the prosecution doesn't prove its case, I would be able to find him not guilty."

He had been kept on, for now.

Of the ten who were excused Tuesday, most had said that not only had they already formed an opinion in the case, they didn't think they could set their prejudices aside. For some, it was no doubt true. Others, savvy from watching TV or movies and eager to avoid spending what might be a major part of the upcoming Christmas season in court, said what they thought would lead to a quick dismissal.

When the circuit judge asked juror number 4 if she could set aside her bias against Grant, she replied: "Honestly, I don't think I can."

Grant stared impassively at her, kept his eyes in check, chin resting on clasped hands.

The judge excused her.

Later, outside the courtroom, she was greeted by waiting reporters. "My personal opinion is, there should be an eye for an eye," she said, identifying herself as Peggy Przybylski.

Day after day it went on, each day a mind-boggling droning of the same questions and responses. After the eighth day of jury selection on Thursday, December 6, there were still 120 left in the original pool of would-be jurors. Each time it seemed the jury was filled, one side or the other would use a preemptory challenge, boot one off, and in they'd bring another.

Judge Druzinski made news, herself, on Thursday. Up until then, one still camera and one TV camera had been allowed into her small courtroom to shoot the proceedings, rotating the duty among the various print and TV outlets. The TV stations were not allowed to show the pool footage until after court ended for the day.

The week before, WDIV Channel 4 and WXYZ Channel

7 had filed a motion asking her to lift the ban against showing footage while the court was in session.

Instead, in a ten-page order, the judge announced that henceforth there would be no cameras of any kind allowed in the courtroom.

"A criminal proceeding is not a game," she wrote, denying that the action violated the constitutional right of a free press and didn't restrict the public's right to an open courtroom. "The right of access is the right to attend," she said.

Lawyers for the TV stations argued that the small number of seats open to the public, fifteen, weren't enough to ensure the right of access.

She disagreed. She said the ban would limit the sensationalism that had been part of the coverage since Tara had been reported missing, pointing to, in her words, "promotional teasers, editorial comments, tickers at the bottom of the screen and break news headlines, presumably for the benefit of television ratings."

The area's courtroom artists, who had fallen on hard times in recent years as Michigan had opened up its courts to TV and print cameras, were joyous. For them, for several weeks at least, happy times were here again.

Friday morning, at 9:30, to nearly everybody's surprise and Koz's joy—it was almost as good as shooting a duck out of the sky—Rabaut announced he was satisfied with the jury. He had more than half of his eighteen challenges left but wouldn't be using them. The jury was made up of six men and ten women. They included two registered nurses, an ambulance driver—given the medical nature of the upcoming testimony, Rabaut might have been expected to try for fewer medical professionals on the jury, the general premise of defense attorneys being that the dumber the jurors, the better— and one lover of mystery fiction.

KILLER SEX

At 10:15 A.M., at long last, the trial commenced with opening arguments.

Amber Hunt had one of those leads in Saturday's *Free Press* you dream about as a reporter, perfectly crafted to capture the drama both of the proceedings and what had happened in the Grants' home in February.

The story ran under a bold two-column headline above the fold on page 1 that had the paper flying out of newsstand boxes:

**Grant killed,
then sought
sex, says
prosecutor**

Hunt's lead was:

> As Tara Grant's dead body lay in their bedroom, her husband sent a text message to the couple's teen-age au pair.
>
> "You owe me a kiss."
>
> A naked Stephen Grant then left a note on the au pair's pillow as a reminder.

"Have you ever wondered what goes through the mind of a man who's just murdered his wife?" Macomb County Prosecutor Eric Smith asked a panel of jurors Friday morning.

Smith paused, then answered his own question: "Sex."

Smith's opening was masterful, nothing Rabaut could do in his opening to get those images out of everyone's minds.

Almost lost in the imagery was the tactical news of the morning: Grant pleaded guilty to the charge of mutilating a body, admitting he'd cut his wife into pieces, an unusual move for a man about to go on trial for murder, but a move seasoned courtroom watchers had expected.

This wasn't, realistically, a trial about guilt and innocence, it was a trial about what kind of murder had been carried out—first degree, second degree, or manslaughter. No sense having the jury hear lengthy arguments on that issue, though the pleading lost some of its tactical advantage when Judge Druzinski ruled earlier that the jury would be able to hear and see evidence about the mutilation, including photos.

The plea by Grant—before the jury entered the courtroom, the judge asked him to explain what happened, and he said simply: "I mutilated and carried away a dead body"—carried a sentence of up to ten years in prison.

William Hughes, the police officer who'd taken the missing person's report from Grant that began all of this, was the only witness of the day. He told of talking to Grant for ninety minutes, making a note of the scratch on his nose and of his demeanor.

Most husbands who report their wives missing are eager to have them back.

When asked how Grant's demeanor differed, Hughes growled in imitation of Grant: "He said, 'I don't know if I want her back. In fact, I don't care if she ever comes back.'"

THE AU PAIR RETURNS

For a trial whose outcome had been a foregone conclusion, there was more than its share of drama.

The tape of Grant's confession had been chilling, but the media had got transcripts earlier and had reported on it heavily before trial, so there hadn't been an air of excitement about its admission. But there was an air of excitement in the court on Tuesday, December 11. (Mondays were reserved for other court business.) A rumor began circulating in the press that the au pair, Verena Dierkes, would be testifying after all, that supposedly she had flown in the day before from Germany.

She'd been on the witness list Smith had compiled, but the prosecutor himself had said it was unlikely he could get her on the stand, that he couldn't subpoena her, and if he went through other legal channels he'd be bogged down forever. For months, reporters had been leaving messages on her phone and sending her e-mails requesting interviews, but she'd never answered. In Germany, the tabloid press had hounded her for months.

First, though, there was drama aplenty with Alicia Standerfer's appearance. She and Erik stepped off the elevator into the second-floor hallway at 8:15 to face what seemed like a horde of media, filming and clicking and writing away. Stoic, they walked over to a bench outside the courtroom and sat down, pretending to be oblivious to the continual clicking in their faces.

Alicia was the first witness after the judge had taken her seat. She told of growing up as Tara's younger sister, of Tara's skills as a mother and executive, of the last, long phone call she shared with her sister on the day she disappeared, and of the message Stephen had left on her answering machine to let her know his sister had gone missing. " 'Can you call me when you get a minute? It's no big deal,' " she recounted.

Her testimony ended with an odd anecdote, but one so perfectly fitting for Stephen Grant. She said her brother-in-law called her on March 2, about an hour before his house would be searched and he would go missing, himself.

He had, he told her, released a videotape of the family to one member of the media. The problem was, he had promised it exclusively to another reporter. Could she do him a favor and say she released the tape instead, keep things copacetic between him and his reporter pal?

"I said, 'I'm not going to lie for you,' " she said.

Lou Troendle, Tara's boss, was next. He told of hiring her in 1994 and of constantly being impressed by her skill and dedication. He said he and his wife were social friends with the Grants, as well, and last had spent time together as couples when Stephen came down to Puerto Rico for a weekend the month before Tara was killed.

Troendle said Grant told him Tara was missing on Monday morning, February 12, and called back that evening to ask if she'd shown up. Troendle said he asked Grant if he had contacted the police. "The answer was that he had not. It was a strange discussion. He kept asking things like 'When is someone legally considered missing? Is it forty-eight hours?' "

Troendle said he couldn't understand why Grant hadn't yet reported Tara missing. "My exact words were, 'Do you want me to come up there and go with you?' I kept telling him, 'You need to do this.'"

The last time he talked to Grant was the day Tara's torso was found. Grant had called him to see if Tara's health insurance was still in effect, that one of the kids was sick.

After lunch Judge Druzinski ruled that the e-mails between Deena Hardy and Grant were admissible, and Hardy then took the stand.

She looked about as mortified as you'd expect when the series of sexually suggestive e-mails was read into the public record, in front of a packed courtroom.

Hardy said she'd known Grant since childhood, and that they'd dated in 1992 and 1993. She said they'd talk on the phone once a year or so just to catch up, but that the tenor of things changed at the end of January 2007. He called, flirted a bit, and asked for her e-mail address. The salacious e-mails had gone back and forth on January 25, and they'd talked on the phone ten times or so, too.

During one of the calls, she asked him if he still worked for his dad. No, he said, he had a job that required a lot of travel.

Hardy said Grant called her after the *Detroit News* ran the story about the e-mails. "He was a little upset about the e-mails being published," she said. But pleased with himself, too. "He bragged that a reporter from *Dateline NBC* kept calling him."

A buzz went through the court when the prosecution announced its next witness: Verena Dierkes, who had returned willingly, at county expense, to help see justice done. A blonde when she was last seen, her hair had been dyed a dark brown.

She told Tobin she was twenty now, studying English and theology as she prepared for a career as a teacher. She had, she said, enjoyed her stay at the Grants,' her weekly schedule including Wednesday nights and weekend nights socializing with her fellow au pairs.

Things changed between her and Stephen in January. She'd come home and Stephen had asked her to read some e-mails. They were between Tara and an old boyfriend and clearly showed Tara was still in love with him. He told her he was hurt, at a loss, didn't know what to do, but that as a product of a painful divorce himself, he hated to put his kids through it. He seemed crestfallen. Her heart reached out to him.

The next day, she told the courtroom, Stephen came into her room as she was preparing for bed and told her, out of the blue, that he loved her and wanted to make love to her.

"I started laughing," she said. "I didn't know how to react." They talked for hours but there was no physical contact.

The next day, while she was at the computer doing e-mails, he came up behind her and invited her to join him in the shower. She declined. That was followed by a sheepish phone call from his dad's machine shop. "He said he was so happy I was still talking to him," she told the court. "He said he was afraid I'd pack my suitcases and leave."

A few days later, Grant sent her an e-mail from his bedroom computer. "For what I'm thinking I know I'm going to hell," he wrote, the "going to hell" line one of his favorites from college days.

On a roll, he sent another e-mail, saying he'd been looking at her breasts, that he hoped she was "itchy." Dierkes said he explained what he meant by that, saying that "scratching the itch" was his favorite code phrase for sex.

Those last two messages came while Tara was still at home. The next day, as Tara was on her way to San Juan, Grant sent Verena a text during one of her classes at Macomb Community College. "Do you want me to do your laundry to see if you are itching."

In the context of all that had happened since, there was an enormous yuck factor in hearing Verena recount the language in Grant's e-mails. There was a shuddering effect, just a slimy feel hearing those words coming from the mouth of the young woman, looking over at Grant and knowing what he was about to do as he wrote them.

After Verena got back from class, there was an e-mail waiting for her. "If you come downstairs, I've got you. If you stay in your room, I'll understand that you hate me."

Dierkes testified she went down and told him: "I don't hate you, but you don't got me, either." He hugged her and she joined him on the couch to watch TV. Later, as she prepared for bed, she got a text from him asking her to come out into the hall. When she opened her door, he was standing there. "He told me he wanted to have sex with me, but I said no."

Grant led her to her bed, laid her down, lay down next to her, and they fell asleep. An hour later, he got up and went to his own room. The next morning, Grant asked her to come to his room. When she entered, he stood up, pulled down his pajama bottoms "and said we could now have sex because I knew what he looked like."

One can only imagine what was running through her mind as she'd glance nervously from time to time at the crowded courtroom, everyone entranced with her disturbing story.

Thursday, February 8, Grant had a beer, said it made him feel dizzy and that he was going to bed early. Verena decided for an early lights-out, too. As she was getting ready for bed, Grant opened her door, stuck in his head and told her, as she recounted it: " 'Good night. I love you.' "

He came in, told her again that he had fallen in love with her. They began to cuddle. He asked her if she would spend the night with him in his room. She demurred. He asked again. No. A third time. He stood up, took her by the hand and led her to his bedroom, and his bed.

"We had oral sex. He did me," Verena told the court.

At seven in the morning, her alarm went off across the

hall in her bedroom. She ran to shut it off, came back and climbed into bed with Grant. She left the door open. A few minutes later, Lindsey walked in on them. Verena, hoping she hadn't been seen, buried herself under the covers.

All day long, Grant texted her, asking her how she felt about him. Her continued response? "I don't know."

That night, at Mr. B's, while she was out dancing with her fellow au pairs, Grant kept texting her. "It was annoying," she said. "The girls were wondering what was going on."

At 10:30, she got one last text from Grant, which, she said, went: " 'Tara is going to be home in a few minutes. You owe me a kiss. Make a noise when you get home so I can get my kiss.' "

Was Tara already dead then? It was impossible to know for sure.

When she got home half an hour later, Tara's car was in the garage, Grant came screaming down the stairs, telling her he thought she was Tara coming back. He told her about their fight, that Tara had left in a car and he was going to file for divorce on Monday.

"He said it was going to be hard, and he would understand if I wanted to leave. But he said he needed me," she said. He told her not to tell anyone they'd had sex, that he would lose the kids during the divorce proceedings if it came out.

He then said he had to do some chores in the garage and went out there with a flashlight.

Verena said they slept in separate beds that night, and on Saturday night, Tara still gone, they spent the night together again. This time, she said, there was no sex.

On Tuesday, four days after Tara's disappearance, Grant told her he had called Tara's boss and family about her disappearance. "He kept wanting to know my feelings. He said he was in love with me. He said, 'Are you falling in love with me?'

"I said, 'Yeah, maybe.' "

On Friday, February 16, Verena's counselor at the au pair agency, Sue Murasky, told her that because of Tara's disappearance, she needed to leave the Grants' home immediately. Grant got on the phone with Murasky and asked if it was okay if Verena stayed one more night. Murasky said it was. That was the last night they slept together. "I slept with him in my room, kissing and cuddling," she said.

Dierkes broke down in tears when asked why she had lied to police early on about the relationship. "I wanted to protect him." Tears harder, now. "I believed him. I believed everything he said."

She walked past Grant and out of the courtroom. He looked at her, controlling his eyes, as his attorneys had counseled. She stared straight ahead. Their eyes did not meet.

A THIGH FIRST, THEN THE HEAD

On Wednesday, December 12, jurors began hearing the gruesome details of Tara Grant's dismemberment and how and where her body parts were recovered.

Detective Sergeant Larry King, who headed up the second search at Stony Creek Metropark and was one of eight witnesses on the day, told of how they found a thigh first, and then, under a snow-covered log, her head. And then, in quick order, her right hand, a femur, her left hand, a foot.

Working from photos, he pointed out for the jury members some of the finds. He showed them a photo. "Here we found a blue shop rag frozen into the ground," he said. "When we opened it up, we found what we believed to be flesh."

The jurors and courtroom were shown on a large screen the videotape of the search of the Grants' home, including the now notorious green Rubbermaid bin along one side of the garage. As the Standerfers and Mary Destrampe watched stoically, the video zoomed in on the bin. A gloved hand could be seen pushing aside black plastic to reveal what looked like flesh.

At that point, Judge Druzinski ordered the video turned off, saying that letting the jury see any more would be more prejudicial than probative. Stephen Grant was stoic throughout, too.

Giving some context to Stephen Grant's choice of a disposal site, Mike Zanlungo, whose yellow truck Grant had used on his wild, meandering escape north as the search of his house was in progress, told the jury that three weeks before Tara went missing, Grant had told him about the increasing number of coyotes that called Stony Creek home.

Zanlungo described falling for Grant's version of events as the story grew, and then broke, right up until the time he gave him his truck keys. "I thought he didn't do it," he said. "It was the worst decision of my life, but I believed it."

Zanlungo said that he'd had no idea the Grants' marriage was so troubled. On the contrary, he said, he and his wife thought the Grants had "the perfect life together. My wife and I envied their relationship."

The last bit of drama in the day? Judge Druzinski ruled that, despite objections by the defense, she would allow the jury to see three photos of Tara Grant's head when medical examiner Daniel Spitz took the stand Thursday.

Rabaut claimed that would be prejudicial, but Druzinski agreed with the prosecutors that the photos would augment Spitz's testimony and counter possible claims by the defense.

The main coverage of Wednesday's proceeding was penciled in for Section B of Thursday's *Free Press,* but the judge's ruling made for a headline above the fold on page 1A, too, one sure to sell newsstand copies:

**Jurors
will see
photos
of head**

A MATTER OF TIMING

Spitz's testimony was a linchpin for defense. He was by far the most important, and compelling, of the nine witnesses called Thursday. Despite vigorous—and at times even angry—cross-examination from Gail Pamukov, he stuck to his conclusion that it had taken at least three and a half minutes for Tara to die. The timing was crucial. Grant attorneys were shooting for manslaughter or second degree, her death unplanned, a tragic result of a moment of rage.

The longer that moment went on, the easier for the prosecution to argue that while the attack could have begun on the spur of the moment, as it went on there was time for Stephen to stop. At some point, it could—and would—argue, the continuation of the attack was the result of a conscious decision to kill. That you can't strangle someone slowly to death without at some point wanting them dead.

"It could have taken three minutes?" asked Pamukov.

"I wouldn't agree with that," said Spitz.

"It could have taken less than three and a half minutes?"

"I wouldn't agree with that, either."

"But you cannot say to this jury exactly how long it took Tara Grant to die, can you?" asked Pamukov.

"You testified there was an altercation. During an altercation, doesn't the brain demand more energy?" Pamukov continued.

Spitz agreed it did.

"The fact that Mrs. Grant's brain needed oxygen could have shortened the time it took for her to die, wouldn't you agree?"

Again, Spitz agreed.

"So, you can't say how long it took for Mrs. Grant to die?"

"Well, as a general rule—"

Pamukov cut him off. "I'm not asking for a general rule. You can't tell the jury how long it actually took Tara Grant to die."

"I wasn't in the room witnessing the strangulation, but you have to take what is known about the physiology of the human brain," said Spitz, managing the last word on the topic.

And if it took at least three and a half minutes, in his opinion, for Stephen to strangle his wife, how much additional time did it take to inflict the other injuries Spitz described in detail? Besides the fracture to the thyroid cartilage in her Adam's apple caused during the strangulation, those included a bruise on her jaw, a fractured breastbone, a scratch on her nose, a large bruise on the back of her head, and large bruises on her lower back.

Then there was Spitz's graphic recounting of how Tara's body was dismembered, at the neck, elbows, shoulders, knees, ankles, and wrists.

The three photos of Tara's head weren't shown to the jurors, but they were entered into evidence, as were photos of the bruising on her back. Should they choose to view them during deliberations, they would be able to.

The jurors *were* shown photos of some of the tools used to dismember Tara, found in the snow by police in their second search of Stony Creek, including band-saw blades, a fillet knife, scissors, and a bow saw.

* * *

The first full week of testimony concluded Friday with the courtroom hearing much of the more than three-hour recording of Grant's interview with Kozlowski and McLean in his hospital bed the previous March 4, the evening of his capture in the snow of Wilderness State Park.

At one point during the interview, McLean, Kozlowski, and Grant shared a laugh, the two of them laughing at him, Grant laughing because he thought he was a funny guy.

The Grant in the courtroom thought it funny anew. Erik Standerfer happened to be staring at him at the time and was enraged to see Grant laugh out loud in accompaniment to his laughter on tape. After he finished laughing, he had a smug, self-satisfied look on his face. *We're going to knock that smugness out of you,* Erik thought.

These are the first two paragraphs of Amber Hunt's deliberately understated page 1 story in Saturday's *Free Press:*

> Stephen Grant's voice was calm and steady as he described how he killed and dismembered his wife.
>
> He praised detectives for being so nice. He asked which body parts they still needed to find. He laughed about whether a store clerk might suspect he was making crystal methamphetamine with the coffee filters and rubber gloves he bought while on the lam from police.

The note to his kids that was found in the Zanlungos' yellow truck as police closed in on him was read to the court. Grant bowed his head, his lips quivering, his face growing red as he listened.

"I know you don't understand what happened to Mom . . . Just know that I love you more than anything else. I was afraid of losing you two, so I ended up taking Mom's life in panic. I'm sorry."

Trial was recessed until 8:30 the following Tuesday.

HE'S TELLING THE TRUTH,
EXCEPT WHEN HE ISN'T

Tuesday, day six, began with jurors hearing the end of the recording of Grant's interrogation in the hospital, followed by more direct testimony to shed doubt on his veracity, in his own words. The jury heard increasingly angry voice mails Grant left on Tara's cell phone after she was dead, and either stuffed in her car or cut into pieces that were scattered in the snow at Stony Creek.

"Tara, next time I call you, you better pick up your phone," he said sternly in one. "Call me or the kids!"

The jury also saw a montage of news clips showing Grant pleading teary eyed for Tara to return to him and the kids.

"I've been up sick worrying about my wife," he said in one of them.

The most important testimony of the day contained an irony that may have been missed by Grant's defense attorneys, but not by Amber Hunt, after the defense's key witness had taken the stand.

As she summed it up in Wednesday's *Free Press:*

> After defense attorneys spent a week trying to show that
> Stephen Grant was telling the truth when he spoke to police

after his arrest in his wife's slaying, their own medical expert threw Grant's credibility into question Tuesday.

The claim by their client that the defense wanted the jury to believe? That his attack on his wife had been unplanned. The claim that needed to be ignored? That Grant knew, or strongly suspected, that Tara was dead because he'd strangled her for so long.

Bader Cassin, another of the prominent medical examiners that Michigan seems to turn out the way the Dominican Republic turns out major league shortstops—he had served for years in Wayne County, was then the medical examiner in nearby Washtenaw County, and had been serving as an expert witness in murder trials across the country for decades—said that Grant's account of the attack couldn't be trusted and that the time it took for Tara to die might have been far, far less than what Spitz had claimed.

Cassin was the first defense witness and the last witness of the day. The prosecution had concluded with a long appearance by Kozlowski, the twenty-eighth prosecution witness, who had recounted his involvement in the case from the day Grant walked into the police station, to his and McLean's interrogation of him in Petoskey.

"I don't believe that what you just read was what went through his mind," said Cassin of Grant's version of events. He was talking to Assistant Prosecutor Therese Tobin, who while Koz had been on the stand had read some of Grant's statement to him and McLean.

Cassin said he doubted, for example, that Grant would have covered his wife's eyes with gray cloth, as he claimed: "I suspect he would have pushed it into her mouth," he said. Cassin said that Grant's state of mind during the attack would have made it difficult to adequately gauge the passage of time, that he likely would have been in a deep flight-or-fight trance as he strangled his wife, an extended state of panic akin to a blackout that would have divorced him from reality and any sense of the passage of time.

As for the passage of time, Cassin said Tara could have passed out as soon as ten seconds after the strangulation started and been dead two minutes later. But the time it took Tara to die was in fact, he said, "irrelevant," because Grant was in such a frenzy he would have had no sense of time.

Cassin, considered something of an odd duck by his peers, reacted oddly on cross-examination by Therese Tobin.

Tobin satirically asked Cassin if he was a psychologist, given his testimony about Grant's state of mind. He was not, he admitted.

So, she asked, he had not treated Grant?

Cassin said he didn't remember.

"You wouldn't remember if you'd treated him?" she asked.

"I do a lot of things I don't remember."

"Are you testifying to this court that you don't remember whether or not you've treated Grant as a psychologist?" asked Tobin, thrilled no doubt at how Cassin was responding.

"I've answered your questions."

Later, much later, Kozlowski would say of Cassin: "It irks me to say his name. Grant blacked out? What kind of bullshit is that?"

The defense wrapped up Wednesday, and both Smith and Rabaut made their closing arguments to the jury. Rabaut's included a request that they find his client guilty of voluntary manslaughter and not the more serious charges of first- or second-degree murder. That carries a fifteen-year maximum, compared to the life without parole for first degree. Second degree can be up to life, but with a chance at parole

Rabaut began with a phrase not much uttered by defense attorneys about their client. "This is a pathetic individual," he began, but one who "had no pre-thought plan to kill Tara Grant. Who plans strangulation?"

Rabaut asked a perplexing hypothetical. He wondered if first-degree murder was "more typically a poisoning or by more forceful means?"

More forceful? As if grabbing someone around the throat, breaking her larynx and breastbone, and choking her till after she was dead wasn't particularly forceful?

Smith, to no one's surprise, urged they return with a verdict of first degree. He told the jury that the night she returned home for the last time, "Tara Grant had no idea what she was walking into," said Smith. "He was laying in wait for her, naked, like a coiled snake. He wanted a new family, a new wife. The only thing that was in his way was Tara. With no conscience or speed limits, he executed his plan."

The highlight of Smith's one-hour presentation was a bit of theater with a stopwatch. He stared the watch, stared at its face, and after fifteen seconds said: "Tara Grant is now unconscious," he said.

He stared at the stopwatch for another three minutes and forty-five seconds, Spitz's best guess. It seemed as if he'd been staring at the watch for ten minutes. "Tara Grant is now dead," he said. "Stephen Grant had a choice between life and death. He chose death. Make him pay."

Smith told them that under the law, even if an attack began in unpremeditated fashion, if enough time passed to allow for a conscious decision to cause death, the standard for first-degree murder was met. The long passage of time on his stopwatch, he said, made it clear there was time for Grant to make sure his wife was dead or to stop things before they'd truly gone too far.

He chose "too far."

"He had the entire time to think, 'She's alive. She's alive. She's alive.' But he squeezed," said Smith.

The jury—after four of the pool of sixteen were dismissed by draw, six men and women were left—began deliberations after lunch, at 12:30. As five o'clock approached, they asked the judge if they could review certain pieces of evidence. Instead, Druzinski sent them home for the day.

DELIBERATIONS

When jury deliberations began on Wednesday, a poll by the foreman showed that nine of the twelve were in favor of a first-degree conviction, and an automatic sentence of life without parole. Gary Hafner, an avid reader of murder mysteries who had been elected foreman, and Richard Schnur, a computer services worker for Ford Motor, were adamant that the prosecution had failed to prove premeditation. (Interestingly enough, the jury, which had crucial medical testimony to mull over, still included two nurses and a paramedic.)

When Thursday came and went without a verdict, most observers felt more than a sense of surprise. It seemed all the more shocking for the level of violence that had been part and parcel of the testimony for two weeks.

Jurors asked for and were given during their deliberations the autopsy report, photographs of Tara's injuries, photographs of Grant's minor injuries taken the night of February 14, his handwritten statement to police, copies of phone records, and his initial missing persons report.

It became clear by midmorning Friday, after fifteen hours of deliberation, that the holdouts wouldn't be swayed. The rest agreed to go along with a verdict of second degree. When word went out that the jury was ready, the courtroom quickly filled with family members, courtroom observers lucky enough to get passes, attorneys and witnesses, including Spitz, King, and Grammatico.

Stephen Grant was led in, hands and feet shackled, pale instead of his normal ruddy color. He looked briefly at his sister, then stared at the jurors as they walked in.

Hafner handed the verdict form to the bailiff, who handed it to the judge, always a high tension point at a trial, the moment of denouement.

Druzinski read the form and had it passed back to Hafner, who read the verdict: "guilty of murder in the second degree."

It was a huge disappointment to Hackel and his crew, to Smith and his, and to the Standerfers. Kozlowski was enraged. Mary Destrampe reached behind Erik's back and squeezed her daughter's arm. Grant visibly relaxed and leaned over to thank his attorneys. The verdict meant the possibility of parole at some point for Stephen Grant. Later, Grant would say he felt like he'd hit the lottery.

After the verdict was read, Smith met with the jurors to discuss their decision. Later, he told reporters that when he reiterated the legal point that someone doesn't have to plan out a killing for it to be first degree, half the jurors pointed at the other half and said, "I told you so."

The holdouts convinced him, though, that nothing would have changed their minds. "The jury has spoken," he said. Was he second-guessing anything he or his staff had done during the trial? "I don't think we would have done anything differently. I still think it's first-degree murder, but we're going to keep him off the streets as long as possible. He's had his fifteen minutes of fame, and now we can put him behind us."

"We believe today that the right result was achieved," said Pamukov, despite the jury rejecting defense arguments for a verdict of voluntary manslaughter. "As I said at the beginning, there are no winners here. We hope the families can move on with their lives."

At the press conference following the verdict, for the first time since she'd first appeared on the scene, Alicia Standerfer's veneer of stoic calm, of a strength reporters could only marvel at, shattered. She broke down in tears as she talked about her sister, the trial, and the verdict. As she broke down, normally equally stoic members of the press were spotted wiping away their tears, too.

"We thank God that a portion of this horrific nightmare is now complete with the conviction of my sister's murderer," she said. Tara was, she added, "a wonderful mother, loving wife and a professional woman who was well on her way to a very successful life and career. She did everything in her power to provide for her family, and her smile and personality will forever be in our hearts and minds."

Haltingly, fighting the tears, she said her family would somehow recover but perhaps not as easily now. "With first degree, we could forget about him." Now, though, she said, she'd have to worry about one day having to confront the reality of her sister's killer out as a free man. She would, she said, do her best at sentencing to convince the judge to put him away for as long as possible.

And she would, she promised, channel her anger into fighting domestic abuse. "I promise you that I will be your voice," she told Tara.

Surprisingly, even Kelly Utykanski said she was glad the jury didn't return with the lesser verdict of guilty of voluntary manslaughter. "The whole time, we've said we've wanted him punished," she said. "We're glad he wasn't convicted of manslaughter because that would have been a slap on the wrist."

As for first degree, she said: "I couldn't see him sitting around all day thinking about killing someone. He was a loving person," she said.

Tough love, apparently.

THE CUSTODY BATTLE ENDS

The same day the verdict came down, the Standerfers filed a motion asking Macomb County Circuit Judge John Foster to reconsider a previous decision allowing the Utyklanskis to have the Grant kids for two days over the upcoming holidays.

The motion contained reports by the kids' psychiatrist that they were suffering from adjustment disorders, anxiety and depression. Seven-year-old Lindsey, it said, suffered from nightmares and physical complaints and doctors were considering giving her medication for post-traumatic syndrome.

The motion contained what was purported to be a quotation from Lindsey: "When I go to visit Aunt Kelly, it reminds me when Mommy died." The motion also said that during a visit to the Utykanskis in September, Lindsey asked her aunt: "Why didn't you tell me Dad killed my mom?"

Foster wasn't swayed. He ruled the visitation would remain in effect.

Amber Hunt of the *Free Press,* always deeply sourced, broke the news on Friday, January 4, that the Standerfers and Kelly Utykanski had reached a deal after months of acrimonious battle over custody of Lindsey and Ian.

Because of a judge's order, neither party was able to disclose details, but Hunt's sources told her that Alicia was given primary custody and Kelly was given visitation rights. That deal came on Thursday, a day after Grant relinquished his parental rights.

A mediator at the Macomb County Friend of the Court brokered the deal. Circuit Judge John Foster had urged the two sides to work something out at the time Grant terminated his rights.

Surprisingly, it was Utykanski who acted the happiest when Hunt talked to her. She was upbeat. "There's two little kids involved," she said, saying she was happy with the outcome.

Alicia Standerfer declined to say whether the deal made her happy or not, but she said she was relieved the battle was over and that she was happy that the children "can now move on and lead productive lives."

Hunt asked her if the custody battle had been more difficult than the trial itself.

"Yes," said Alicia. "More than you could know."

It would come out during the next month that during jailhouse conversations, either in person or over the phone, Stephen Grant and Kelly had connived for hours over how she could get custody of the kids, from portraying the Standerfers as friendless types who wouldn't be able to get babysitters and as the owners of a home Grant claimed had numerous code violations to exaggerating Kelly's interaction with them over the years.

But the weeks of plotting had come to naught. As it was preordained. There was no chance in hell that any court in Michigan was going to give custody of two kids to their killer's sister when their dead mom's sister and best friend was eager to take them in.

That Stephen Grant thought he could help his sister from jail to manipulate the system and influence where his children would grow up was just another in a string of a lifetime of delusions.

JAILHOUSE SEDUCTION

On February 7, a reading and watching public who thought the Stephen Grant story had been about played out and had no more surprises left were proven wrong. There was at least one weird—extremely weird—surprise left.

Prosecutor Smith released excerpts from twenty letters Grant had written to female inmates at the jail, including several to another infamous killer, Jennifer Kukla. She was the woman who took a butcher knife to her two young daughters and slaughtered the three family dogs and the girls' pet mouse. The woman who told police when they came to her home that she was waiting to be taken to hell in a hearse made of bones. Who had gone as far off the deep end as anyone has ever got on the Super Bowl Sunday before Grant sawed his wife into pieces.

Nice to have something in common when you're starting a relationship.

The letters—notes, really, often passed under food trays and left in doorways—began when Kukla was still at the county jail, in the psychiatric unit, as was Grant, and continued after she was transferred to the Huron Valley Complex in Ypsilanti. He shared one thing in common with his pen-pal relationship that he had with his previous relationships in the outside world: he lied about his work habits, claiming not only that he was Mr. Mom but that he worked full-time at his dad's shop. He lied to her, too, about being a proud college graduate.

On June 30, 2007, he kicked things off.

"Hi, Jenny. Linda said you might like someone to write back and forth with, so I am offering. I have often seen you outside the A doors . . ."

Oct. 1, 2007:

"Hi, Jenny . . . It has been nice writing to you these last couple of months. I still laugh when I remember your one note. You asked: 'Are you scared of me?' (LOL) You are too nice to be scared of. I just wish we could arrange a rendezvous in the closet one of these days."

(His notes were peppered with LOLs.)

"I hope you realize you will be okay no matter what happens. I'm pretty sure you are stronger than I you think. You are. Don't let me down."

In his letters, Grant was full of braggadocio, an object, at least in his own mind, of endless desire. He wrote in one letter that "the women in their holding cell were hooting and hollering at me. A lady [deputy] came over to me and told me to stop enticing the women. It's weird. Wherever I go, people point at me and whisper or yell at me."

AND THEN IT GOT WEIRDER

There are signs scattered around the visiting center at the Macomb County Jail warning inmates and visitors that their conversations are being recorded, and so are prisoners' conversations during their collect calls to the outside.

Either Grant and his sister, Kelly, never noticed them, or once embroiled in conversation forgot about them, or didn't care. Grant, never one to hold his tongue, didn't care. Neither did Kelly. Or maybe he was just every bit as dumb on a daily basis as he was the night he'd meandered all over the state trying to get to Wilderness State Park, ending up in a snowbank in 14-degree weather without a jacket or shoes.

This was, after all, a guy who unburied his wife's torso and put it back in his garage moments before the cops showed up with a search warrant. Police are hoping to find trace or microscopic evidence three weeks after he's had time to get rid of the big stuff, and her torso's in a Rubbermaid bin in the garage?

The tapes had been a matter of contention before the trial. When fifty hours' worth of recordings of seventy-one conversations were handed over to the defense a month before the trial began, defense attorney Stephen Rabaut asked to be removed from the case, saying there wasn't enough time to listen to them all before the trial. Judge Diane Druzinski refused the request.

It became a moot point. The tapes weren't introduced at trial, the prosecution feeling their case was so strong, there was no need to give Rabaut and his team a possible appealable issue.

The media had been told that the recordings were explosive, filled with more of the you-can't-make-this-up stuff that had characterized the entire case. On February 1, 2008, twenty days before sentencing, Assistant Prosecutor Bill Cataldo announced that in response to several Freedom of Information Act requests, the department would soon make available CDs of some fifty hours of recordings made since Grant was arrested the previous March.

The media didn't have to wait for its headlines, though.

Patrick Simasko, one of Alicia Standerfer's attorneys, had listened to all fifty hours and he briefed the media on what they could expect to hear. Grant, he said, had joked about his wife's death and dismemberment and had schemed with his sister to figure out a way to do a book deal that would circumvent state law—and the $50 million judgment awarded Alicia the previous May that gave her any money Grant made while in jail—and let Kelly benefit from the proceeds instead of his children.

"The jokes are beyond horrible," said Simasko. "You won't believe what's on those recordings. It'll turn your stomach."

For example, he said, just before Tara's burial, Grant and his sister joked about whether all her body parts would be buried in one casket.

Later, he seemed preoccupied with a 5K run and fundraiser in Tara's memory at the same Stony Creek Metropark where he'd scattered those body parts. Grant told his sister she should enter the run so she could pick him up a souvenir T-shirt, said Simasko.

Grant and his sister were recorded talking about a book deal on several occasions. "On the tapes, Stephen and Kelly talk about how they've already got an agent in California to peddle a book deal," said Simasko. "They also talked a lot about how Kelly can charge a management fee for being Stephen's manager, and there was definite discussions about how, if Kelly was the manager, any money they made from the book wouldn't be garnished."

Not to worry, said Simasko. He'd go after any money anyone in the Grant family made from any book deal. This was, after all, the same attorney who'd filed in Macomb Circuit Court the month before to collect the $24.71 Grant had accumulated in his jail account.

Standerfer had listened to the tapes, too. "It's pathetic," she told reporters. "It gives you an insight into the minds of the people who were involved."

On February 8, the day after Smith released Grant's letters to Kukla, his office released three CDs of Grant's jail-house conversations. They lived up, or down, depending on your point of view, to expectations. He tells his sister that while his lawyers have had him practicing a more relaxed look, getting rid of the pop eyes, his buddies in jail love the look. "They say, 'Do the Stephen Grant look,'" he told her.

In one conversation, Grant for one rare moment expresses remorse. "I never thought my life would turn out like this," he said.

Kelly consoled him. "It's not like you're Jeffrey Dahmer."

Well, there is that.

When he tells her that he's afraid he'll spend the rest of his life in jail, she consoles him again. "Well, I guess we'll spend our retirement together, then."

Lieutenant Darga had the chore, unpleasant, of listening to Grant's tapes almost in real time. "There were some conversations that would just infuriate you," she said later. "You're listening to people who have so much hatred." She couldn't listen to the tapes late in the day; they'd piss her off so much she'd carry the anger home to her family, and that wasn't fair to them. So she'd listen to them earlier in her day.

Kelly's first visit to Grant on March 8, the same day Rabaut stirred up controversy with his appointment as trial attorney, was innocent enough. Grant and his sister sat on opposite sides of a bulletproof barrier and talked by phone for more than twenty minutes.

Grant: "So, how's everybody?"

Kelly: "Everybody's pissed off at you. I'm pissed off at you. I love you. I'm pissed off at what you did. I can't ask what happened to make you snap, even though I want to. You can tell me later."

She apologized for telling the police the night he fled north where he was heading. "I didn't want you to die," she said.

Grant: "That's okay."

Kelly: "Don't be mad at me. I didn't want you to die in a snowbank."

Grant: "I was close. It was 90 degrees, my body."

Kelly: "I saw you helicoptered out. I was pretty stressed out."

Grant: "So, how much of it was on the news?"

Kelly: "It was all over the news."

A little later, Kelly: "When the kids left us, the story was they knew their mother was dead. I used a counselor to tell them. They were too young to understand that you did it. They're not supposed to be told until they are ten and eight . . . Am I allowed to bring you pictures of Ian and Lindsey?"

Grant: "Yeah, but I don't want to see them right now."

On March 14, another visit from Kelly, where they start off talking about being able to communicate in a fashion that can't be recorded:

Kelly: "What about your book on sign language, can you . . . ?"

Grant: "Yeah, probably."

Kelly: "Okay. I'll buy the same book."

Grant: "Okay."

Kelly: "I don't see any reason why they wouldn't let you have it."

Grant: "Yeah. Well, maybe not."

Kelly: "Well, Chris's sister's deaf."

Grant: "Okay."

Kelly: "So, what if she comes to visit you?"

Grant: "Okay."

Kelly: "They're having another fund-raiser, too. It just seems like a big money grab to me."

Grant: "They're having a fund-raiser? They've had more than one?"

Kelly: "Well, they opened up a trust fund at Warren Bank that, you know, the public is contributing to. And now they're having a fund-raiser."

Grant: "How big is this out there? Because, I mean, I don't see anything. I don't see any news."

Kelly: "I'll start getting the paper, and then I'll start sending you some clips."

Grant: "Okay."

Kelly: "Some people are really bashing them for having a trust fund. They're like, 'Isn't that stupid?? They don't have life insurance and stuff?' She has a life insurance policy, and once it gets out, she's really going to get slammed . . . It's like a big money grab."

Grant: "Right. You're looking at like a million bucks, by the time those kids are eighteen. At least."

Kelly: "Like Chris said, it will double or triple. Even if you took a hundred grand out, that's still gonna leave 550."

Grant: "Right."

Kelly: "You know, by the time they get to college, or a car at sixteen, I mean, that's ridiculous. If they get custody, they're going to piss it away . . . Erik set up that trust fund at Warren Bank, and somebody has to be set up as the manager of the trust fund. And the manager of the trust fund gets to take an allowance. So, he could be paying himself sixty grand a year to manage the trust fund."

Grant: "Nice."

Kelly: "So, he could be taking that right now, and taking a leave of absence from his job."

Grant: "Nice."

Kelly: "What does Erik do for a living?"

Grant: "I think he's, like, one of the operators of the paper mill. I think he's like one of the managers."

Kelly: "Does he have lot of debt?"

They then discuss at length more strategies for Kelly getting Ian and Lindsey. They're going to argue that Kelly's house is bigger and that she has a much larger circle of reliable friends, including a friend of her husband who is a cop, than Alicia and Erik have. That way, if Kelly ever needs a babysitter, she'll have a better chance of finding one. She tells Grant someone from social services is coming out in the next few days to look at her condo.

Kelly: "I'm moving the litter box to the half bath in the basement."

(As if, all things being equal, litter-box placement could decide the kids' future.)

Then Kelly brings up her suspicion that Alicia might try to auction Grant's clothes off on the Web.

Kelly: "I want to dispose of all your clothes. I don't want them to end up on eBay."

Grant: "I've got three nice suits, brand-new suits, one's black, one's charcoal gray. And I've got a white, brand-new, nice white shirt and a nice cream shirt. Then I've got ties. Lots of them."

Kelly: "Although if she decided to put them on eBay, that would make her look really bad. But still."

Grant: "You might want to hold on."

Kelly: "Well, I'll put them in Rubbermaid containers and put them in my basement, then."

Grant: "There's lots of Rubbermaid containers at my house."

Bah-dah-boom-bah-da-bing.

Grant: "Sorry."

Kelly: "I'm going to tell her, like you know, I want your pots and pans because you were a gourmet cook and I'm a gourmet cook, those kinds of things. I'm not going to squabble with her over a television set or a sofa or something like that."

Kelly: "Can I have your iPod?"

On March 21, a visit from Kelly and their father, Al.

Stephen: "Dad . . ."

Al: "I'm so sorry."

Stephen. "Hey, that's okay. Shit happens."

Shit happens?

Stephen: "Kozlowski apparently came out and said I was abusing Tara. Is that true?"

Kelly: "Yeah. Everybody's saying that, by the way. Turning Point, the abuse place, they did a vigil at Stony Creek, and they all said that you were an abusive husband for years and years and years. And it culminated in the murder."

Stephen: "Well, you should have told them it was the other way around. That's what you should've told them."

Kelly: "Well, I can't. I'm trying to get the kids. I can't bash the dead woman right now. Yeah, she was the most emotionally abusive bitch I've ever met [but] I can't really say that. She was the puppetmaster. I can't really say that right now."

Stephen: "People want my autograph."

Kelly: "Well, you're famous."

Stephen: "I had someone offer me a whole box of donuts for my wristband."

It was Al's only visit to see his son. He cried at the funeral service for Tara, he cried when he visited his son. One wonders what he thought as he listened to his offspring—spawn?—as he listened to their patter.

A hint would come later in sad, dramatic fashion.

March 28, a visit from Kelly.

Grant: "Did anyone mention me at the whole funeral?"

Kelly: "No. It was like you did not exist."

Grant: "So, it was like I just disappeared."

Kelly: "There were no pictures of you. No wedding pictures. No nothing."

Grant: "That's fucked up."

Kelly: "Oh, and they released purple balloons. And they all wore purple ribbons at her funeral, because she was a beaten woman."

Grant: "Okay, somebody should tell me what the evidence is that I beat my wife. She was never even verbally abused."

Kelly: "I saw her be the puppetmaster for twelve years, dude."

Grant: "And I kowtowed down."

Kelly: "He [a mourner at the funeral] made me gag. He's like, 'She's being buried in a maple casket because she liked to make maple syrup.' I'm like, 'For the love of Christ, are there any barf bags in the pew?' They could not have sapped it up any more. Mom says, why didn't you just put the whole body in the trunk at the airport?"

Grant, joking, with exaggeration: "Because I didn't do it, Kel. That's why. I had nothing to do with it?"

Kelly, mentioning someone's fantasy league basketball team: "Somebody named their team Tara's Torso."

Grant, laughing: "That's sick. That's twisted."

Kelly: "What I want to know is—and this is very disgusting, I realize that for the tape recorder—if they put her back together again, in the coffin."

Grant: "They probably laid her out that way."

Kelly: "Did they dress her, too?"

May 24, a call to Kelly.

Grant: "We had this internist in here. She was with the nurse. She was a bitch. She was fucking hot!"

Kelly: "Hot, you said?"

Grant: "Yeah, there's only so many you can look at in here."

Kelly: "Yeah. At least eye candy."

Grant: "I have a chick from up on six, seven, who's writing me letters. She's a little bit freaky."

Kelly: "Do you know what she's in there for?"

Grant: "No, I have no idea. She gets out in August, probably probation violation. She wants to have my baby."

Kelly: "Oh, fantastic."

Grant: "I know. Ain't that nice of her? She wants to write me a freak letter."

Kelly: "I told you that Jeffrey Dahmer guy had sex by the water cooler so he could have a kid."

Grant: "No. That was the other guy."

Kelly: "Oh yeah, I forgot who."

Grant: "That's my second one. That's just funny. It's weird to me. The guys in here give me a hard time. 'You've got a fucking stalker, man.'"

June 6, a call to Kelly, where Grant talks about a deposition the day before in the custody case. Before it began, he told his attorney that he wasn't going to answer any of the opposition questions.

Grant: "He [Grant's attorney] is like, 'It's not our money.' And I'm like, 'I'm not answering an questions.' He's 'You're right.' So I sit down and there's big fat Michael Smith, right?"

Kelly: "Yeah. He's that new guy."

Grant: "So, he's sitting there and I'm at the table and he's there and the big video camera is in front of me. And this guy's got like probably a $5,000 video setup, right?"

Kelly: "Is Alicia there, yet?"

Grant: "She's sitting there just fucking glaring at me. So, I'm so happy right now. I'm like about to piss my pants. So, I clip the little fucking microphone on and I sit down."

Kelly: "You can't just call the deposition off?"

Grant: "Wait, hold on. No, I don't want to. It would be more fun my way. So, Smith says, Michael Smith here representing Alicia Standerfer and then Simasko is here representing the estate of Tara Grant. And then the stenographer said, 'Mr. Grant, can you identify yourself for the record?' And I said, 'No.' I said, 'On my attorney's recommendation, this thing is over.' And I walked out."

Kelly: "What did Smith do?"

Grant: "Smith goes, 'This isn't over until I say it's over.' "

Grant: "And I'm like, 'This is over. I'm not answering any more fucking questions. Have a nice afternoon.' And I walked out. Fuck him. It's so funny—$1,500 worth of lawyer time."

Kelly: "Yep. He's lucky you didn't jerk off for the camera and be more than happy to have a little porn film to sell on eBay."

Grant: "They were about to fuck me, too. They had this whole list of questions about fucking all kinds of crazy shit."

Kelly: "Fuck you and me and the kids."

Grant: "And Donovan, [he said] 'What are you asserting?' I said, 'I'm not even answering that question.' 'Are you asserting a fifth-amendment right?' I'm like, 'I don't have to answer questions. We're done.' I said, 'Get a court order.' What can they do? Jail me for contempt for not answering a motherfucking question? Go ahead, jail me for contempt."

They then talked at length about a local legal commentator on Fox TV, an attorney named Charlie Langton.

Kelly: "He said, 'You know, if you're willing to take the stand and say that you'll give [the Standerfers] court-mandated [visitation] like in a divorce. Every other weekend, four weeks in the summer, every other holiday, and they'll choke on her words before she'll sit up on that stand and say I'll do the same thing.' Because she won't.

"He said, 'You know, [the judge] will terminate the rights to you. There won't be a three-day trial, and that saves the court money. Everybody will be happy. You'll get the kids to raise and she'll get them for visitation . . . Charlie Langton also said Simaski was an idiot. He said, 'You know, your side has been very quiet.' And he says, 'Keep doing that.' He said,

'You're carrying your side with grace and dignity. Keep doing that.'"

June 11, a call to Kelly.

Kelly: "Did you hear anything about the judge you got, this lady?"

Grant: "No, who is it?"

Kelly: "It's something like Druzinski, or something."

Grant: "You're fucking kidding me."

Kelly: "No."

Grant: "Kriznowski?"

Kelly: "No, it's not her. It's not the lady you didn't want."

Grant: "Not hanging Mary?"

Kelly: "No. It's not her. It's like Druzinski or something. Druzinski or Trazinski. But it's not the one you didn't want. But it is a lady."

Later:

Kelly: "I'm scared that if Alicia gets custody, she will bad-mouth you all the time and she won't support if the kids want closure, and she won't support if the kids want to forgive things. You know, I'll take the kids to mass every Sunday, and if they do want to forgive you or if they do want closure, she won't support that when they're eighteen."

June 12, a visit by Kelly where they discuss her efforts to get custody of the Grant children and what value it might be for her case to denigrate Tara's parenting. They discussed the various au pairs the Grants had used and who might say what.

Grant: "Simona, she's from Brazil. I don't think you ever met her. She was never around. She was there for like two weeks and then Yanna was there for like three weeks."

Kelly: "All the changes."

Grant: "And the one from the Ukraine. She didn't try to bite me on the ass, by the way. Viktoria."

Kelly: "How many of them are going to say they fucking

hated working for Tara because she was such a fucking tyrant?"

Grant: "Viktoria, maybe. But she's going to say bad shit about me."

Kelly: "I would say they all would say that Tara was a bitch to work for."

Grant: "No, they wouldn't."

Kelly: "They could all say she was a fucking, you know."

Grant: "Yeah."

Kelly: "That she was strict."

Grant: "Lonnie would say that, but I don't know how to get hold of Lonnie."

Later, while discussing firing the attorneys working the custody case against Alicia:

Grant: "Malpractice. Oh, I'm going to sue him for $100 million. He fucked me. That's malpractice."

June 22, a collect call to Kelly, who's on the cell, in her car, driving Ian and Lindsey for a swim at her pool.

Kelly: "Say hi."

Ian and Lindsey together: "HI!"

Lindsey: "How are you?"

Grant: "Good."

Kelly: "Wave, because we're passing."

Grant: "What?"

Kelly: "We're passing you right now."

Grant: "Oh, thanks. Nice."

Lindsey: "Can he see me?"

Kelly: "No. He can't see you."

Kelly, to Grant: "They worry about you a lot. They say they understand you must have been really mad to do what you did, because you're a really nice guy."

June 27, a visit from Kelly, and a discussion of her brother's ongoing appeal to women.

Grant: "Yeah, I swear to God I'm going to shock her. And she's like, 'Come here, baby.' And I'm in the hallway right in front of the women's cells. There's one women's holding cell."

Kelly: "Are there like bars you could have like stuck it through?"

Grant: "No. There's like a food chute. And she's reaching out, kind of like grabbing me. So, she's reaching out trying to grab me. I'm like, 'What the fuck?' I'm backing up, and she's like, 'Come on, baby. I love you.'"

Kelly: "Does she, you know, like your notoriety?"

Grant: "It's ridiculous in here."

BOMBSHELL: WHAT THE KIDS SAW

On Friday, February 15, just six days before Stephen Grant was scheduled to be sentenced, the Prosecutor's Office dropped a bombshell. The Grants' children, Lindsey and Ian, hadn't been sleeping when their mother was killed, as everyone had thought. They'd been awakened by the arguing and Lindsey, at least, had witnessed their mother's brutal slaying.

On Christmas Day, according to a forty-page sentencing memorandum released to the public, Lindsey, now seven, had broken down and admitted she and her brother had seen their dad kill their mom. Smith said he had first heard of the news in January.

In the memo, Prosecutor Smith urged Judge Diane Druzinski to exceed the probation department's recommendation of forty to sixty years. His recommendation? Fifty to eighty.

Alicia Standerfer told details of that holiday confession to *Free Press* reporter Amber Hunt. It was about dinnertime that Lindsey wanted to talk about something important, so Alicia and Erik took her into the bedroom and locked the door to keep out any of the other kids in the house. Lindsey, to their shock, began to reveal her long-kept secret.

"We sat there in complete, utter disbelief. Christmas Day

was Shellshock Day," said Alicia. A few minutes later, under gentle questioning, Ian, now five, confirmed his sister's story.

"She kept it in for a reason, and that reason was fear," she said.

Lindsey's story conflicted with what her father told investigators, said Alicia, but she declined specifics.

Alicia said that while she would have liked the information to come out at trial, the only way it could have done so was by having one or both of the children testify, and there was no way she would have let them take the witness stand and have to face a cross-examination and a room full of strange faces.

Because of rules about hearsay evidence, the Standerfers' recounting of the children's revelations would not have been admissible. Still, she hoped that the news would have a bearing on the judge's upcoming sentence.

Smith's filing was timely. On Thursday, defense attorney Stephen Rabaut had filed his sentencing memorandum, asking for a sentence of fifteen to twenty-five years, which meant, with time already served, Grant, now thirty-eight, would be able to ask for parole when he was fifty-three.

In his memo, Rabaut argued that there was no evidence that Tara had "suffered extreme or prolonged pain," one of the conditions under state law for a judge to tack on extra jail time.

Smith had countered in his memo that bruises and cuts in and around her face and chest and the amount of time it took to strangle her, several minutes, did in fact constitute extreme suffering.

"The length of the act in minutes demonstrates the cold, calculated brutality of this defendant," he wrote. "This, together with the dismemberment of his wife's remains, speaks of a level of intensity of hatred far beyond the imagination of a civilized society."

Smith said Grant showed no remorse when he matter-of-factly described the chain of events in his hospital interview with Kozlowski and McLean, had spoken disparagingly of his wife in jailhouse conversations with his sister, and had been a frequent troublemaker in jail.

Rabaut, in his memo, had anticipated Smith's charges. "A court is not permitted to consider the lack of remorse of a defendant because the appellate courts have found that this determination is not an objective and verifiable factor," he wrote.

Lost in the drama of the horrible image of two young kids watching in secret while their dad killed their mom, the other news of the week got lost. The Macomb County Board of Commissioners had approved a payment of $25,000 for a county contingency fund to help the cash-strapped Prosecutor's Office fund the Grant prosecution.

DAY OF RECKONING:
LOTTERY REVOKED

February 21, 2008. Ten TV trucks parked outside the Mt. Clemens courthouse, a record as far as anyone could remember, their satellite dishes aiming skyward, told casual passersby this was no ordinary workday. Those at home watching local early-morning TV news knew what was up: it was reckoning day for Steven Grant.

Up on the second-floor hallway outside Judge Druzinski's courtroom, technicians duct-taped cable to the floor. A couple of cameramen shot interior b-roll, to be edited later into the juicy stuff to come.

A bailiff announced instructions loudly. Media were told to sign up. They would be let in to the small courtroom, first come, first served, for a total of fifteen. Fifteen members of the general public would be let in. Members of the media who tried to pass themselves off as members of the general public would be dealt with harshly. Five friends of both Tara and Steve would be let in. There would be no print photographers allowed inside, following the judge's rules during trial.

People continued to come into the hall from the stairs and elevator. Print media with their thin notebooks, radio reporters with tape recorders, still photographers with their digital cameras, TV reporters with coiffed hair done just so, court regulars, retired folks or those who worked afternoons and midnights and caught all the trials, big and small, that they could, filled the benches that lined the hall and wandered back and forth as best as they could in the throng.

Dateline was there. Court TV, *20/20. Dateline* loved the Grant case so much it was rushing a show to the air; it'd be on in eight days. Loved it so much they were going to start it about 9:50 P.M. in its two-hour block of time, that way keeping viewers through the bewitching time of ten, when otherwise they might be apt to pick up the remote and do a little channel hopping.

At 8:30 A.M., Alicia and Erik Standerfer arrived. The still photographers flocked to them as they were led to the closed courtroom door, which was opened to let them in and then closed again.

At 8:45, the doors opened again, and the signees who made the cut were invited in. So, too, were two courtroom artists, as dying a breed as car modelers for Ford or General Motors who still work in clay.

Prosecutor Eric Smith, who had released Grant's jailhouse tapes, could be heard jokingly complaining that they were getting lost in the brouhaha over transcripts of more notorious conversations that had been released to the press. He was referring to a story that had recently exploded across the headlines and the airwaves, a recounting of the lurid, graphic text messages that had gone back and forth by the thousands between Detroit's Mayor Kwame Kilpatrick and Christine Beatty, his chief of staff, friend from high school, and longtime mistress.

What made this more than just a tawdry tale of two prominent office holders betraying their spouses and children was that the year before, the two had denied under oath in a whistle-blower lawsuit that they were lovers or ever had been. The suit had been filed on behalf of a Detroit internal-affairs detective investigating persistent rumors of a wild party at the city-owned Manoogian Mansion, a stately home on the Detroit River that was a perk of the mayor's office.

According to the rumors, the mayor's wife, Carlita, unex-pectedly came home, found a stripper in action and beat her up, requiring her trip to a nearby hospital. While investigat-ing those rumors, the internal affairs officer was ordered fired by Beatty, who also swore under oath that she hadn't ordered his dismissal.

Their text messages showed otherwise. The ensuing head-lines had enthralled the city for weeks and would continue to do so for months. Something had finally knocked the Grant story from the top of the fold. The *Detroit Free Press* would eventually win a Pulitzer Prize for breaking the story, and the mayor and his chief of staff would leave their offices in disgrace and serve four months in the Wayne County Jail for perjury and obstruction of justice.

At 8:54, a door that led to offices adjacent to the court-room opened and the Standerfers entered and took their seats at the front of the spectators' area, near Smith.

Stephen Grant was led in from another door, shuffling in shackles at his ankles, in a blue short-sleeved jailhouse jump-suit, blinking repeatedly.

The bailiff told all to rise, and Judge Druzinski entered.

"Are the people ready to proceed?" she asked. "Is the defense ready to proceed?"

They were.

"This case has generated strong emotions by everyone in-volved. Today, the court will not tolerate any outburst in court. If there are any, that person will be evicted and arrested for contempt of court," she said, the same stern, no-nonsense judge she'd been throughout the trial.

First on the agenda was a presentencing report by the cor-rections department, a pro forma bit of business that was in reality irrelevant to what was coming. Grant had been scored on a variety of variables related to the crime, and state-mandated sentence guidelines added time to the basic sen-tence based on how the defendant scored.

Defense attorney Stephen Rabaut objected to a finding

that while in the county jail, Grant had violated a rule by being found in possession of gambling paraphernalia.

"My client says that is not true. It's not accurate and I ask that it be stricken," he said.

Smith recounted the basis for the charge. The judge let it stand.

Next, Rabaut objected to a finding that there had been aggravated physical or emotional abuse in Tara's death. It struck observers as silly, at the least. He'd carved her into pieces but hadn't committed aggravated physical abuse?

"It is clear an altercation occurred," said Rabaut. But, he argued, since death had occurred so quickly once Grant started strangling her, it didn't constitute aggravated abuse, just abuse.

The judge let stand the maximum of 50 points.

Next came impact statements from Tara's friends and family. Her boss, Lou Troendle, was first.

"I remember when she came in fourteen years ago, just out of Michigan State and looking for a career and long-term commitment," he said. "First impressions are everything, and she made a good first impression. And she proved to be hardworking and dedicated and learned our business quickly. She only ever asked for two things: respect, and to be offered equal opportunities with those with whom she worked.

"Her untimely death was shocking and horrific. She will never be forgotten," he concluded. "Her loss has created a void which will not be filled. I've heard it said that time heals all wounds. I truly believe this is one wound time will not heal."

Erik Standerfer was next. He got up from his seat near the front of the courtroom, holding a prepared statement in his right hand, and walked up to the podium. What he had to say would be electrifying and headline inducing. It was the expected impact statement and so much more.

"Good morning, your honor," he began. "As a result of Stephen Grant murdering his wife in February 2007, Alicia and I were thrust into extremely life changing circumstances. Once we learned of Tara's fate and of Stephen's capture, our main focus quickly became Lindsey and Ian, the living victims of this terrible tragedy. Their life was completely devastated by Stephen Grant. Their entire security blanket including their parents, friends, school, house, neighborhood, etc., were immediately stolen from them. Our effort to give them the security blanket and chance at a normal life through the adoption process over the last year has been nothing short of horrific, as well, for my family."

Erik told the court about Tara and what made her so special, and what was special about her relationship with his wife, the bond between them so unique it "cannot be described in words. While the two lived many miles apart in their adult lives, they would routinely pick up the phone and start a conversation as if they had lunch every day of the week and lived across the street from one another."

Erik told them about Tara's attention, despite her travel and her job, to her kids, calling them daily no matter where she was, leaving cards on their pillows to tell them she loved them before she'd leave. "I believe the horror of leaving her children was the last thought that went through Tara's mind that fateful night," he said.

"While I will never be Tara's blood relative, I will miss Tara Grant terribly for the rest of my life and have etched the beautiful image of her as a young mother, sister-in-law and professional in my mind forever. Her legacy will live on through her children, but I often wonder where she would have ended up, being such a determined and talented person. Her success in almost all aspects of her life remains incredible to me. Tara is not your normal victim, if there is such a thing.

"Stephen was her Achilles' heel," he said. "I never liked or trusted Stephen. I cannot begin to express how many times my family and I were betrayed or belittled by this man. Stephen Grant was the relative that everyone tolerated only because he was married to Tara . . . He literally siphons the energy from those around him only to make himself more powerful."

What came next got everyone's attention, not that anyone's thoughts had been drifting. Reporters, in particular, perked up.

"I still remember vividly the time I kicked him out of my son's room as he forcefully tried to get him to lay in his crib. For my eighteen-month-old son recognized Stephen Grant as a monster," he said. "I remember it clearly, because this represents the only time I allowed Stephen Grant to interact one-on-one with my own kids, and it was a complete disaster. I should have banned him from my family then. Maybe the end of this tragedy would have been different."

Erik told of a long history of family events and holidays ruined by Grant. "The majority of any family functions in the thirteen years I have known Stephen have been extremely difficult due to his controlling presence," he said. "There were so many times during those years that Tara would ask us to do something together, such as go in together for gifts, take family vacations or come and visit. Often, we decided we just could not, solely because of Stephen. Even on the day of her death, Tara was reaching out to our family to consider a vacation rental with them, an arrangement my wife Alicia and I were unwilling to enter due to our extreme dislike and distrust of Stephen. We celebrated the births of our children, winter holidays and other fun times together, but typically, there was some type of controversy that involved Stephen, resulting in the fun coming to an abrupt end.

"Deep down, I know Tara was embarrassed of him and his actions, but she was too proud to say anything negative about Stephen or leave him behind. I witnessed her come to Stephen's aid on more than one occasion, yet she would not allow others to help with her innermost struggles, concerning how to remove herself and her children from the grip of Stephen Grant."

Erik implored the judge to sentence Grant harshly. "I stand before you today and ask you to deliver the absolute stiffest penalty possible to Stephen Grant. It is my opinion that he should NEVER be a free person, again. I firmly believe Stephen Grant represents a life-threatening risk to my immediate family, specifically my wife, our biological children and especially to his biological children, Lindsey and Ian. He is not capable of rehabilitation, nor does he deserve a chance."

The biggest moment of drama in Erik's impact statement was at hand. "Lindsey has described to Alicia and I in detail what she witnessed that horrible night. Lindsey became overwhelmed with fear and guilt the night of December 25, 2007. After nine months in our house, Lindsey shared a secret that was eating her up from within. She provided a chilling, detailed account of the tragedy as seen first hand, through her own eyes. Based on her description, Lindsey supports the fact that Stephen conducted a calculated, thorough beating and ultimate killing of Tara. One that directly conflicts with the argument concerning travel, as Stephen suggests. It was absolutely brutal to listen to Lindsey describe that night, watching her dad scream directly into her mother's ear to 'Quit looking at me!'

"Alicia and I had to convey to Tara's parents that Stephen killed Tara and then proceeded to cut her up and spread her remains in Stony Creek Metro Park. This was the second hardest thing I have ever done in my life, only behind telling Lindsey and Ian in the presence of a psychiatrist the truth about their dad murdering their mother. Only months later did I learn I was telling Lindsey something she already knew. How terrible it must have been for Lindsey to keep her secret for all this time.

"I have sat and listened for many hours as Lindsey described the mental abuse he inflicted on Tara and the children over the years. I have listened as Lindsey described the night Tara was killed, what she saw, what she felt, what she heard, what she tried to do to make it stop. And it is nothing short of terrifying."

The next line of the printout Erik held had a line crossed

out, Erik realizing what effect it likely would have on the radio, TV, and print coverage. What he had originally written next, but decided to skip was: *"My wife and I began to weep as she described checking her mother's still warm eyelids to see if she was dead or alive after Stephen left the room."*

Instead, he continued with: "How she observed undetected as her father rolled her mother's lifeless body to the door.

"My hatred for this man is indescribable. He is living proof that the devil lives and works among us. I pray to God and ask that you exercise your power and oversight in this case to deliver the toughest penalty possible."

He was nearly done. "Finally, I would like to personally thank you for your persistence in moving this process along smoothly to the best of your ability. Your professionalism and dedication in handling this case has no doubt allowed our grieving and constant life strain to be lessened. As your final act, I ask you to protect my family, including Lindsey and Ian, by sentencing Stephen Grant to the longest term possible. What Lindsey and Ian witnessed that day and the impact of Tara's murder on our family knows no sentencing guidelines and is everlasting. Thank you for your consideration in this extremely difficult matter."

"You're very welcome, Mr. Standerfer," said the judge.

Tara's mother, Mary Destrampe, was next. Erik took his seat and she walked to the podium.

"What I have to say is mostly to Stephen, if you don't mind," she said.

"You're not technically allowed to address the defendant. Address them to me, and I assure you he will hear," said the judge.

"He turned to me in this courtroom and to say, 'I am so sorry.' How could he say that when he squeezed the life out of her and mutilated her so badly her father and I couldn't touch her. I will never forget February 9, 2007, when Tara was violently ripped from our family. I will never forget

February 13, when Stephen Grant called and told me Tara was missing. He was crying and playing to my emotions, which he always did.

"I can't forgive you for what you have done to my family," she continued, switching to "you" from "he," the judge letting her continue. "My family will get through this terrible loss with love. I will be surrounded by love. But I hope you live the rest of your life alone."

Then came Alicia. In January, she had been named conservator of Tara's estate. Six days earlier, on February 16, she had been told final adoption papers had been approved for the Standerfers to adopt Lindsey and Ian. Now, this. She was hoping for more good news today. First, she had two drawings Lindsey had made for her therapist handed to the judge. One showed her mother being buried. Unlike the real burial Lindsey had attended in the Upper Peninsula, the drawing of this one included her father hiding behind a nearby rock. The other drawing had the words: "My dad thinks he has power."

"Tara had a beauty that could light up a room," she began. Observers couldn't help but be struck by her resemblance to Tara, whose headshot had been on the TV news and the front pages so often it had become a familiar face, and here it was having come alive in front of them. Only the hair was different, the curls softer. There was almost a feeling that Alicia wasn't just speaking for Tara, but embodying her, too.

She, too, told the court of the Christmas Day Lindsey, to her horror, had told her what she had seen and heard the night Tara was killed.

"She not only saw her father choke her mother to death, but she heard her last breath," she said.

"Stephen is a master manipulator, a narcissist and a psychopath. This entire year has been the most horrific year I ever hope to be involved in," said Alicia, who told the court of the insulting shock of listening to hours of taped conversations between Grant and his sister, including his mocking the release of the purple balloons at the funeral service. "I stand before you today, numb, not really believing I'm addressing you."

She finished with another anecdote, of explaining to Lindsey soon after her mom's death that it was God's plan, that he knew her mother had had a horrible home life and the only way to free her from it was to take her.

"'Why didn't he just take the person who caused it?'" she quoted Lindsey as responding. "I had no answer for her. He's not worth being called a human being. He's the devil in the flesh."

A four-minute video tribute was played for the judge. The courtroom couldn't see it, but could hear it. As a guitar played softly, family members told of their love for Tara. The room seemed especially silent when the video ended. Alicia walked slowly to her seat, all eyes on her.

It was time for more formal business to resume. Prosecutor Eric Smith went over the probation department's sentencing-guideline assessment, reiterating the reasons why Grant deserved extra time added to the minimum for second degree. Points had justly been assessed for Grant's having caused psychological damage to his family, clear by what the kids had told their therapist and the Standerfers, he said. Points had justly been assessed because he had interfered in the police investigation. Points had been assessed for his misconduct in jail.

Smith recounted examples of Grant's behavior in jail—telling his sister he wanted Channel 7 to do an attack story on Tara to get her off her pedestal; how it would be funny if his sister ran the 5K in honor of Tara so he could get one of the race T-shirts; that he thought he would be able to use the power of his name to sell a bike on eBay for a premium price; that he was looking forward to a movie and book deal; that he'd been signing autographs in jail for his fellow prisoners.

How remorse seemed a foreign concept.

"Your honor, there's a time for moderation and forgiveness. This is not one of them. This is the time for justice. Moderation is not justice," said Smith, who sat down.

Rabaut stood up, playing as empty a hand as any poker player who ever sat down at a Texas hold 'em table. He said that the state-mandated guideline for second-degree murder called for a sentence of between 225 months and 375 months, eighteen to thirty-one years.

He said that a lack of remorse couldn't be used to tack on extra time, based on a decision by an appeals court, and that the probation department had erred in recommending added time on the other issues. "There are no objective or verifiable reasons to exceed the guidelines," he said. "I don't believe there's any reason for the court to exceed the guideline range."

"Objective and verifiable" was legalese, a requirement under the law that if there were circumstances that led to an increase in a sentence, they couldn't be willy-nilly or capricious, but codified under statute.

Rabaut had to say something. But he might as well have said there was no reason for a palm tree to bend in a hurricane.

"Does Mr. Grant wish to address the court?" asked the judge.

"One moment, please," said Rabaut, who leaned over his client and whispered something to him. Grant whispered back.

"At the advice of counsel, he has decided not to make a statement," said Rabaut.

"Is that right, Mr. Grant?" asked the judge.

"Yes."

"Will you please rise, sir?" she told him.

He rose.

The judge explained that there were two possibilities when sentencing for second-degree murder, a life sentence with eligibility for parole in fifteen years. Or, a sentence requiring a minimum amount of time served within the guideline range plus an aggregate of months for other related factors, factors that were—and she was careful to use the phrase—"objective and verifiable. The reasons that justify a departure should keenly and unmistakably grab the court's attention," she said. "Under the circumstances of this case, the court does not believe the defendant should be eligible for parole in fifteen years," she said. "This case has grabbed the court's attention like no other."

And then she proved how much her attention had been keenly and unmistakably grabbed. She pronounced her sentence. "On count one, on the charge of second-degree murder, fifty to eighty years." There were gasps in the courtroom.

"On count two, for obstruction of justice, six to ten years." Under Michigan law, that sentence would be served concurrently with the first.

Adding insult to injury, she ordered Grant to pay $180 in fees to the state and the county and to pay $41,663 in attorney's fees.

The lottery ticket he won with the verdict had been proven counterfeit.

Late in the afternoon, the Standerfers took Ian and Lindsey out to eat at a restaurant in downtown Mt. Clemens. Alicia broke the news to them about their father's sentence. How long did you want him gone? she asked Lindsey.

"Forever."

A CHAPTER CLOSES

Grant was led from the courtroom. All rose, and the judge left. The crowd slowly made its way back into the hallway outside the court. Reporters were led to a nearby room, where cameras had been set up in front of a podium.

Smith and his fellow prosecutors, Therese Tobin and Bill Cataldo, walked in and went to the podium. "I want you guys to look like you're alive behind me," he joked to his team, staff, reporters, and radio guys still jostling for position.

After a pause, Smith began: "Nothing will bring back Tara Grant. But nothing will bring back Stephen Grant, either. The next step by Mr. Grant will be an appeal, and that will be denied. Stephen Grant will be serving his fifty years. He's thirty-eight now, he'll be eighty-eight when he's up for parole. Not getting released. Up for parole. And I'll be ninety-one, then, and I'll have them wheel me in and I'll object."

("And if Smith can't make it, I guarantee you, Brian will," said Darga later about Koz making any possible parole hearing for Grant when he's eighty-seven.)

Smith was asked if, once it came to light that Lindsey had witnessed her mother's murder, he had considered putting her on the stand. "We'd never do that," he said, adding that if he had to choose between putting the young girl on the stand

and getting a conviction for first degree, or keeping her off and getting second degree, "I'd choose the latter."

And what would happen to Grant, now? Where would he be going and when? "He'll be moving to Jackson immediately," Smith said, referring to Michigan's first prison, which opened in 1839 in the city of Jackson in the south-central part of the state. By the 1920s, it had grown to house six thousand prisoners and for a while was the largest walled prison in the U.S.

"They've been preparing for this at the county jail for a long time. They'll have the skids greased," said Smith. He said what Grant could expect was to be on lockdown for twenty-three hours a day for several years, then, depending on his behavior up to that point, he might be let into the general population.

What were possible appealable issues?

The confession up north, had there been enough probable cause to justify the search warrant of his house, not moving the trial to another county, said Smith.

The Standerfers came to the podium.

"As you know, normally I have something prepared to read," Alicia began. "I don't have something prepared today. I didn't have the energy. The sentence she handed down was perfect. It's for the rest of Stephen's natural life, and we're so happy with that. It sits well with us. It's been a horrific nightmare I still haven't woke up from."

Had she been surprised when Grant chose not to speak?

"I was quite surprised, quite honestly. We all know how much Stephen likes to hear his own voice."

Alicia thanked Sheriff Hackel and praised Kozlowski and McLean, who, she said, "have shown through your words and actions what it means to be dedicated to your profession. Your relentless, detailed pursuit contributed to the ultimate conviction and sentencing delivered by Judge Druzinski today."

She finished with some comments about domestic violence.

"Even though Tara's life was ultimately taken due to

physical violence, she suffered years of mental abuse, which permanently scarred her, and in many respects, mental abuse is much worse because the scars are invisible. But the pain goes deeper than any of us could ever know. Domestic violence is an epidemic in our country that all too often is dismissed as a fact of life. It is imperative that my sister's death not be in vain, but in fact serves as a lightning rod for additional educational resources aimed towards the prevention of potential future tragedies.

"Each of us is likely to be influenced by domestic violence in our lives to a certain extent; I struggle with how Tara, being such a strong, proud woman, could have been overcome by it. My family will forever be influenced by this tragedy, but we *will* recover. Individuals do not have the right to control or abuse other human beings and there are ways out of violent relationships. As a society we must continue to bring awareness to domestic violence through organizations like Turning Point here in Macomb County and in our school systems through education, starting at a very young age.

"Tara, you will never be forgotten. You and your children will never be influenced by Stephen Grant again."

Mrs. Destrampe was next. "I prayed for this day," she said.

She explained the circumstances behind Lindsey's revelation about what she'd seen. The family had come north for the trial and Mrs. Destrampe asked Lindsey if she knew why they were in Michigan.

" 'I don't know,' " said Mrs. Destrampe, recounting Lindsey's response.

" 'We're here for your father's trial and I just want you to know he'll be in jail a long time.' "

"Lindsey then described the scene," she said.

Did Lindsey know the sentence, yet?

"We'll tell her later in the day."

She looked out at the press, paused and said: "This is closure on another chapter."

POSTSCRIPT

Right after the Grant case, Koz pulled duty on another weird one, mile or two from the Grant house. Mary Jou Johnson, an Asian woman who married money, lots of very expensive jewelry. Hires a handyman named David Wright to do some plumbing work, he takes a shine to her jewelry, kills her, ties her to a big rock, rows her out to the middle of the lake behind her house and dumps her over.

Doing life for first degree.

Koz helped break the case. "I got him to flip. He was substantially more difficult than Grant."

These days, Koz looks a far cry from the sorta chubby, maybe mistake him for soft, brush-cut detective who worked the Grant case. He runs a six-man undercover team and is part of a multijurisdictional SWAT team, too. If there was such a job as full-time SWAT, all day, every day . . . dream job, man. Meanwhile, he'll do SWAT when needed.

His head is shaved, a black bandana covering his scalp and pulled low over his forehead, a thick, bushy, Z Z Top beard fighting for attention with the tattoos that run up and down his heavily muscled arms. He has three thick silver rings on his right hand, a thumb ring on his left.

"I've done so much time saddling up with the bad guys, I

won't say I've developed a friendship with them, but it does give me some understanding of them," he says. Drug bad guys. B&E bad guys. Not wife-killing bad guys. Grant, he'll never understand. Drug guys, sometimes it seems they aren't really hurting anyone but themselves, and popping them doesn't always give him a sense of accomplishment. Home-invasion guys? That's another story. Loves following them around, waiting for them to hit a house, catching them wide-eyed with his gun drawn when they come out loaded with stuff.

His office is miles away from the sheriff's department, on the second floor of a warehouse-looking building in an industrial park. A big, soft leather chair confiscated in a drug raid awaits visitors. There's a model of a ninja warrior on his desk, the big poster of Denzel Washington behind him, looking nearly as fearful as Koz in his black Ghetto Dogs T-shirt with the skull on the front.

Despite Koz's gruff demeanor and tough-guy looks, McLean sets the record straight: "Koz doesn't want people to know he's really just a big, soft teddy bear. Don't put that in the book. He'll be over at my desk saying, 'What the fuck, Pam!'" The last said in a deep voice mimicking Koz's, and then she breaks into laughter.

On Friday, July 27, 2007, the Grants' home in Washington Township went up for auction in Macomb County Circuit Court, with bids starting at $221,468.73, the amount owed the bank, which had not got a payment since Grant's arrest in February.

Home auctions were a novelty then. Sadly, they soon would become a fixture in the U.S. and southeastern Michigan, in general, and in Washington Township and other fast-growing townships in northern Macomb County. The housing boom had turned cornfields into sprawling subdivisions filled with so-called big-foot houses. Loans were easy to come by, houses sold faster than they could be finished, and developers were only too happy to build on spec, not needing a buyer before they started, sure they'd find one before they finished.

The housing market began to crash in late 2007, and after the devastating fall of Wall Street investment banks and the freeze of credit markets in the fall of 2008, housing and commercial development imploded. Foreclosed houses and auction signs became ubiquitous. Bankers stopped being surprised when house keys showed up in the mail, customers not even trying to sell or refinance, knowing it was hopeless. Bankers stopped demanding that auctions start at the price they were owed; they began taken offers for pennies on the dollar.

On March 6, 2008, Macomb County Circuit Chief Judge Richard Caretti approved Grant's application for an appeal on his conviction for second-degree murder and for a court-appointed appellate attorney. His appeal is still pending but is considered to have little chance for success, given that Michigan's appeal-court judges stand for election and are traditionally very reticent about granting appeals for new trials.

On October 17, 2008, Alicia and Erik Standerfer were held in contempt of court after denying Stephen Grant's mother, Susan Brown, access to Ian and Lindsey. They were ordered to pay $500 in attorney's fees to Brown and to arrange visitation within ninety days.

Lieutenant King retired in January 2010 after more than thirty years with the department. He spends as much time as possible at his place in Grayling, one of the towns that played into Grant's wild ride around the state on his way north the night they found Tara's torso.

The same month, McLean started another high-profile homicide trial, this of a beefy forty-two-year-old scumbag named Timothy Prince, charged with killing an eighty-seven-year-old woman named Dorothy Cezik who lived across the street. He'd befriended her a few months earlier, started asking for favors, like rides somewhere or other. She was a feisty old lady, a former farmer who still drove her own truck.

On March 7, 2009, Prince asked her for money to feed his twelve-year-old son. When she refused, he beat her up, stabbed her and slit her throat, then drove in her truck to the northern edge of the county, east of Stony Creek, and tossed her battered body onto a bike path. He then drove home and set her truck on fire.

In January 2010, he was found guilty of first-degree murder, kidnapping, armed robbery and arson.

Chad Halcom, the *Macomb Daily* reporter whose call to Sheriff Hackel triggered the first search for Tara at Stony Creek Metropark, is now a business reporter at *Crain's Detroit Business,* part of Crain Communications, which owns niche business publications around the world and is one of the rare thriving print operations left standing.

Halcom's work area is on the other side of a short divider from that of a certain business reporter who moonlights as a true-crime writer for St. Martin's Press.

Amber Hunt continues to cover crime and courts for the *Detroit Free Press* and now writes true-crime books for St. Martin's, too. She helped with this book.

True to her words at the press conference after Grant's sentencing, Alicia took up the fight against domestic violence. Stephen Grant may have tried to bury Tara under the snow and fallen trees of Stony Creek Metropark, but in an ironic and wonderful twist, her memory and her spirit live on there. She loved running its trails; now, each fall, several hundred participants run or walk 3.1 miles, or five kilometers, over those same trails in the annual Tara Grant Memorial, a fundraiser for Turning Point, a shelter for abused women in Mt. Clemens that Alicia thought perfect as a beneficiary.

Her husband, Erik, an avid runner himself, races the 5K hard. Alicia walks it. Sheriff Hackel can be counted on to finish near the top. A certain true-crime writer and his black Lab mix run as hard as Hackel, but not as efficiently or as fast. A handful of county deputies, who normally run only after fleeing suspects, enter out of respect for Alicia, whom they'd grown to like.

In 2008, Hackel pulled a hamstring muscle during the race, but still hobbled to sixth place. The next year, healthy again, he finished sixth again, in 23:26. The reporter kept him in sight for a change, finishing eleventh in 25:02, then rounding up Alicia, Erik, and Sheriff Hackel for a photo in front of the banner proclaiming the Tara Grant Memorial 5K. There's a big picnic and a series of short sprints for kids.

Hackel runs each year with Vince Viviano in a friendly but competitive rivalry, rubbing it in if he happens to out-kick him. Viviano was a manager at Warren Bank, a small community bank, and helped get the race organized and helped the Standerfers with various financial matters and probate issues after Tara's death. He also set up the kids' trust fund and the Turning Point abused-women's shelter's Tara Grant Liberation Fund. Alas, the bank fell victim to the mortgage meltdown of 2008 and was closed down by federal regulators in October 2009.

Hackel, an adjunct professor at Macomb County Community College and Wayne State University, teaches the Grant case to his students. "It's got everything," he says. A missing body, real leads and false trails, a manhunt, a frenzied media horde, what steps you need to take in the first forty-eight hours of a possible murder, how savvy street cops can read a suspect, how important a sixth sense can be, such as his feeling they ought to search Stony Creek—if that won't keep a class's attention, what will?

He remains close to the Standerfers, particularly Alicia, and they stay in touch, through e-mails, phone calls, and Christmas cards.

"She was just such a dignified person," he says. "Her composure thoughout the whole thing was so important to us."

One of the many touching photos that ran in the dailies was of Hackel and Alicia embracing after the press conference the Standerfers held when Tara's body was found. You could clearly see the emotions running through both of them, victimized sister, career cop. "How do you not get emotionally involved?" he asks.

In March 2010, the Michigan Supreme Court turned down Grant's appeal for a new trial.

Hackel won reelection easily in 2008, the top vote getter of all candidates running for office in the county. On November 2, 2010, Hackel was elected to be the chief executive of Macomb County and stepped down as Sheriff at the end of the year.

Captain Anthony Wickersham was appointed to replace Hackel as sheriff. Wickersham then promoted Elizabeth Darga to captain and Brian Kozlowski to lieutenant.

The park is a favorite running and kayaking spot for this writer and his dog. When the second search of the park turned up most of Tara's body parts, but not all of them, the writer's wife demanded the two run elsewhere for a while. The dog, who runs off leash, is proud of her ability to find and retrieve bones, usually deer femurs or bird skeletons, eager to be praised for being a good hunter as she drops the bones at the writer's feet.

There is a wonderful holiday run every July 4 in the northern Michigan resort town of Beulah (setting of another true-crime book published by St. Martin's Press, *Afraid of the Dark*) known as the Firecracker Run. It starts and finishes just off the beach of impossibly beautiful Crystal Lake.

The writer and his wife and dog run that race some years. Erik runs it every year. "It's a yearly event for Erik and his cousin," says Alicia. "They are very competitive with each other, which makes it fun. There are several other relatives that run as well, and then a handful of us that run the first two hundred yards, then walk. It is fun and we always have a good time. It is a way for the adults to get together on the Fourth of July morning and not worry about anything except finishing the race.

"It won't be long before Lindsey will want to participate. Then it will become a true family event for the Standerfers."

Two days before Father's Day, Friday, the thirteenth of June, 2008, William (Al) Grant, Stephen's father, called the St. Clair County Sheriff's Department at 1:40 P.M. He wanted to report a suicide.

Whose? the dispatcher asked.

"Mine." He gave an address and hung up.

A deputy was sent to a house in small Emmett Township, forty miles northeast of Detroit. By coincidence, the township shared a sound-alike name with Emmet County, where Al's son was caught in the snow.

As the deputy got out of the car, he heard a gunshot coming from the garage. He found Grant, sixty-six, on the concrete floor, a rifle at his side.

He was still alive. He was taken to Port Huron Hospital, where he died.

"It was so sad," said McLean. "Al was such a nice guy. Even when we were serving search warrants on him at his business. The second one we served, he said, 'Do what you need to do. Take your time. I'll get out of your way. Call me when you're done.' My heart went out to him. He was such a nice guy, and to end up raising a psychopath."

One might wander if Stephen Grant's reaction was:

Shit happens.

ACKNOWLEDGMENTS

Special thanks to Lieutenant Brian, make that Koz, Kozlowski. He was a very reluctant participant at first and grew to be extraordinarily helpful and entertaining. And special thanks to Sheriff Mark Hackel, without whose blessing this book would be, to the extent it might be interesting, far less so. I still think I can give him a run for his money one of these years at the Tara Grant Memorial 5K. Thanks, too, to John Cwikla, the able and responsive media relations manager with the Macomb County Sheriff's Department; to Captain Elizabeth Darga, a fellow softball junkie and cop extraordinaire; to Sergeant Pam McLean, another fellow lover of Labrador retrievers; to Captain Larry King, whose wit was much appreciated and his supply of photos at below market rate (free) even more so; and to new Sheriff Tony Wickersham, who helped pave the way and who is another of the sheriff's department lifers who make it such a good outfit.

I want to give a hearty thank-you to *Detroit Free Press* reporter Amber Hunt, who covered the case like the bulldog she is and who provided valuable assistance *and* who is a new true-crime author for St. Martin's Paperbacks. Hunt had an interesting engagement with Kozlowski in defense of the First Amendment during a court hearing that preceded the trial.

As part of a motion made by the defense to toss out Grant's hospital-bed confession, Judge Druzinski wanted to talk to a doctor at Northern Michigan Hospital, Michael Johnson, to hear his assessment of Grant's mental condition the day he was found in the snow.

Johnson couldn't make the trip to Detroit, so Druzinski arranged for a phone deposition to be taken in her chambers, with attorneys present. Alas, in violation of the law, reporters weren't notified and the call was not open to the public.

Hunt got word and stormed into the courtroom in a lather a few minutes after the deposition started.

Koz, who was in the courtroom, barked at her that the session was closed. She barked back: "Maybe you ought to worry about protecting the First Amendment."

"Thanks for the lesson. Maybe you ought to worry about proper courtroom attire," countered Koz, thinking she was dressed a tad too casually.

The judge granted Hunt access to her chambers to serve as a pool reporter and she was able to get a transcript of the fifteen minutes she missed. Johnson said Grant's mental faculties were just fine by the time the police interviewed him, and the confession was allowed into the record.

After the trial, Koz and Hunt made up, bonding in a modern way. Hunt went in to a Mt. Clemens parlor for a new tattoo. Koz was already in a chair getting an addition to his eye-catching collection.

Thanks, also, to Chad Halcom, my fellow reporter at *Crain's Detroit Business*, who provided the tip that finally set in motion the cinematic series of events that made this a book; and to other TV, radio, and press accounts of this sad story from which I could borrow, including the *Detroit Free Press* and the *Detroit News*.